Women of the Outback

Sue Williams is an award-winning journalist and columnist who has written for all of the country's leading newspapers and magazines. She is the author of ten books, including *Peter Ryan: the Inside Story*; *Mean Streets, Kind Heart: the Father Chris Riley Story*; and *And Then the Darkness*, about the disappearance of the British backpacker Peter Falconio, which was shortlisted for the prestigious Golden Dagger Award in the UK for the international True Crime Book of the Year, and shortlisted for the Ned Kelly Awards in Australia. Born in England, Sue spent many years travelling and wrote *Getting There – Journeys of an Accidental Adventurer* before settling in Australia in 1989. She now lives in Sydney with her partner Jimmy Thomson.

For more information please visit
suewilliams.com.au

Women
of the
Outback

SUE WILLIAMS

MICHAEL JOSEPH
an imprint of
PENGUIN BOOKS

MICHAEL JOSEPH

Published by the Penguin Group
Penguin Group (Australia)
250 Camberwell Road, Camberwell, Victoria 3124, Australia
(a division of Pearson Australia Group Pty Ltd)
Penguin Group (USA) Inc.
375 Hudson Street, New York, New York 10014, USA
Penguin Group (Canada)
90 Eglinton Avenue East, Suite 700, Toronto, Canada ON M4P 2Y3
(a division of Pearson Penguin Canada Inc.)
Penguin Books Ltd
80 Strand, London WC2R 0RL, England
Penguin Ireland
25 St Stephen's Green, Dublin 2, Ireland
(a division of Penguin Books Ltd)
Penguin Books India Pvt Ltd
11 Community Centre, Panchsheel Park, New Delhi – 110 017, India
Penguin Group (NZ)
67 Apollo Drive, Rosedale, North Shore 0632, New Zealand
(a division of Pearson New Zealand Ltd)
Penguin Books (South Africa) (Pty) Ltd
24 Sturdee Avenue, Rosebank, Johannesburg 2196, South Africa

Penguin Books Ltd, Registered Offices: 80 Strand, London, WC2R 0RL, England

First published by Penguin Group (Australia), 2008

7 9 10 8 6

Design by Karen Trump © Penguin Group (Australia)
Cover photograph by Bill Bachmann
For inset photography credits, see picture section
Lyrics from 'Tell These Hands' by Sara Storer on page 88 reproduced
with the kind permission of ABC Music Publishing
Typeset in 12/17.5pt Fairfield by Post Pre-Press Group, Brisbane, Queensland
Printed and bound in Australia by McPherson's Printing Group, Maryborough, Victoria

National Library of Australia
Cataloguing-in-Publication data:

Williams, Sue, 1959–.
Women of the outback: inspiring true stories of tragedy and triumph / Sue Williams.
ISBN: 9780718104948 (pbk.)
1. Rural women – Australia – Biography. 2. Ranchers' spouses – Australia – Biography.
3. Frontier and pioneer life – Australia.

994.0099

penguin.com.au

To Selwa,
for making anything possible

CONTENTS

FOREWORD

Outback women have proven over the years to be the very backbone of Australia. From the first days, Outback Aboriginal women were among the finest hunters, gatherers, trackers and providers to have ever walked the earth. Later, when Europeans arrived on the continent, women were again usually the hardiest of the pioneers, battling an untamed country, the ferocious elements, crushing isolation and often unimaginable hardships to keep their families alive on the land.

Today's Outback women continue that fine tradition of caring for their families, their communities, their land and their country in some of the most far-flung places in the world, well away from the services, support and levels of comfort that most of us take for granted. I'm delighted that, with the publication of *Women of the Outback*, we are now able to recognise the achievements of a number of them, and celebrate their successes.

The difficulties these women have often confronted have been many and varied. For some, it's the harshness of the landscape itself, devastated in places by seven long years of drought. For others, it's stock falling sick or having to be destroyed, crops failing, tourists staying home or prices for products slumping to ruinous levels on world markets, far beyond anyone's control.

Because, while Australia's Outback is a place of incredible beauty, vast horizons and wild nature in all its glory, living on the world's last untamed frontier can also be indescribably lonely, constantly challenging and with only one certainty: its uncertainty.

The women of Australia's Outback often end up with far more than their fair share of both joy and sorrow. There have been terrible accidents, and deaths of husbands, fathers and sons, which have left some women alone on the land, facing the decision to quit their homes and opt for a safer, more secure life in a town or city, or staying put and battling to make a go of things by themselves.

There have been doubters and naysayers who've often contended the Outback is no place for a woman, making it even harder for those who choose to dig in and work incredibly long hours to prove they're more than a match. Then there is also the terrifying isolation, the seasonal swarms of rats, beetles, mice, cats and wild dogs, and the vagaries of the climate: from dust storms to droughts to monsoonal rains to bushfire; from scorching hot days to bitterly cold nights.

Some women have found it hard-going to school their small children, but later even harder to send their teenagers to boarding schools, usually many hundreds – if not thousands – of kilometres away. Some have found it tough to combine caring for families and communities with running successful businesses, doing both against a heavy backcloth of guilt, feeling they simply aren't giving enough time to either. Others have struggled to maintain friendships when they live so far from everyone, and have no one to ask for help when it's most needed.

Some of the women in this book were originally city slickers who came to the Outback either by accident or design, and loved it so much they ended up making it their home. They might not have been able to tell a cow from a bull when they first arrived, but with determination, hard work and a passion for their new lifestyles, they've become experts in their fields. And, along the way, they've enriched everyone else's lives with their presence.

All the women profiled in the following pages are great examples of the inspirational courage, resolve, true grit and daring that have long characterised Outback women.

I've always believed that it is extremely important for each one of us to be an active participant in life and what's going on around us, rather than simply being a spectator. These women do exactly that. Despite the almost overwhelming odds each one has encountered at times, they've all managed, with perseverance, determination and daring, to make a real difference to the world in which they live.

With their care of the land and love of the Outback, they've also shown those who have no experience of their world the fierce beauty of the place in which they live, and how important it is for all Australians.

Janet Holmes à Court AC

INTRODUCTION

When I began this book, by far the biggest problem in writing about women in the Outback, I soon discovered, was that all the women live . . . in the Outback. And there's nothing like trying to visit them to really start appreciating the tremendous isolation that dominates their lives.

While so many have overcome incredible hurdles and shown astonishing courage in the face of almost unbearable odds, it's the vast distance most of them live from their nearest towns, cities or even neighbours that is simply staggering. As someone who lives right in the middle of a city, close to a supermarket that stays open until midnight and two minutes from a twenty-four-hour coffee shop, it's difficult to understand how many of these women can possibly survive in such remote, lonely, distant parts of Australia.

'But what would I want with a city?' one of the Outback women asked me, baffled. 'All those people, and that traffic, pollution, noise . . .' Another, when I marvelled that life could even exist in such a harsh, dry, barren swathe of the country, followed my eyes and said, 'I felt much the same when I first came here. But you learn to love it. When I arrived, I looked out and saw nothing. Now, I look out and see nothing but wild, savage beauty.'

After a while in the company of these fabulous, hugely enterprising and inspiring Outback women it was my privilege to meet and interview during the writing of this book, I began to understand a little of the lure of Australia's wide open places. Just a little. Because that isolation still throws up remarkable challenges.

For me, it was hard enough simply visiting them. Gradually, I completed a series of long journeys around Australia: a flight to Brisbane, then an agonisingly long drive to drop into the homes of two; a trip up to Darwin and a slow fanning out from the city; a flight to Adelaide, then Coober Pedy, then further and deeper still.

Eventually I was left with four women to visit whose homes were so far from anywhere that I despaired. Local travel bureaux advised me I'd have to find convoys to travel in, to even be sure of arriving at any of them safely. Another scoffed when I said I'd probably be able to change a burst tyre if I had trouble in a particular area. 'Last time I drove that road, I had six in one hour,' he snapped.

In the end, I had the bright idea of chartering a plane to visit them. The plane companies seemed as eccentric as the places I was trying to get to. One sounded promising but the receptionist said they'd have to get back to me on a price as the pilot was at his own birthday party. 'Nice,' I replied absentmindedly. 'Yes, it's very special,' the woman responded. 'It's his eightieth.' I chose another company.

While, yes, it was expensive, it probably saved me many weeks of driving and possibly months of standing by the roadside, struggling with tyres. It also provided a very special glimpse into the loneliness of many of my subjects' lives.

There's nothing like flying over thousands of miles of the undulating red sands of the Simpson Desert to reach a homestead to understand the enormity of one woman's decision to take on the running of her vast station when her husband was killed. It's a stunning experience, too, to fly hour after hour south of Alice Springs to capture a sense of wonder that another was able to live happily for so many years, completely alone, in a tiny house out back of nowhere.

Similarly, you begin to appreciate the staggering challenge it must have been for another to take on the task of turning a tiny speck on the map, amid vast plains of encrusted dried salt lakes, into a place that's become renowned around the world for its natural attractions.

I've learnt so much about the aching distances of the Outback after travelling around 18000 kilometres – the equivalent of Sydney to New York – to visit the women. But this unbelievable isolation produces women of courage, daring, resilience, enterprise and stubborn good humour in the face of all the terrible lows and dizzying highs that life hurls at them.

And apart from that, what do all the women in the following pages have in common? When I approached each of them, they all in turn said they didn't feel qualified to be in this book, among such august company. Thus the final quality they all possess in spades can't possibly be underestimated either: humility. This book is a celebration of their lives in the hope that they'll finally be acknowledged for what they are: the real heroes of a sunburnt country, our inspiring women of the Outback.

Sue Williams

1

Never Many Tears

GAYLE SHANN, *Moranbah, Queensland*

When 24-year-old Gayle Atkinson married 21-year-old Mac Shann, it was the happiest day of her life. The couple were surrounded by family and friends as they solemnly made their vows to each other in a picturesque whitewashed chapel overlooking the ocean on Queensland's dazzling Capricorn Coast.

'It really was a fantastic day,' smiles Gayle, her grey-green eyes shining with the happiness of the memory. 'We weren't too worried about it being perfect, which made us both enjoy the day. As a result, it really *was* perfect!' She stops and gazes at a photograph of the pair. She was gorgeous in a slim, elegant white silk gown, her honey-blonde hair pulled back off her face with a traditional veil and headdress, and Mac standing proudly beside her in a dark formal suit. Both look totally enrapt in each other.

Today, they still have that same look when they're in each

other's company and exactly the same soft smile; it's just that everything else has changed. For between that day and this, the devoted couple have been to hell and back following an horrific accident that almost cost Gayle her life and Mac, everything he held most dear. And it's an accident that continues to cast a dark shadow of pain, frustration and, occasionally, misery. But never any self-pity.

'No tears,' says Gayle, suddenly looking back up from the photograph. 'There's not been many tears, really. There never have been.'

One moment, Gayle and Mac were happily working together, building a new steel fence around the rundown homestead on an Outback Queensland cattle station they'd put all their time and every spare dollar into making a beautiful home and economic success. The next, Gayle's work glove caught on a release pin on the drive shaft, spinning the post-hole digger Mac was operating from the back of the tractor, and she was flung, like a rag doll, into the machinery and spun around and around.

The following few seconds were a blur of pain and panic. Realising how terrible Gayle's injuries would be, Mac raced for the phone in the house, knowing her only hope of survival lay with the Royal Flying Doctor Service. Not even sure whether she was dead or alive, he pleaded feverishly with the doctors to hurry. Meanwhile, a friend who'd been working with them lifted the unconscious woman carefully off the digger and carried her to the back of the house, placed her on a bed and covered her up with a blanket. He then took over on the phone.

Mac rushed immediately to Gayle's bedside, following the trail of blood, his heart sick with terror at what he might find. Before him, his beautiful wife of just two years was lying on the bed, her face ashen, her body writhing in agony. 'What happened?' she was asking in a soft moan. 'Help me! I'm in so much pain. Help me, can you move my right arm?' Mac leant over to catch her words and carefully lifted the blanket to help her. It was only then that he discovered the morning's shocking toll: the arm was completely missing.

But the torment didn't end there. In the two long hours it took for the Flying Doctors to reach the remote station, four hours inland from Mackay, Gayle could have died at any moment from the massive loss of blood from her injuries. And even when they arrived for the emergency airlift to hospital, they weren't sure she would live.

'Come and say goodbye to her, mate,' they told Mac gently before take-off. 'She might not make it.'

Gayle herself, perhaps fortunately, doesn't remember a thing from that time. 'I was conscious for much of the two hours until the flying doctor got here, but I don't remember it at all,' she says. 'Really, I wouldn't have imagined someone could possibly live for two hours while losing so much blood.' Incredibly, with her last breath before blacking out again, she told Mac to call a neighbour on a property 15 kilometres away who'd once been a nurse. That neighbour, Robyn Newbury, realised as soon as she saw Gayle that she was in danger of bleeding to death, and pinched her blood vessels together with her bare hands until the blood clotted.

When the doctors finally arrived – in a helicopter from Mackay, a plane from Townsville and an ambulance from Moranbah – they assessed Gayle's injuries as critical. Her right arm and shoulder-blade had been torn from her body, her left arm was broken in four places, four of her ribs and her left leg were broken, her nose was smashed, and she had cuts all over her body, including a gash across her face. The doctors operated for two hours at the house, sealing off Gayle's blood vessels in the hope she might survive the flight to Brisbane. Just before they put her into an induced coma to heighten her chances, they told Mac to say goodbye – just in case.

'I kissed her and said goodbye, which was so hard because in the back of my mind I knew that could be the last time I ever saw her,' says Mac softly. 'Of course, you're hoping that's not going to be the case. It was a scary moment and very worrying, but I didn't have much time to think about it – it all happened so fast.'

Once in the air, the doctors decided to change their route. 'Because my leg was really badly broken, it was blocking the blood to my foot,' says Gayle. 'They were worried I was going to lose my leg because the foot was turning blue, so they switched des-tinations to Townsville. That was very lucky for me. If I'd have gone to Brisbane, I probably would have stayed there and not had specialist treatment, but because Townsville didn't have a lot of neurosurgeons they later moved me to Sydney for treatment.'

By the time Gayle woke in hospital in Townsville and discov-ered the surgeons weren't able to sew her right arm back on, things still didn't look too bleak. With Mac sleeping on the floor in her room, she felt instantly comforted, even though she still couldn't move her left arm. A natural left-hander, she simply assumed it would recover in time, along with all her other broken bones. She underwent scores of tests and scans, and the doctors remained outwardly optimistic. But eventually, they broke the worst news imaginable to her family: Gayle's remaining arm was completely paralysed. The accident had wrenched all the nerve roots of her left arm out of the spinal cord, and it was unlikely she'd ever be able to use it again.

'My family didn't want to tell me straightaway and I never even assumed,' says Gayle, now thirty-two. 'I couldn't move it at all, but I think because it was very badly broken I didn't *try* to move it. Then eventually one of the nurses slipped up and said something in front of me and I asked "What do you mean?" My dad replied, "No, nothing," but I was saying, "No. Stop. What do you mean?" So then they told me.

'I think for Mac that was a breaking point. I don't think it was so much for me; maybe because I was on so many drugs! In some ways that's probably not a good thing, because you tend to bottle things up and it takes years to come out. But that's the way it was.'

Indeed, being told that Gayle had lost the use of her remaining arm was very tough for Mac. 'That was definitely the hardest thing to handle, for us as well as her,' he confirms. 'We were just about coping with all the injuries she had and then, all of a sudden, that came up. We all took it very hard.' The shock was so great, Gayle's mother Alison feared Mac might not be able to cope. 'Mac was devastated,' she says. 'But by the next day, he had put himself into gear and was just a tower of strength from then on. He could remember more than any of us what the doctor said, all the medical terms. It was really hard to select a time to tell Gayle about the second arm, but she overheard things that were being said, so then we had to tell her. She was devastated too for a short time but, like Mac, she took hold and accepted it. It was a really tough time for her.'

Nothing more could be done for Gayle in Townsville once she'd been stabilised and her immediate injuries had been treated, so she was flown down to Sydney's North Shore Hospital by the Flying Doctors. She'd lost such a huge amount of weight, the doctors had to constantly urge her to eat and the family brought in titbits to tempt her. Eventually, she got back onto her feet, after about two months in Sydney. 'It was just wonderful to see her walking again – I'll never forget that day,' says Alison. Mac and Gayle celebrated their third wedding anniversary in hospital, with the nursing staff holding a little party for them in the waiting room.

'Looking back, I think I did handle it all very well,' says Gayle. 'There wasn't ever any huge breaking point for me. All I could think about was the horse side of things – not being able to ride. It wasn't just the campdrafting that I'd always loved, but our daily life's work, mustering cattle and all that, revolved around horses.

'It wasn't really until I came home for the first time, out of the hospital system and away from the nurses doing everything for me, that I realised I had a lot more to worry about than just the horses! Daily care and hygiene and all those things had been taken away from me. And then those concerns took my focus away from me thinking about never being able to ride horses again. It was a big reality check.'

Growing up the third of four girls on the stunningly beautiful wetlands property Valley of the Lagoons, 180 kilometres inland from

Ingham, between Cairns and Townsville along the upper reaches of the Burdekin River, Gayle spent her childhood surrounded by horses and cattle. It ran in her blood. Both her mother, Alison Lethbridge, and her father, Alan Atkinson, were the latest in the line of long-time farming dynasties. Alan's great-grandfather James had been at the forefront of the legendary migration of pioneers, arriving in northern Queensland by bullock dray three years after he'd set out from the Victorian goldfields. His son Bob bought more grazing properties to add to the burgeoning empire, then his son Monty, Gayle's grandfather, developed the hardy and extremely successful Droughtmaster cattle breed. Alan was another chip off the block, breeding horses and becoming a part-time jockey. At the age of twenty-two, he was sent by his father to manage the Valley of the Lagoons, where Gayle and her sisters Kylie, Sherri and Robyn were all born.

'It was the most unbelievably picturesque, scenic property to grow up on,' says Gayle. 'I had the most wonderful childhood. The four of us would disappear on our horses for hours on end. We'd all ride down to the river and spend hours building cubby houses, racing, building cross-country jumping tracks on the sand, swimming and lighting a fire and cooking mussels for lunch. We had such a beautiful setting, and the freedom we had to enjoy it in was just wonderful.

'It's a very natural setting for me. I just love being on the land. Maybe when people have seen a lot of the city, they might be inclined to want to go there, but when you've been born to this lifestyle, you always want to go back to it. I just love it.'

Life wasn't completely plain sailing, however. Gayle's second eldest sister Sherri contracted polio at the age of fourteen months, and had to undergo a series of operations on her legs. Then it was a long time before the youngest, Robyn, started talking. At first, the doctors thought she might be deaf. Later, they discovered she had a severe intellectual disability. 'It was very hard,' says Gayle's mum Alison. 'As a mother, you can't help wondering what you've done wrong. Sherri was so sick as a baby, then Robyn had so many difficulties. It's heartbreaking watching your children struggle.'

For Gayle, the biggest trauma of her childhood was still in store – being sent away at the age of eleven to boarding school because there was no high school near, wrenched away from the land and confined to a classroom. For a child who'd revelled in her freedom and had become used to only her sisters for company, being surrounded by hundreds of other children and being forced to live by a strict timetable was a real culture shock. 'I was very shy, so it was terribly difficult for me,' says Gayle.

She began living for holidays when she'd return to her beloved Valley. Since there were no sons to help their father, each of the girls was taught to do everything around the property, and Gayle grew up strong and independent, breaking in and shoeing her own horses, and mustering cattle. 'It was wonderful work,' she says. 'Dad instilled a good work ethic in us all. He did everything using horses rather than helicopters and motorbikes, so it meant more people were needed to cover the big areas. He'd have big camps of workers and we'd go mustering. We'd spend two weeks at a time camped out in our swags, cooking meals on a fire, and one camp was close to a waterhole where we'd have a bath. In the middle of winter it was a bit chilly! But it was all such a great experience. It was one common to generations before us, but most people my age don't get to experience it today.'

Picnic races were also a big event in Gayle's life. The family would take horses to race meetings around Queensland, arriving two weeks before the start in order to train the horses. The last five or six days, when the crowds arrived, everyone would mix with other families.

Too soon, school would resume again, and Gayle would reluctantly leave home. She started out at Townsville and, when her parents separated and her mother left to live in Rockhampton, Gayle transferred to a school in the area to be closer. 'I remember at boarding school one particular term, I was feeling very homesick. It was in a very bad drought and I remember telling myself that if I didn't cry all term, it would rain. Even though I didn't cry, I don't think it did rain, but there've never been many tears from me since.'

Gayle did well at school, and her mum secretly hoped that she'd pursue her interest in agricultural science further. 'I tried to encourage her, but all she wanted to do was get back on the land,' says Alison. 'I think it was just in her blood.'

As soon as she was seventeen, Gayle left school and returned to the Valley to help her dad and her sisters run the property. Alan wanted them to have a variety of different farming experience, so they each left at various times for jobs on other properties, Gayle working with cattle all over Queensland. 'She was always a really hard worker,' says sister Sherri. 'She was passionate about horses, about cattle, and about life in general.'

In her spare time, Gayle began to go campdrafting, the traditional rural Queensland sport that has its origins in the early days of the Australian stockman. Then, horseback drovers had to 'cut out' a beast from a mob of cattle to put it in a separate yard, blocking its attempts to return to the mob. These days, the sport demands that riders separate out a beast from the yard, follow it through a gate into an arena and steer it around a course of turns before finally guiding it through a gate at the end. Points are scored by the campdrafter both for horsemanship and knowledge of, and skill with, cattle. The winning horse gains in value as a good stockhorse.

'You get terribly nervous when you first start doing it but as soon as you've had a go you want to have another,' says Gayle. 'Having that competition is quite appealing, wanting to succeed together, and it's a great feeling of achievement when you've bred the horse yourself or bought the horse young and broken it in and trained it. A lot of work goes into it.

'There are a lot of variables, too, because there's a beast involved. There can be bad luck with it doing the wrong thing, but much of it comes down to the skill of the horse and the skill of the rider. There are some quite serious accidents, though, which is often just very bad luck. The surface might not be great and the horses can slip over. We went to one event recently and they had three very serious falls – one girl broke her leg badly and two other girls were knocked out. But it's family-orientated, much more so than rodeoing, and kids go and compete. There's always a big party afterwards. It's great fun.'

It was campdrafting that brought Gayle one of her most cherished moments: meeting her soul mate, Mac Shann, at an event in March 1998 in Charters Towers. The pair were instantly attracted to each other. Mac, then nineteen, was taken with the 21-year-old immediately. 'She was obviously very beautiful,' he says, 'the most beautiful girl there. She was also very outgoing and friendly, and was from the same sort of background as me.' The feeling was mutual. 'He's so charismatic,' says Gayle. 'He was always laughing, giggling and being silly, and making everyone else laugh. His humour instantly appealed to me.' They seemed to have so many interests in common and both shared a deep love of the land.

The couple started dating regularly – or as much as was possible living seven hours' drive apart: Gayle in the Valley and Mac at Myall Springs, 170 kilometres west of Collinsville, on the southern reaches of the Burdekin. They filled in the gaps with phone calls usually a couple of times a day, with Gayle spending a small fortune on the pay phone her dad had installed for the girls and staff. 'I liked Mac from day one,' says Alison. 'Right from the beginning, he was like a son, the son I didn't have.' They soon also realised another link: Alison's mother and Mac's grandmother on his father's side had been close friends as teenagers, writing to each other all the time, and riding the two days to each other's properties.

Gayle and Mac met mostly at campdrafts, and then visited each other and helped out on the properties. 'Most of the time, I'd be in the truck with horses, which would turn it into more like an eight-hour trip to see each other,' says Gayle. 'I'd stay a couple of weeks and help with whatever they were doing at the time, whether it was cattle work or anything else. Then I'd come home and Mac would come to me and work for a couple of weeks. When we were mustering, we'd camp out, and he'd come to all of those because it was such a great experience.'

In addition, for a bush bloke, Mac seemed to be exceptionally gentle around women. 'He was very perceptive and thoughtful towards females,' says Gayle. 'He's the very opposite of a male chauvanist. Look, he's no angel either, but he'd always help me prepare the meals after working all day, and my sisters used to marvel at him. I was very happy to find someone like him!'

The couple got engaged in February 1999, eleven months after they'd met, and were married that October. Just before their wedding day, they had the chance to go skiing with a group of eleven friends in New Zealand and, short of money like any young couple starting out, they agreed that would serve as their honeymoon. It left them free to enjoy the whole wedding evening at the resort where they and their guests were staying at Yeppoon, and the next day before everyone left. 'It was a great wedding,' says Alison. 'They were very well suited.' 'We were both so happy,' beams Gayle. 'We had the most perfect day . . .'

For the first year, Gayle and Mac lived at his parents' place at Myall Springs, returning regularly to the Valley to help with mustering. Then Gayle's father sold the Valley and in September 2000 bought another property, Cantaur Park, on the Suttor River, 100 kilometres north-west of Moranbah, and asked Gayle and Mac to manage it. They moved in within the week. It was everything they'd dreamed about and worked towards for so long: a property to manage on their own, working side-by-side, to create the perfect home and business.

When the rains come, the 117-square kilometre Cantaur Park is a stunning property, rich in green pastures and well able to support upwards of 3000 cattle. In drought, the deep ochre of the earth strains through, a vivid contrast against the sapphire sky. Beneath that crust lie deep seams of black and yellow gold.

The area within the Bowen basin, in the hinterland south-west of Mackay, is rich in natural resources. Today, the road west from the coast is pitted with vast mines all opened up and extended as part of the current boom in resource prices to power the industries of China. On closer inspection, a black and tawny mountain range in the distance turns out to be a row of massive slagheaps. Gold was discovered in nearby Clermont in 1861, also the site of the first copper mine in Queensland, and the Blair Athol coal mine, 22 kilometres to the north, produced its first coal in 1864, and is now Australia's largest exporter of thermal coal. These days, the drone of light aircraft over the area, constantly looking for fresh resources to exploit, strikes fear into every dedicated farmer's heart.

The mining companies didn't approach Gayle and Mac, so they were left alone to care for 2500 cattle and around twenty-five horses on the gently undulating hills of their property. As a result, they were able to throw themselves completely into improving the place. 'It was very run-down when we came,' says Gayle. 'We did a lot of work and put a lot of time into the basics that weren't done. Structurally, the house was good, but it had been badly neglected, so we sorted that out. There was a real shortage of water here too, and we had five very big dams put in within the first six months. We then laid pipes for water since there was no water to the garden, the sheds or the cattleyards, and we brought our own Droughtmaster breeding herds down from up north. We've also done a lot of improving of the soil, light ploughing to aerate it and planting seed to create hardier and more fattening pasture. The place was set up enough with the fencing that we could muster all the paddocks on our own.'

While the couple worked hard, they also played hard. They wanted to continue campdrafting and, in order to fit that in, usually travelled at night to venues after their work was done for the day. They'd load the horses onto the trucks at 7 p.m., arriving at their destination at midnight or 1 a.m. Then it would take a couple of hours to set up electric fences for the horses and feed and water them, before they were finally able to lie down themselves and snatch a few hours' sleep, camping on the ground or in the back of the truck. 'You'd have a late night travelling, then a late night partying, but we had plenty of energy,' says Gayle. 'Life was very busy and quite chaotic, but it is for most people today. And we couldn't complain – after all, the campdrafting was self-inflicted!

'We had a big responsibility put on us to manage Cantaur Park, but that was exactly what we wanted. We'd worked in this industry all our lives, although it's a bit different when you're in charge of everything that's going on. The book work, for example, was a bit of a shock to the system! But we liked the responsibility. It was exactly what we wanted. There was just the two of us, and we worked well together. We were very happy. We felt we couldn't be luckier.' That luck was finally to run out, however, early on the morning of 9 August 2002.

Returning home to Cantaur Park from hospital in October 2002 was excruciating – and not just because of Gayle's injuries. More than 4000 hectares of the station's land had burnt out at the end of 2001 and, with Australia in the throes of its worst drought in a hundred years, there'd been no chance for any new grass to grow. In addition, there'd been prolonged periods of much higher temperatures than had ever before been experienced, so the soil was bone dry. There was enormous heat stress – and hunger – among the animals, and the gross value of farm production was forecast to fall by around 20 per cent that year. Badly drought-stricken, yet with so many head of cattle, Cantaur Park wasn't being spared. Feed prices were sky-high and there was nowhere to send the animals, since the whole of Queensland and New South Wales was in exactly the same position. The survival of the fittest demanded drastic measures, and Mac embarked on a heartbreaking program of shooting cattle.

For Gayle, on top of everything else she'd endured, it was acutely depressing. The tears still didn't come, however – perhaps it might still rain if she didn't cry. From someone who treasured her independence so dearly, she was now totally dependent on Mac for everything: from getting her up in the morning to helping her shower, dress, clean her teeth – even putting on her make-up. Usually, she'd manage to laugh at the mini-disasters during Mac's 'training'; the occasions when her make-up came out a mess, as well as the times when she longed, like any other woman, to restyle her hair after an unsatisfactory trip to the hairdressers, but had to put up with it instead. Only rarely did she think of giving up.

'There were probably times when I did; more so when I was in hospital, and then soon after, but never seriously,' she says. 'You have those thoughts but I never got to the point where I was consumed by that. Everybody would have those thoughts at some stage. Before I got hurt, I remember that at times I would see someone in a wheelchair and think that if something like that ever happened to me, I wouldn't cope, and most people would probably think the same thing. But I really believe that people don't realise how strong they are until something goes wrong. It's easy to say, "No, I wouldn't cope, I'm fiercely independent, I wouldn't let my husband do anything for me". But when you don't have any other choice, you either cope or you give up altogether.'

Gayle's family, friends and neighbours rallied round, buoying her spirits enormously. A working bee was held on the property to finish the garden fence Gayle and Mac had been erecting when the accident happened, and the women of the neighbourhood called by to clean the house from top to bottom. After a month of Gayle being home, everyone from the region then organised an event they christened the 'Moranbah Muster' to raise money for the young couple. An astounding 400 people attended the function and bid in a silent auction for a variety of donated items, from jewellery to artwork. Country singer/songwriter Graeme Connors provided the entertainment.

'I've never cried much ever, but there were tears when Graeme got up to sing,' says Gayle. 'He sang one song about a young girl, born and bred in the bush, who went home and worked in the mustering camps with Aboriginals. So many things were similar to my life that it was very emotional for me. It was the most wonderful evening. It really made me feel better about everything.'

She wasn't the only one. The local community had aimed to raise $60 000 from the event. They ended up with over $200 000.

Today, five years on from that time, Gayle Shann moves easily around the house at Cantaur Park, opening the large sliding drawers in the kitchen with her bare feet, doing the accounts on the computer with her toes on the oversized keyboard on the floor or with a voice-activated program, and carrying her pack of pills in her teeth to Mac. He takes them gently from her mouth, pops a pill from the silver paper and places it on her tongue, pouring water into a special cup, with a straw, for her to drink. At meal times, the couple sit close together at the end of the table, Mac feeding her a mouthful from his plate, then himself, then her. It's an intimate scene; in any other circumstances romantic even: two people working in perfect harmony to build as good a life as possible with each other, for each other.

With the funds raised from the Moranbah Muster, the house was gutted and completely rebuilt around Gayle's new needs; plus time, material and labour was donated from businesses all around the area and co-ordinated by the industrial organisation Masterbuilders. 'I saw a piece in the local paper about them having trouble finding tradesmen to work on their house, so we thought we would help out,' says Wayne Pelling, the regional manager of Masterbuilders, North Queensland. 'We went out there and realised we'd have to completely make-over the house, so in the end, members went out all the time to help. I think Gayle's courage and her fighting spirit touched everyone. Lesser people would have crumbled and thrown in the towel, but it was obvious that she was drawing on inner strength which was so impressive. And the thing that touched us the most was the wonderful relationship and tremendous caring and love that Mac demonstrated. It felt such a worthwhile project to help them.'

As a result, the rebuilt homestead is airy, light and open plan, with a screened outdoor area, sensor lights that go on at night when anyone steps out of their bedroom to use the bathroom, doors that push open when anyone leans on them, and user-friendly taps that turn on easily by foot.

Just outside is a new lap pool where, with a little help, Gayle can float in the water, free of pain, looking up at the sky and the birds, and dream. One of her most devoted companions is her little dog Tuffy who, ironically, has also learnt to live with a dis-ability. He was scampering around the garden one day when a woman employed to help around the house was mowing the lawn, and a sharp stone flew straight into his eye. Like Gayle, he copes. It isn't easy, though. This afternoon, Gayle has a slight cold and has to keep sniffing as her nose is running. As soon as Mac draws near and notices, he wipes her nose for her. The rest of the time, she manages as best she can.

All around the walls of the house are photos of Gayle and Mac, Mac and Gayle. There's the beautiful photograph of her winning a campdrafting event, steering her horse with skill, a fierce determi-nation and passion. There's a picture of the couple brimming over with happiness on their wedding day. And there are trophies and cups the two have won in easier times.

Yet, as far as she can, Gayle tries to lead a normal life. The pair still argues – 'Yes, we're like any normal couple, we have our fair share of arguments, but the only difference is, I don't storm off to the pub afterwards!' says Mac – and they still go camp-drafting. They've just bought a big live-in trailer they tow behind the truck to make the experience more comfortable. 'Originally, I didn't want to have anything too flash, because then you're expected to do well,' she laughs. 'When you turn up in an old bomb and you do well, then you surprise people, although it didn't always work out like that! But it has improved our life ten-fold.' She attends now to support Mac in the events, who often rides her horses. Sometimes, she's called on to be a judge too, something she's only just starting to get used to. 'It's scary; I don't really like it,' she confesses. 'I wish I was more confident at it, but maybe that'll just take time. Everyone hates the judge . . .'

Above all things, Gayle has learnt patience. She's had to endure a series of long operations on her left arm, one surgery a world-first. Sydney's North Shore Hospital neurosurgeon Dr Michael Biggs carried out exploratory surgery for nine hours, then worked for seventeen hours to swing the – ironically – healthy nerves from her right side by her missing arm, across the top of her chest to her left side. There, the nerves were all dead from having been pulled out of the spinal cord, so the living right-hand nerves were attached to her damaged left arm. As a result, from having no sensation or movement at all in her arm, Gayle can now flex her elbow a little and move a couple of her fingers. 'She'll undergo a few more orthopaedic procedures to enhance the feeling, and there's a chance that will help,' says Dr Biggs. 'You never know. There's always hope.'

The doctor was inspired to do the very best he could by Gayle, so impressed was he by the way she was coping. 'She's a very unique woman,' he says. 'I was just amazed. I thought she was going to fall apart psychologically from the trauma, but that never happened. She always remained so optimistic about the future, and strong and resolute. She's a wonderful person.'

While she still doesn't have much movement in her arm, Gayle is nevertheless happy that it's a lot better than anyone thought it might ever be. 'Before, my arm completely flailed; it was a dead weight over which I had absolutely no control and it used to dislocate out of my shoulder if I took it out of a sling, whereas now it's got some of its own muscle to hold it in place,' she says. 'So the surgery was successful in a lot of ways. But it still makes it difficult to be as active as I want to be. Realistically, I don't think I'm ever going to get much function out of it, but they are doing surgery now to get the absolute best out of what's working.'

As a thank you gesture to Dr Biggs, Gayle named a horse after him when one of the mares foaled the day she had the first gruelling operation. He was pleased, although looked bemused when, twelve months later, she had to break the news he'd just been castrated.

Debilitating headaches were another problem, until doctors found fluid leaking from Gayle's spine where the nerves had been torn out. Three more operations fixed that up. 'But nerve pain is my number one problem,' she says. 'I get phantom pain in the amputated limb, but that's nothing compared to the neuropathic pain in the paralysed limb. The nerve roots were pulled out of the spinal cord but my brain still tries to send messages to the nerves and then it can't work out what's going on and thinks it's a problem, so it creates pain signals.'

Unfortunately, that pain, and the periods during which it's particularly intense, may never cease. Medication helps control it and Gayle has also tried listening to relaxation tapes to help her sleep. Since the accident, due to the bouts of pain, she's never slept a complete night through – which is particularly hard to bear when she remembers how she always used to sleep like a log. As one tactic, she's had a TV installed in the bedroom to help her distract her mind. 'I'd often wake up early and not be able to go back to sleep,' she sighs. 'If you've got nothing else to think about, you start concentrating on the pain and it intensifies.'

Around the property, Gayle helps out where she can. The couple are getting more involved in breeding Droughtmaster stud cattle and horses, like her grandfather before her, and, since their first Monty Atkinson Genetics Droughtmaster sale in December 2002, that part of the business has grown tremendously. She's been back on a horse too, although she has to be extremely careful at this stage. She's even able to help muster on a four-wheeled motorbike, modified so she can steer with her feet.

'The vehicle gave me back some independence as it's hard not being able to go outside on the land otherwise,' she says. 'Frustration is my biggest enemy, because it's difficult to sit back and watch other people do everything. I was never that sort of person but now I don't have any choice. But what can you do? You want to be happy. You can't be down in the doldrums all the time. What I struggle with the most is when Mac's really busy and I feel like I'm making his life busier by loading him with extra things. I have to be patient and just do what I can.'

Yet Gayle still counts herself lucky in the scheme of things. She's relieved the couple didn't have to move house, closer to the city or, as she most feared, that she wasn't put into a nursing home. At first, she was even a little anxious Mac wouldn't stand by her. In hospital, one woman she spoke to who also lost an arm in an accident was dumped by her fiancé the very next day. 'Those kind of things are always at the back of your mind, but I was fairly confident that Mac would stick around,' she says. 'Now I am optimistic about the future. The fact that Mac has taken on the care involved has enabled us to both stay where we are, where we've done so much together. A lot of husbands might not have.'

While the pair planned vaguely to start a family, that may never happen now. 'We haven't made a final decision but I just feel it would be very, very difficult,' says Gayle quietly. 'I would need someone full-time to help and I think the frustration of that would put me over the edge in a lot of ways, watching someone else hold my child when I couldn't. It would put more pressure on Mac as well. We'd never talked about it; I just assumed that somehow we would do it and even when we were modifying the house I had in the back of my mind to make it easier for kids. It wasn't until we both actually talked about it three years down the track that Mac said it wouldn't be the end of the earth for him if we didn't have children. I just assumed naturally that he would want to – and of course he does – but he just feels the same as me that it would be too much. But you never know!'

It's inspiring to be in Gayle's company. Cheerful and upbeat, she's always looking for the bright side, for the laughter, in her situation. A vague acquaintance who hadn't heard what happened saw her with her paralysed arm in a sling one day, and didn't notice the other was missing. 'She made a joke about Gayle breaking her arm, laughing about it, and Gayle just went along with the joke,' says her sister Sherri. 'The woman still didn't work it out, but Gayle didn't mind. She's very confident and content in herself. I don't think she gives a blue hoot about what anyone else thinks.'

One exception, however, was when Gayle and Mac featured on ABC TV's award-winning *Australian Story*, and their tale was subsequently voted the all-time best show, on the tenth anniversary of the program in 2006, by all the people who'd also featured on it over the years. She was completely overwhelmed. 'I think everyone was touched by such a beautiful love story between a young married couple in the face of so much suffering,' says the show's executive producer Deb Fleming. 'There's something transcendant about the pair, with Mac so dedicated to Gayle, and Gayle just so luminous. It struck the deepest chord within us all.

'Despite being the most urban nation in the world, people do seem to look to the bush for higher virtues of inspiration and for overcoming adversity and real spirit. There's a marvellous Outback tradition of people who show exceptional stoicism and resilience.'

Of course, even though Gayle is tremendously resilient, it must still be hard to keep smiling at times. But she nearly always manages – in public at least. 'I always knew that Gayle was strongwilled, but the way she's coped has been absolutely amazing,' says her mum. 'To see Gayle and Mac now, totally involved in a social life, in everything that's happening around them . . . They've never sat at home feeling sorry for themselves. She's incredible.' Sherri agrees. 'Gayle just doesn't have down days at all,' she says. 'She keeps very busy, running the business and doing a lot of office work on her computer, so she never gets bored. She is extraordinary.'

Gayle herself begs to differ. The rehabilitation centres she attended after her accident made a lasting impression. 'Some of the people you see there make you realise there are many worse off than you,' she explains. 'One particular young fellow, he was nineteen at the time, had meningococcal disease and had lost all four limbs. They'd put some sort of acid on all his remaining body to kill the disease and he looked like a burns victim. He's one who sticks in my mind. He'd been through hell and back. Also, some people I met there had no one, no family. I couldn't imagine what being put through that system would be like if you didn't have someone there. I was lucky. I had Mum, all the other family and, of course, Mac.'

Mac has always been the solid, quiet presence that gives Gayle so much strength. His voice grows gentler when he talks about her. 'In the early days, she would get a bit overwhelmed at times, but certainly in the last four years, she doesn't have many down times – not that she shows anyway,' he says. 'She's certainly very courageous. No doubt she gets frustrated at times with the things she can't do, but she's great to handle things as well as she does. I think this has made us closer; you can count the days on two hands we've been apart in five years, and I don't think there'd be many relationships like that. Gayle's still basically the same person I met, fell in love with and married. She's very special.'

But his wife still insists there's nothing particularly special about her. 'No, I don't think so,' she says, shaking her head. 'People don't give themselves enough credit for their strength until a situation arises when they need it. But I do think people who are born and bred in the bush might be a bit tougher because they see gruesome things in their lives, like the death of animals. But for us, we're lucky in that we have each other. Without Mac, I'd be lost. I picked the right one there. We're very happy.'

2

A Deadset Legend

MOLLY CLARK, *Old Andado, Northern Territory*

After crossing thousands of kilometres of undulating red dunes, the tiny plane dipped down somewhere in the middle of the vast Simpson Desert and bounced along a stony airstrip. The passengers clambered out, the fierce heat punching the breath out of them, wondering where on earth they were.

Around them, they could see nothing but coarse red sand, rolling off into more endless dunes, sprinkled with clumps of wiry spinifex, stretching all the way past the horizon. The air was still but for the buzz of a million flies descending on the thrill of fresh prey. There was nothing, and no one, in sight.

Eventually, the faint drone of a car engine sounded somewhere in the distance. Slowly it came closer until finally there was a crunching of the brake and the creak and slam of a door. 'There you are!' called a voice. The group of four started. 'You're late!' it scolded. 'I thought you were never going to get here.' The four stood silent, in a state of shock, as an elderly woman slowly hobbled into view.

'Well, what are you waiting for?' she barked impatiently. 'The chops are on and they'll burn unless you get a move on.'

It was their introduction to the legendary Outback pioneer Molly Clark, who'd been living alone in the middle of the desert in a ramshackle 1920s homestead for the past twenty years.

It was certainly never Molly's intention to end up living on her own, completely isolated from any kind of civilisation, deep within one of the most barren deserts on earth. More than 330 kilometres south-east of Alice Springs – yet with no connecting road – and close to the very centre, geographically, of Central Australia, it wouldn't be many people's idea of a habitable location. 'But you never know what life's going to deal you,' says Molly sharply. 'And you just get on with it.'

Molly Clark first came out to Andado as a 33-year-old in 1955 with three young sons. She hadn't wanted to take the job she and husband Malcolm, known as Mac, had been offered managing the property that, at around 10 850 square kilometres – the size of Lebanon – is the largest privately-owned cattle station in the southern hemisphere. But after two years at another property in Tennant Creek, Mac felt it offered a welcome challenge and boundless potential. The owners had offered the further induce-ment that if the couple could make a go of it, they could pay the dividends on the place or buy shares into it. That tapped right into Molly's dearest dream: to one day own a property of their very own. 'Because they said that, we knew, one day, we might be able to own it,' remembers Molly, now eighty-five. 'That was very smart of them. It makes you work harder. You turn yourselves inside out to make something a success.'

At first, they looked right on track. There were years of half-decent rains in Australia's driest desert, and the 5000 head of cattle fattened up nicely on the grasses. The old tin-roofed homestead, nestling among the dunes on the Finke River floodplain, was sweltering in the summers and freezing cold during winter nights, but it served them well enough. For the kids it was a childhood idyll: a backyard bigger than anyone else's in the world.

When the rains came, however, they would sometimes settle in, and a few times the homestead ended up completely surrounded by water, cut off from the old timber saddlery, bakehouse and equipment sheds nearby. Each time, the foundations would grow a little weaker, and the whole place become a little more difficult and costly to maintain. As a result, Molly and Mac decided to build another homestead, a bigger one but still pretty basic, on higher ground, 18 kilometres to the west. They transferred the Andado name to this new building, and moved there in 1960.

Life in such an isolated spot was hard, but no harder, Molly insists, than for any other Outback woman looking after a family and around fifteen station hands at any one time. 'The challenge was to stay alive. Isolation never bothered me; you just worried if anything happened to the children, would you be able to get through? Otherwise, it's exactly the same as in any other place. You get good days and bad days, the weather can be very frightening, with big storms and things, and you wonder if you're good enough to be able to cope with it all. But that's no different to any other woman in any station. You're not just the woman back there, you're a mother, a housewife, a cook, a nursemaid, a companion, and a help maid to every jackaroo and probably half-a-dozen Aboriginals every day. Then you're a governess and a teacher as well.' Molly, with the help of the School of the Air, taught her three sons herself: Graham, born in 1947, Kevin in 1950, and Philip two years later, only sending them away to school for the last three years of their education.

'We didn't see it as tough or otherwise. It was just a life, a lifestyle; it's what you wanted to do. If you choose to be a minister's wife, then you lead the life of a minister's wife. I happened to choose to be the station wife, so there we are. You're cooking, cleaning and washing and looking after everybody. But that's a valuable position.'

As if she didn't have enough on her plate, Molly also hatched an ambitious plan to bring in money to help tide the family over during drought time. The old homestead, now rechristened Old Andado – meaning 'stone knife' in the local Aboriginal language – had begun falling down, so she decided to shore it back up and restore it to its original state, for it to be opened to passing tourists as an example of a real pioneer home. 'People told me I was mad, that it wouldn't work, that I couldn't do it,' says Molly. 'They said no tourists would want to see it, and it was just all rubbish. But I wanted to give it a go.'

For Molly was nothing if not determined. When she had an idea, she was dogged about seeing it through, often badgering other people until they'd agree to join her. Always sharp-tongued and quick-tempered, she would never put up with any nonsense or much human failing, being so capable herself. 'She's just a genuine pioneer,' says long-time friend Chris Tudor, the head teacher of St Philips College in Alice Springs. 'She's very determined, but also very smart. If something goes wrong, she deals with it, and if there's something to be done, she gets on with it.' This time was no different. Whenever she had a spare few hours, she'd drive down to the site and put in as much backbreaking work as she could manage. Slowly, very slowly, she was recreating the home she now remembers so fondly.

It was in 1975 that all Molly's hopes and dreams began to fall apart. Her middle son Kevin had a terrible car accident that left him fighting for his life in hospital; he only just survived. Then, three years later, Mac suffered a heart attack while flying his light plane to check on cattle. He made an emergency landing and sustained no injuries in the crash, but his heart became too weak to keep him going. He died the following week.

Nine months later, tragedy struck once more. Molly's eldest son Graham, thirty-three, was driving a truck across a railway line at Pimba, south of Woomera, one evening with his little daughter Meegan in the cab beside him. His wife, six months pregnant with their second child, had driven on ahead. Too late, he suddenly noticed the freight train bearing down on them, and he attempted to swerve away. The train caught his side of the truck. He died two days later in hospital in Adelaide.

Yet, even in her grief, there was little reprieve for Molly. Across Australia during the late 1970s and 1980s there was an increasing awareness of diseases among cattle, most notably TB and brucellosis. The government feared that infected herds could easily spread the illnesses to healthy animals – particularly in the Northern Territory, where cattle were often allowed to roam unfenced – and thus jeopardise future beef export prospects. Brucellosis especially was an invidious disease. The bovine strain multiplied bacteria in cattle's reproductive organs which in males often reduced fertility, and in females triggered abortion, stillbirth or the early death of calves. It could also spread to humans, known as undulant fever. The Commonwealth, State and Territory governments embarked on a rigorous program to slaughter herds they believed to be infected, and eradicate the disease.

When the order arrived at Andado that Molly's entire stock be destroyed, she argued vigorously that her cattle were free of the disease and that the frenzy to slaughter stock was more to do with politics than the health of livestock. The United States wanted a greater share of the meat trade for itself, she claimed, and to halt the decline in exports from Argentina. 'Brucellosis has been in stock since pussy was a cat,' she says. 'But the dirty work went on and Australia, like idiots, went into the campaign and nearly ruined their whole industry trying to sort it out. It was a load of hogwash. They just didn't know how to handle the situation. It was a load of crap!'

It's understandable why Molly was, and remains to this day, so angry. All 5000 of her cattle were shot, and she was ordered not to keep any more on her land for another three years, until the government could be sure there was no more risk. Just two years off owning Andado outright, she was suddenly ruined. The value of the station plummeted and, with no stock to keep, she had nothing to do, no income and no prospect of any for the next three years. 'I asked the government, "What are we going to do?

If we can't have cattle, what is there for us?" They said, "Oh, you can take a job." But how can you take a job when you are hundreds of miles away from where there might be a job?' The only thing to do was to sell Andado to try to recoup some of her losses.

But even that was an extremely hard ask. 'I had to sell it, but I couldn't sell it,' she says. 'What did they expect you to do: starve? It wasn't real funny to have a place you've worked on so long just taken away from you. No one wants to buy a place, especially in the middle of a campaign like that, particularly somewhere with no stock and a place you can't put stock on. It took us three years to sell, taking all my savings, and finally it was bought in 1985. The boys tried to find something else they could do, and somewhere to live; one of them had a family, the other one didn't.

'So finally it was just me left here. It had been our lives for over thirty years, and then you've not got anything – you're just left standing.'

Fired with rage and burning with disappointment, Molly travelled 1830 kilometres up to Darwin to confront the Chief Minister about the situation. It was too late for her stock, but she felt it wasn't too late for her. She argued vigorously for compensation, with little success, but then asked for approval for a Special Purpose Lease for Old Andado, to allow it to be used as a full tourist operation. That was immediately granted. 'I suppose it was better than a kick in the pants,' she says wryly.

When Molly had sold Andado, she was careful to retain ownership of a 45-square kilometre block around Old Andado. She moved all her possessions back into the old homestead and set up residence there, among all the old keepsakes on display. It was

1986 but, apart from electricity and a Royal Flying Doctor Service radio for contact in emergencies, she was living as if she was back in the 1920s.

When tourists found out about Molly at Old Andado, many were keen to meet her and see a perfect working replica of a traditional homestead. Molly erected dongas, demountable cabins that worked as a bunkhouse for visitors to stay in, and an area with facilities for campers. It added hugely to the allure that Molly was actually living in the home, and would cook breakfasts, lunches and dinners for visitors, or sit down with them for a cup of tea, as well as giving them a personal tour of the house. 'I'd cook whatever I'd got,' she says. 'Chops, spaghetti on toast, anything. I don't have a corner store so I can't go and get anything from there. They have to make do.'

If visitors were lucky, and she was in a good mood, she'd also talk about her past – growing up in Mount Barker in South Australia, a nursing career cut short by a bout of TB, going wool-classing in Outback New South Wales, then taking a job as a governess at Mungeranie Station on the Birdsville Track where she met and married ringer Mac.

Pilot and photographer Damon Smith has dropped in on several occasions over the years, often waiting on the airstrip for Molly to drive over and pick up her guests, depending on what she was busy doing, or cooking, at the time. 'You'd usually get a roast or corned beef, mashed potatoes, overcooked vegetables – whatever she had in the freezer or in tins in the pantry – and endless cups of tea,' he says. 'She'd cook on her wood stove, even in summertime, so it could become very hot in there, and she'd do eggs and bacon for breakfast.

'She was quite set in her ways, and you'd have a bit of a dig at things and try to get her revved up a bit. She had very firm views on life and how things should be run, and opinions like all politicians being bloody no-hopers. People dropping in was part of her life, and Molly made the place. She was its heart.'

The corrugated iron and timber house itself, originally built by grazier Robert McDill for his new wife Eleanor Lucy in 1922, is fascinating. With a dark eat-in kitchen, lounge room and couple of bedrooms, it's instantly evocative of another era. In the long, narrow kitchen is the big old range, fired by wood, to cook and heat water, with a huge selection of tin pots on top, next to an ancient kerosene fridge. The pantry is still replete with a selection of ancient jars and tins, and clumsy, free-standing wooden cupboards hold plates, cups and cutlery. At one end, by the only windows, is a table and chairs all around, and an old wooden highchair for a baby stands against the wall. Cabinets tacked perilously to the walls contain prized items of china along with a variety of novelty salt and pepper shakers, while oil lamps share space with Akubras hanging off the walls.

The small lounge room similarly has walls of bare corrugated iron, without any windows to let in the light, and a fireplace with an old clock, family photographs, a vase and a selection of kitsch ornaments on the mantelpiece. An overstuffed lumpy floral-patterned sofa, scattered with cushions, and an armchair sit in front of the fire, while next to it is a straightbacked chair, a mean layer of thin carpet and a small, worn rug underfoot. The main bedroom is barely bigger than the bed, allowing room only for a wooden chest of drawers with a mirror above, its surface cluttered with a hairbrush, hand mirror, more photographs and trinkets sitting on lace doilies. The only addition to the 1920s décor appears to be a small reading light and a main electric light with a modern fitting attached clumsily to the tin wall. A second bedroom is crowded with a chest of drawers and cupboards, as well as a narrower bed.

The place is a real living museum, albeit a little more worse for wear than most. The harsh elements, however, make its survival a minor miracle. The temperature during the summer months often soars well past the 40 degree Celsius mark; there are regular plagues of rodents and beetles; and occasional floods still eat into the foundations – waves were actually slapping against the building in a big wet a few years ago. In addition, the dry, hard red sand periodically assails the walls and then whips through the house in a dust storm, leaving everything ochre in its wake.

But there are hardy materials here. Posts for the fences are made of the extremely hard wood from the rare waddy trees, *Acacia peuce*, which grow only in three locations around Australia: here, in Birdsville and in Boulia, south of Mount Isa. With the trees growing tall – up to 17 metres high – and living for around 500 years, the quality of their wood made them the choice of 1880s surveyor Augustus Poeppel when he was putting in mile posts to mark out the borders of South Australia, Queensland and the Northern Territory in the Simpson Desert. A protected grove of waddy trees lies 30 kilometres to the north-east of Old Andado and is named, in memory of Molly's lost husband, the Mac Clark Acacia Reserve.

Regular visitors include the Outback Camel Company, with

its tourist treks across the desert. Owner Andrew Harper likes to use Old Andado because of the atmosphere of the place and its history as the starting point of explorer Dr Cecil Madigan's camel expedition across the Simpson Desert from Andado to Birdsville in 1939. 'I think Molly likes having the camels around as a link with that history,' says Andrew. 'She's a very decent person, obviously hardworking, and someone who likes people who get stuck in and have a go, which probably reflects her life.'

Close by the house, there's the pretty timber and hay roof saddlery that has been left distinctly leaning by the floods, an old butchery for slaughtering cattle, and the ruins of a turn-of-the-century wagon next to a variety of rusting old vehicles. Molly's red Landcruiser also sits nearby, the vehicle she always drove when going to Alice along an Outback track she herself pioneered – a journey that could take her anything from four hours to fourteen, depending on how many times she became bogged.

Local photographer and musician Barry Skipsey has a fierce respect for her driving skills, born out of experience and sheer terror. Back in 1994, he agreed to follow her from Old Andado to Alice but, even in a much later-model four-wheel-drive, he found he just couldn't compete with the then 72-year-old. 'I quickly learnt that she drives like a bat out of hell,' he says. 'We tried to keep up, but her dust trail seemed less evident with every kilometre. I just didn't feel comfortable driving at her speed so I ended up slowing down to a much more moderate 100 kilometres per hour.'

Molly's new business venture steadily became a huge success, particularly as four-wheel-drive tourism took off, and now, astonishingly, around 1000 visitors, mostly day-trippers, call in a month at the isolated outpost. 'You know most of that fuss is because you're alone, and people can't get over the fact that a woman can be out there on her own,' says Molly. 'But I had the Flying Doctor radio, I could put out the SOS if there was something really wrong and somebody would come. It might take a few hours but it would be okay. You think, if something went wrong in Melbourne, it could take you hours to get to hospital and then you might wait hours for a doctor to see you. So out there, it's often easier.'

Her granddaughter Meegan Sullivan, who survived her father's fatal crash and is now thirty-three, vividly remembers staying with Molly during holidays, spending her days playing in the sand dunes and the afternoons often helping make tea for visitors. 'She was very busy with tourists and we loved to be left alone to explore,' she says. 'Then we'd help Nanna make pots of tea and wash up afterwards. Nothing had changed there in so many years. It was always the same from the time we first went, even to now.'

In 1993, the homestead was given a heritage listing and a Northern Territory Tourist Commission Brolga Award. 'It showed all those people who said it couldn't be done,' Molly says with satisfaction. 'People are interested in our history. They want to see.'

Yet Molly wanted to do more to demonstrate how people survived in the Outback. Throughout the 1980s, she'd become captivated by the massive national fundraising effort to establish the Australian Stockman's Hall of Fame at Longreach, central-western Queensland, which was finally opened by the Queen in 1988. On a visit there, however, she was shocked to find how many men were honoured, but how few women.

'There was all this talk of Mr this and Mr that, but where were all the Missuses?' she declared. 'It's high time we recognised that

Australia was built by men *and* women working together. Living in the Outback, it doesn't matter whether someone is killed or there's an accident or a bite, burn or kick – they all come back to the women. At times like that, you're the one who has to deal with it. You read about the building of Australia and how Mr Smith done this and that, out droving, selling stock and fixing fences, but there's no mention of Mrs Smith who was left behind and kept things running. Without her, most of the work in building wouldn't have been done, so how about telling her story?'

She felt the Hall of Fame had largely overlooked the trials and triumphs of pioneering women in the bush, so came up with the idea of establishing an equivalent hall of fame, this time exclusively for pioneer women, in the Northern Territory. 'Everyone else was all talk, so I thought, Why don't I do it? It took me a long time to get enough courage to think that I could do it as I haven't got any PhDs or anything like that, so I thought I wasn't qualified enough. But when I spoke to several people about it, they jumped at the idea.'

At a public meeting in Alice Springs in 1993 she outlined her vision, and kicked off her own fundraising effort. 'She had the idea and the concept of how it would work,' says Chris Tudor, who got to know her when she served on the board of the Alice Springs school, originally a residential college for Outback kids. 'She just wouldn't give in to opposition.' Shortly after, another proud Outback tradition was born – 'Molly's Bash' – a fundraising Mother's Day weekend party with plenty of bush music and food, held once a year at Old Andado. With the arrival of the phone to Old Andado finally in 1996, it became even easier for Molly to organise. Its tenth anniversary, in 2003, brought more than 500 people to the remote property. In 2006, it was rained out, but 2007 was another huge success. 'It's now a permanent fixture,' says Chris. 'Kids from the school go out there and help clean up the place and support it. Molly is one of the school's recognised Outback achievers, so we'll always be involved.'

Molly was never so keen on the party, saying she preferred solitude, and she was even less keen on the phone and the progress it ushered in with it. 'I wish I didn't have it now sometimes. We had two little solar panels on the side of the house that operated the phone. Then this new-beaut idea came,' she says sarcastically. 'They wanted to put this huge dish right up against the house. I had a big argument with the workman, and I told him if he didn't shut up and take it where I wanted it, he wouldn't put it up at all. It was a pioneer set-up; I didn't want a great big modern structure like that sitting up against the house!'

Soon after, the National Pioneer Women's Hall of Fame opened in its temporary home of Alice Spring's heritage-listed old courthouse. 'Molly was very determined,' says Helen Joraslafsky, its current manager. 'She gets an idea and runs with it, and often succeeds through the sheer force of her personality. Her brain and her mouth have never slowed down.'

Molly travelled throughout Australia promoting her cause, attending fundraisers, talking to the media, government agencies and anyone who might listen – and make a donation. As a result, the hall started getting bigger and better, with exhibitions commemorating the contributions of more than one hundred women, including Deborah Wardley, the first female pilot for a main airline; Rosie Kunoth Monks, the first female Aboriginal film star; Edith Cowan, the first female member of an Australian parliament; and

Peg Christian, the first veterinarian to establish a practice in the Territory. Other notables are Ida Standley, who in 1914 was Alice Springs' first schoolteacher, and widow Isobel Price who drove sheep 800 kilometres with her four teenage children and set up a station in a rough bark house in the 1920s. The hall is also acquiring and maintaining an archive of individual pioneering women's histories, literature, historical records, photographs, manuscripts and oral history recordings, as well as a collection of pioneering women's art and crafts and a library of reference books. The databases now contain the stories of more than 1200 women.

The museum was finally moved to its permanent home in the town's old jailhouse and re-opened officially on International Women's Day, 8 March 2007, as one of only three women's museums in Australia, besides the Pioneer Women's Memorial Folk Museum near Brisbane, and the Pioneer Women's Hut at Tumbarumba, New South Wales.

'It's a good feeling to see it get out of the courthouse because we had so many exhibits we couldn't display,' says Molly. 'The displays here are beautifully set out.' As befitting the occasion, Molly was also presented with a special achievement award from the government for her sterling contribution to Australia's pioneering heritage. 'It's just that women deserve recognition for their part in building Australia,' she says. 'We just get on with the job.'

But the museum is all credit to her, her vision and her resolve to see it through. 'Molly has always been a very strong lady, very determined and she's achieved so much in her life,' says Meegan. 'She has a strong personality and never gives up. She doesn't tolerate fools and has always adhered very strongly to her beliefs. She's quite incredible.' Barry Skipsey agrees. 'Her reputation for being a woman of feisty substance always preceded her, and probably still does. She's never been as media savvy as, say Sara Henderson, but her story is just as compelling. Like many of her time, her life, her tenacity and her character were honed from basic necessity.

'But what an extraordinary life of pioneering! Yes, she can sometimes be a little abrasive and cranky, but she's a deadset legend. I reckon they broke the mould when they made her.'

For Molly, the triumphant opening of the museum was still a bittersweet occasion. While she was thrilled at establishing it, she was heartbroken that, after more than fifty years out at Andado, she was finally forced to leave because of ill-health and failing eyesight. She'd argued that she was still well enough to stay, but friends and family wouldn't hear of it and moved her into a house in Alice Springs where she's able to have help.

Molly still lives in hope, however, that one day she'll be able to persuade a carer to come back with her to Old Andado, so she can once again take up residence in the old place. 'I'd still be out there all the time if I could,' she says sadly. 'I just can't get anyone to go out with me now. There's no TV, and people can't seem to live without TV. I had a radio at night-time – you couldn't get it during the day – but now you can get radios that pick it up at day too . . .'

Sitting in her house in Alice, Molly's face is lined and weathered by all those years in the sun and desert, her hair is a shock of white and her tiny body a little stooped, but her pale-blue eyes still twinkle with delight while looking back on her life. 'She's much frailer now, and it was a tragedy when she lost the sight in one eye, but she'll never give in,' says Chris. 'She's feisty and a real rough diamond, but she's also very kind. When I was sick a while ago, she sent me cards and a DVD – all thoughtful things. From being in the bush so long, she has this real idea of the importance of everyone supporting each other. She's one of those ladies of the bush to be congratulated . . . and occasionally feared!'

These days, Molly has seven grandchildren and five great-grandchildren. Meegan recently moved back to Alice Springs from Adelaide, so she could get to know her grandmother better, and help preserve Old Andado with the formation of the fund-raising Friends of Old Andado. The homestead is still exactly as Molly left it, a caretaker is now installed most of the time, and visitors are asked to leave a small donation towards its upkeep. Molly continues to have sadness in her life – she lost her second son, Kevin, in 2001 – but her mind is as vigorous as it's ever been, and her tongue no less sharp. She's still scathing about city life, and city people.

'It would do a lot of people good if they were sent out to Old Andado to live for a while,' she says. 'They're so soft these days, they can't do anything for themselves. If there's a problem, bush people just get on with it, but city people throw up their hands.' She puts on a high, girlish voice to imitate them: '"What will I do? I can't cope!"' She laughs in derision. 'Look, there are no chal-lenges living in a city,' she says bluntly. 'Most people there don't want a challenge because they wouldn't know what to do with it. They get up in the mornings and go to McDonald's for breakfast. They have to be seen down the street. They have to have every-thing – this and that, always bigger and better and the latest, all the music and everything – but they're never home to use them or listen to it. So why do they want these things? They're just show ponies.'

As for herself, Molly insists she's quite the opposite, and that's plain to see. She still doesn't see anything special about herself; she was merely dealt a certain hand in life and simply did her feisty best. 'I just got on with it,' she says. 'I did the best I could.'

3

Love Can Be Blind

NELL BROOK, *Birdsville, Queensland*

The beautiful young South African wrote to her Australian pen-pal to tell him the exciting news that she was about to visit his country. 'I'm flying to Perth,' she penned. 'Is it easy to pop over to Birdsville from there?'

Nell Schulenburg had absolutely no idea what she was in for when she fell in love with a man living in the most remote town on the Australasian continent. When he finally flew her there in his own plane and pointed out the family cattle station, sprawling over a vast area of 8000 square kilometres, she still couldn't quite comprehend what she was seeing. Even when she learnt that the only means of communication was by letter or telegram, that there was very little bitumen on the roads and the electricity supply was erratic to say the least, she still refused to be put off.

'They say love is blind,' laughs the woman who has today

become a key player in keeping the local Birdsville community surviving and thriving. 'I was so excited about everything. I think they must have been right: love is indeed blind.'

From the air, it's a tiny speck interrupting hundreds of kilometres of absolutely nothing in the middle of nowhere. As one of the most isolated places on earth, slap-bang in the middle of the vast burning emptiness of Central Australia, Birdsville truly is out back of beyond. Where four of the most barren deserts on the globe all end – Sturts Stony Desert, the Simpson, the Tirari and the Strzelecki – it's a town quivering on the edge of the Never Never, the very last frontier to oblivion.

But down on the ground, Birdsville, together with its legendary pub and races, is an icon that looms large in Australian imaginations; a haven since the late-nineteenth century from the harsh desert that surrounds it, and a symbol as weatherbeaten as the Outback over which it presides.

For 23-year-old Nell Schulenburg, that vision of extreme isolation in the far south-western corner of Queensland, close to the borders of South Australia and the Northern Territory, held no terror. After all, she only had eyes for David Brook, the man born and bred in the town, whose grandmother had once owned the renowned Birdsville Hotel.

They had a lot of catching up to do too. They'd actually met when Nell was fifteen and David seventeen, a long way away from both their homes, each on their own school trip to Europe. The two groups ate in the same restaurant halfway through those 1965 excursions, then went on the same night tour of Rome, Nell sitting behind David on the bus. David still has his diary entry from that evening, saying how he'd met some beautiful South African girls, one of them named Nell. The next day, there was a call to the girls' hotel: David would like to write to Nell, could he have her address? Nell, who loved writing anyway, gave it and from then on a long-distance friendship was born between the pair.

At first, their correspondence was mostly Christmas cards, but curiosity about each others' lives gradually grew. They couldn't have been more different. Nell was the youngest of four children in a loving bilingual Afrikaans–English family headed by a well-respected surgeon and a nurse, who counted the pioneer heart surgeon Dr Christian Barnard among their closest friends; David was the only child of an Outback stockman, whose mother died when he was just nine years old. Nell grew up an archetypal city girl in a rambling old house in Pretoria, the bustling administrative capital of South Africa, 50 kilometres north of the country's largest city, Johannesburg; David lived with his father behind the general store in Birdsville – population thirty-five – 1200 kilometres north of the nearest city, Adelaide, and 1600 kilometres west of Brisbane.

In addition, Pretoria sits in a well-watered, fertile valley surrounded by the hills of the Magaliesberg Range, 1370 metres above sea level, its city streets lined with brilliant jacarandas. Birdsville, in stark contrast, is one of the flattest, driest, reddest places in the world. And while Pretoria was in the grip of the apartheid regime of the old South Africa, David spent his childhood playing with the Aboriginal kids of the area. As a six-year-old, he appeared in the landmark documentary *The Back of Beyond*, about the old Birdsville Track mailman Tom Kruse, and learnt from an Aboriginal elder how to make animal tracks in the sand with his hands.

But they say opposites attract, and Nell and David kept up their communication for many years. Their long correspondence suddenly switched up a gear, however, after Nell graduated from the University of Pretoria with an economics degree, a year's scholarship in the United States and a job as an air hostess with South African Airways. She'd always loved flying, and David, already a keen pilot of small Outback planes, was by then also doing some work as an agent for Trans Australia Airlines, one of the two major Australian domestic airlines, later sold to Qantas.

Nell wrote to him, saying she might visit Australia, but fell ill with hepatitis and was forced to delay her trip. With time on her hands as she recovered, their letters became more frequent, and more serious. Then, lying in bed one day, recovering, her brother walked in behind an enormous bunch of flowers. The card with them read, 'Get well soon, love, David'.

'Who can they be from?' asked Nell, puzzled. 'The only David I know lives in Australia.' Her brother rang the florist and discovered the flowers had, indeed, been ordered from overseas. 'That's probably the best bunch of flowers he's ever bought,' she laughs today. 'From those flowers, and the letters, I knew I wouldn't be serious about another guy until I'd actually met up with him again.'

Nell and David's next meeting finally came in January 1973, when David visited South Africa to go on safari. The attraction was immediate and mutual. David was charmed by the tall, elegant woman who was, at the same time, so full of life and fun. For her part, Nell was impressed by the good-looking young man, self-assured and articulate, yet well-mannered, gentle and kind. Their next rendezvous was in Perth when she flew in with her job. Then followed a crazy whirl of courtship, with Nell sending telegrams to

David telling him when she'd be in Australia next and where, and he immediately flying to her destination city to meet up. 'It was quite hilarious and busy, but all pretty exciting,' says Nell.

Finally came the big step. 'I think you'd better come and look at Birdsville,' he told her during one visit. 'You should see what it's like.'

Birdsville completely underwhelmed the first European explorer to stumble by. Charles Sturt, after whom the desolate desert to the south-east of the settlement is named, was unimpressed, describing it as a 'desperate region having no parallel on earth'. The hapless William Wills, on the doomed 1860 Burke and Wills expedition from Melbourne to the Gulf of Carpentaria, was only a touch less scathing. He merely noted the huge number of birds in the region, including, startlingly, seagulls attracted to the salt lakes nearby, which ended up giving the place (originally called Diamantina Crossing after the river that sometimes flows nearby) its final name.

It took another twenty-five years for Birdsville to bounce back from this early bad rap. Originating as a depot for surveyors working in the Simpson Desert, a rail head was opened in 1884 at Marree, 520 kilometres to the south. Gradually drovers and station owners in western Queensland realised that this offered the best route for transporting cattle to the markets on the coast. As a result, they all congregated in Birdsville, then took around a month to walk their animals down the Birdsville Track stock route to Marree. To capitalise on this sudden flood of pre-Federation traffic, the Queensland government set up an inter-state customs collection point at Birdsville since it was only ten kilometres to the border with South Australia. By the late 1880s, the town was enjoying boom times, boasting 300 residents, two hotels, three stores, a bank, a doctor and a magistrate.

David's great-grandparents on his mother's side moved to Birdsville in 1885. Then, in the early 1900s, his grandparents managed Annandale Station for cattle king Sir Sydney Kidman, who at one stage owned over one hundred stations and more than 2 per cent of the whole of Australia. When drought closed the station, the couple returned to Birdsville to take up the Royal Hotel and later the Birdsville Hotel and shop. In 1942, their daughter Dorothy Gaffney married a young stockman from Adelaide, Bill Brook, who had begun his working career on the area's Cordillo Downs station – once the largest sheep station in Australia. After leaving Cordillo Downs, Bill worked other cattle properties, regularly riding at the Birdsville Races, and in 1939 bought a 500-square kilometre block of desert country west of the town. Gradually, he added more land until his holding topped 8000 square kilometres. Eventually, Bill was also to buy Cordillo Downs for $1.2 million, the end result of a lifetime's patient and steady accumulation of cattle and land; not at all bad for a stockman who'd started work there being paid thirty shillings a week.

David was born in 1947 and, after his mother's death, Bill sent him to boarding school in Adelaide. Seven years later, at age sixteen, he returned to the Outback, driven by the dream of keeping the family's strong Birdsville legacy alive. He started running the store in town selling groceries, living out the back and, by the time he reached his early twenties, he had taken over managing his father's first property, Adria Downs.

It was early in September 1973 when David and Nell's Birds-ville rendezvous finally took place, the pair travelling together on a commercial flight to Broken Hill where David picked up his plane to continue to Birdsville. It was the time of the renowned Birdsville Races, when horses and spectators came from all over Australia with visitors sleeping in swags under the shade of cooli-bah trees, and thoroughbred horses and their trainers kicking up dust everywhere. Nell was fascinated, while the locals were simi-larly intrigued by her. A friend still has a photo of her at those races, a striking woman in a bright scarlet blouse with sheer sleeves and a vivid green shorter-than-short miniskirt amid a sea of denim and check shirts.

'But the place felt right for me,' says Nell. 'As a child in South Africa, I can remember going to the bush veldt with my family and always loving it. One of my sisters had married a farmer and we often went there for winter holidays, camping in the bush, sitting around open fires at night, which I always liked. And, growing up looking at an atlas, I'd always been interested in Australia; I don't know why.'

As a teenager, Nell had eagerly devoured novels by Australia's pre-eminent romance novelist Lucy Walker, whose stories always revolved around innocent young women – a governess, nurse or an overseas visitor – falling in love with a tall, handsome stockman or property owner. Unwittingly, Nell was becoming a character straight out of one of those books. After three days in Birdsville, David asked Nell to marry him. She didn't hesitate.

David then flew to Pretoria to ask her parents' permission, and preparations began for their wedding in February 1974, just thirteen months after they'd met for that second time. 'From the day we met to the day we married, we probably weren't in each other's company for more than three months,' says Nell. 'I actually worked it out: I guess it was just meant to be.'

After the wedding in Pretoria and a honeymoon on board the ship returning to Australia, Nell, just twenty-four, came to Birds-ville to live. For the first six months the town was totally cut off from the outside world after the Diamantina River rose to record flood levels. She didn't exactly fit in seamlessly with Australian Outback life, either. She still had her smart wardrobe from her days spent jetting around the world and always cut a conspicu-ously chic figure around town. Her cooking for the stockmen became very much an exercise in pot luck, when she invariably chose the wrong cooking method for the various cuts of meats, roasting rump steak, boiling sirloin and barbequing brisket. 'But they were very diplomatic about it,' she reports. She also raised eyebrows the first time she had people over for dinner and served them roast meat with a pot of apricots, in true South African style, in place of the vegetables. Getting used to doing all the cleaning, cooking, washing and ironing for the two men in the house, since they were all tasks left to the servants back home, took a while too.

Even the language presented difficulties. 'To tell the truth, I really struggled in the first six months understanding what people were saying,' she confesses. 'Everyone spoke too fast, mumbled or didn't say anything at all. I also found the bush culture difficult; not opening your mouth unless you had something sensible to say, to keep the flies out. And it took a while to get used to the long silences in stock camps and, just when you were leaving, the issue you'd come for would finally be discussed or decision made.'

But, after a few false starts and regular visits from her parents, Nell adapted magnificently. The family home began to exhibit a real African flavour, with Nell's collection of animal carvings, paintings, photographs and cushions made from traditional patterned fabrics. The community welcomed her, since David and his family were so well respected. 'I just embraced life here,' she says of her arrival thirty-three years ago. 'There must have been times when people thought, Who the heck has David brought to Birdsville? but I was just so excited about this new life. It was nothing like what I'd been used to or grown up with. I could have stayed in South Africa and lived next door to my mother, however, and still been desperately unhappy. But I can't remember ever once sitting down in Birdsville crying and saying I wanted to go back home. I was happy here from the moment I came.'

Living in such a completely different environment did demand a radical mind shift for Nell. There were no regular freight services to the town, with perhaps a delivery arriving only every three months – if you were lucky. There was barely any bitumen on the 1600 kilometres of road within the Diamantina Shire, which, at 95 000 square kilometres is one of the largest local government areas in the world, and twice the size of the entire country of Denmark. The power supply was irregular, there were only two airconditioners in the house, and the summers, with maximum temperatures averaging 41 degrees Celsius, could prove suffocating. David and his father often slept outside on the verandah in order to take advantage of any breeze, but that was a notion totally foreign to Nell after a youth spent in a country where security was uppermost in people's minds because of omnipresent tensions.

'In South Africa we always used to lock the house at night, but they didn't here,' she says. 'That was quite difficult to get used to. It took David six months before he could get me to sleep on the verandah. I just couldn't do it. I guess I was just so used to locking myself up at night.'

There were also the six major dust storms a year. With frequent strong winds and little ground vegetation, the clouds of dust roll in and blanket everything in red dirt. Everyone simply has to sit each one out. Then there were the rat and beetle plagues, particularly difficult to cope with for someone used to living with a modicum of sheltered gentility. 'It's a life of extremes here: extreme heat, extreme dust and extreme isolation,' says Nell. 'I now tell people, if you have any emotional baggage, you're going to have to deal with it. There's nowhere to hide from it here. You've got to be happy within yourself, and happy where you are.'

Not that Nell had much spare time to fret, anyway. She'd been married about six months when the manager of David's general store came to see him. 'Well, you've got a wife now,' the woman said, 'so I'm going to resign.' As a result, Nell immediately found herself behind the counter, serving each day, as well as helping David run Adria Downs, and then a neighbouring property, Kamaran Downs, which David and his father bought the following year. With David also active in local government (elected on the local council at the age of twenty and later to spend thirteen years as mayor), Nell was quickly corralled into all manner of community activities. 'I think in my innocence I was given a lot of jobs, and felt I had to agree to them all,' she says. 'I didn't know much about sitting on committees and things, but I soon got used to it. For instance, David was secretary of the local race club, so I had to become part of that. Because I came to that bush society, I became Australianised very quickly.'

The local community, in turn, warmed to her. 'I like to think I might have been a refreshing change,' she says. 'It was interesting for others seeing this girl come in to join them who wasn't a local. I never really felt that people thought I was different. I guess because I didn't know how people lived in the Outback or what I was expected to do, I just did my own thing. I never felt isolated. I was never frightened of the land. The place just became a part of me. I came to love it.'

There were still the occasional frustrations, however. When Nell went down to Adelaide for a pregnancy check-up in 1975 and discovered she was having twins, the only way to contact David was by letter or by the Royal Flying Doctors' telegram service, where a message would be read on air and recorded by the nurses at the local hospital, and then finally delivered. With the nearest telephone in Bedourie, 180 kilometres away, Nell had little choice. By the time the telegram had been through all the channels, David was pretty much the last person in town to learn the news. He couldn't understand in the interim why everyone was smiling so broadly at him.

The twins Deon and Dalene were the first of six children to be born to the couple, shortly followed by Anthony in 1977, Gary in 1980, Karen five years later and, finally, Jenna, two years after that. With only twenty-one children in the local school, Nell became involved with the Parents and Citizens' Association, serving as secretary for an astounding nineteen years. She also undertook a great deal of fundraising within the local community for the school and for the various charities around the area, as well as for the provision of local services. The group raised hundreds of thousands of dollars – enough money for both a swimming pool and an extra building at the school.

'We made things happen,' says Nell. 'We started a play group, so we were fairly involved with that, and then of course there was the school. I was also involved with the Isolated Children's Parents' Association and was part of the social club and race club. I was quite involved with raising funds for the Royal Flying Doctors Service too, Frontier Services, the hospital . . . I don't think you can live in a small town and *not* be involved with community events. Otherwise nothing happens.'

Under David's stewardship and with Nell's help, the Birdsville Races were also growing to the point where it had become a major date on the Outback calendar. Both David and Nell served on the races committee, with Nell president of the race club for five years. People from across Australia now head to the town for the two-day event, swelling the tiny settlement's regular population of just one hundred up to 6000. The lonely outpost is transformed into a hive of activity, the pub bursting at its seams, the airfield chock-a-block with over 200 planes and swags and horses everywhere; it's become one of *the* sights of Australia.

Friendships have always been important to Nell, with long letters helping sustain her. In Birdsville, one of the first people she befriended was remote-area nurse Jo Laurie, who quickly became a close confidant. She even introduced Jo to builder Kym Fort, who later became her husband. 'Nell always had a genuine interest in other people, and made a real effort to get to know them,' says Jo. 'People warmed to her as she was very open and generous, and had a great presence about her. She also had a great sense of fun. If there was any dancing to be done, she'd be the first onto the floor.'

There was a surprisingly busy social life to enjoy, since a few families had kids the same age. With no TV, movies were flown up from Brisbane for a big Saturday-night showing, and there were regular social functions to attend. Always a close family, Nell and David would spend as much time as they could with their children, taking them down to a Diamantina River waterhole – nicknamed the Wool Wash – for a swim, playing games together at home, visiting Adria Downs or flying off to see friends.

'She's always been a really dedicated, exceptionally good mother,' says another close friend, Adelaide midwife Robyn Davies, who had her child at the same time as the twins, and went on to help at the birth of Nell's other children. 'She's fiercely loyal and loving. She's very supportive of all her children, and of David and everything he's wanted to achieve, to the nth degree. In the same way, she works extremely hard for the community too. At the races every year, they put up around sixty people on their block and feed them and look after them, without ever thinking of themselves.'

Living in such isolation could still be difficult, however. With no high school in Birdsville, the hardest decision was sending the children away to Adelaide to school when they each reached twelve, and then attending their major functions while juggling the needs of the other children back home. 'I don't know if Mum ever got over having to send us away,' says Dalene. 'She would only see us for eight weeks a year at home, and I think that was one of the hardest things she had to do.' While the separation was tough for the children too, they could all laugh about their unusual lifestyle. Early on, when the twins were small, they were on their way to a Christmas tree party at Bedourie. Deon got into his seat on the plane, strapped himself in and asked glumly, 'Why can't we be like everyone else and drive?' 'To him, that would have been much more exciting,' laughs Nell.

But, gradually, life in the town was changing. The arrival of the radio telephone in 1976 made communication much easier and life a lot more relaxed for Nell, with David so often away working on one of their properties. When arriving back late one night after crashing his plane – he was, happily, unhurt – Nell ordered a radio for their home so that she wouldn't have to wait alone in dread, not knowing for hours, ever again.

The Birdsville Hotel has long been a treasured symbol of Australian life, standing up against all the harsh elements and surviving . . . almost. Built in 1884, it had a long and colourful history until burning down in 1979, with an electrical fault thought to be to blame. The day before, an offer entrepreneur Dick Smith had made on the pub was accepted by the owner, but his telex confirming the deal didn't arrive till the next morning – when the bar was just a smouldering ruin – so the sale didn't go through.

Faced with losing the town's only pub and a national treasure with an iconic status secondary only to the Opera House, Harbour Bridge and Uluṟu, a consortium of businessmen bought it, which later came down to a partnership between Nell and Jo's husbands, bringing it back into David's family once more after a fifty-year hiatus. Rebuilding and restoring the gutted building to its original turn-of-the-century facade entailed a huge amount of work, but they used the opportunity to add an eating area and extra rooms, while still retaining its traditional atmosphere. It became a true labour of love. 'It is a wonderful place, and we like to think of it as a real locals' pub,' says Nell. 'It means visitors can come in and really get a feel for what it's always been like. It's important for Birdsville, and for the Outback.'

Nell still had an appetite for new challenges and, in 1984, her long-time love of flying led her to take lessons to learn to fly herself. She saw it as a way of gaining a greater degree of independence, and imagined she'd spend many happy hours flying around the bush, landing on tiny hidden airstrips. As it turned out, she ended up doing more flights to major centres, like trips down to Adelaide, outings to have the plane serviced and flying between properties. At the same time, it did enable her to represent the community at many functions and events, as well as fundraising for local services, and it soon earned her the moniker 'the Birdsville Flying Mum'.

'It was really good for me since it was something only I could do,' she says. 'You are so busy with your children and your family, I suppose, and then all of a sudden I was doing something that only I could study for, only I could fly the plane and only I could land it. It was enormously liberating.'

Just one more thing that Nell did extremely well, believes the former Quilpie parish priest Father Jeff Scully, who became a confidant. 'She was always a wonderful mother and wife, but also a very good businesswoman – she didn't muck around. She could be brusque, and doesn't suffer fools gladly, but she is also a very kind, profound woman. And to have raised such a wonderful family in a place that's the remotest of the remote . . . On the big issues, she's something of a giant.'

The town was soon in for a shock, however. That same year, conservationists began talking about applying for a World Heritage listing of the Lake Eyre Basin in which Birdsville is set. As the world's largest salt pan, covering 1.17 million square kilometres of Central Australia – 17 per cent of the entire continent – some believed the wetlands and their fragile environment should be protected. Most of the pastoralists, on the other hand, felt that a listing would unreasonably limit what they could do on some of the best grazing and 'fattening' land in the country, and could even end up forcing them off. The rows rumbled on until 1993, when the issue was re-ignited by Paul Keating's election campaign promise to have the idea of the listing revived.

Many of the locals, including Nell and David, teamed up to fight the proposal, as well as another to introduce cotton farming on the Cooper Creek, until the government finally ended up backing off. It had been a long and tiring three years, but there was another positive outcome. 'What it did show us was that we had to go out there and tell people how very special this area is and how well we're actually caring for it ourselves,' explains Nell. 'Then David and a few other people got together and said, "Well, we are actually organic because we have no pesticides, and we don't use any chemicals". So we started this process of learning how to market our own beef, and selling it as certified organic.'

It was a stroke of genius for the area. Twenty other cattle producers joined Nell and David, and together they set up the company OBE Beef in 1995, producing organic beef not only for Australia, but for export to Asia, Europe and America. The day they started selling hamburgers to America was particularly sweet.

'We are passionate about it,' says Nell, of what's become the largest organic beef project in Australia, if not the largest in the world. 'We think it's a good thing for the earth and for the human race, and we're able to do it. It's hard work but I think it's also something for the next generation to strive for. Now, you've got all the communications and can travel easily, so you get to know your international markets and learn about other cultures as well. We have Japanese customers that come out every year; we've had a group of women from Taiwan; and we recently went to Hong Kong, Taiwan and Seoul in Korea to talk to them about our beef. It's so rewarding.' Eldest daughter Dalene currently works for the group too. 'It's always been managed very conservatively as farmers are a conservative lot, but it is very successful,' she says. 'We're now in so many markets across the world.'

Everything, once again, was going splendidly. But Nell's happiness wasn't to last.

On the afternoon of Anzac Day 1996, Nell's eldest son Deon called her from Windorah, 390 kilometres east of Birdsville, where he'd had the helicopter he was flying serviced. He was just leaving for the family's Cordillo Downs property to do some aerial mustering the next day, and was then to come home for a friend's wedding. 'Have a safe flight,' Nell wished him. They were the last words she was ever to say to her son.

Around sunset, she received another call; this time from Deon's boss, the station's manager. He hadn't arrived, and he didn't seem to be contactable on the radio. David, Deon's brother Gary and a group of stockmen began looking for him, while Nell stayed by the radio through the night. No one was too worried, though. Deon was an excellent and experienced pilot, and radio problems were all too common. Even if he'd had to make a forced landing, he'd probably simply camped for the night.

The next morning, a full-scale air search was launched and David, Nell, Gary, his elder brother Anthony and a friend took their plane out to look around an allotted area of the grid. To their horror, they spotted the crumpled helicopter below, radioed the rest of the team, then circled until another rescue helicopter landed. The medic scrambled into the wreckage, found Deon's limp body and pronounced him dead. It was just three months before his twenty-first birthday.

'We were looking down, hoping he would appear from a creek and everything would be all right,' says Nell. 'But he didn't. And as terrible as it was, it felt right that we were there together. It felt right. It was a privilege that it was us who found him.' They left the site in silence. 'Nell said later that one of the toughest things she's ever had to do was to not break down, knowing that David still had to fly the plane home,' says Father Scully. 'It wasn't until they landed at nearby Mount Leonard Station that they let themselves enter into the moment.'

From that station, Nell rang Birdsville and urged Deon's friends to continue with their wedding, despite the tragedy. As the ceremony started on the Big Red, the massive sand dune just out of town and one of the largest natural dunes in the world, an eagle swooped down, much lower than anyone had ever seen before, and circled them. 'It was so low, they had to stop for a minute,' says Nell. 'Later on, we all agreed that we felt it was Deon coming to say he was okay.'

The funeral five days later became an occasion for the entire

Birdsville community, with 120 cars joining the procession to the cemetery on a small sandhill just by the town. Deon was buried in a spot with the best view of the Birdsville Hotel. During the ceremony the same eagle returned, and perched nearby, watching. Since then, Nell and David have seen that eagle at least one hundred times. The sight always affords them some comfort amid their ongoing grief.

'The moment Deon died, the life we knew died as well,' says Nell. 'It's like you're reborn into another life. You're like a baby again. The first year, if someone says to you, "Eat!" you eat, and then after about three months you learn to lift your head up, then to sit up, and then, finally, to walk. You have to learn to live again. And you have to do that with your family; you can't forget your other children and your parents who are also grieving. Anyone who's ever experienced grief has been down that pit.

'But at the same time, I think it finetunes your capacity to experience human emotion. It also gives you the resolve to recognise and experience joy, even in a fleeting moment, looking at a beautiful sunrise or sunset.

'After Deon died, I probably got a bit angry at times when I saw people not appreciating what they had. I now try to celebrate every moment.'

Now, Nell, fifty-seven, sits on the ground by Deon's grave, reflecting back over her life at Birdsville. She comes here often to pay her respects to her son, and friends and family often join her and David on Anzac Day every year, to mark the anniversary of his death. As she sits, the familiar eagle flutters down to land on one of the trees planted on what would have been Deon's twenty-first birthday.

Nell isn't maudlin, however. She likes to remember Deon as he was: a spirited young man who loved flying, farming and loved life. His loss in the accident, the cause of which remains a mystery, was a massive blow, but she hasn't allowed it to overshadow everything she's achieved and has yet to achieve.

The death of her father the next year from cancer and her mother's death in 1999 were also blows, but Nell managed to use that grief to reaffirm her commitment both to her faith and to life generally. These days, she's still as vital a part of Australia's most faraway community as she ever was.

She and David, still living in the same house where his parents lived, are dedicated to their family – Dalene, thirty-two, works with OBE in Brisbane; Anthony, thirty, is back on the land managing Cordillo Downs with his wife Janet and their three young children; Gary, twenty-seven, is the executive officer at the School of Natural and Built Environments at the University of South Australia; Karen, twenty-two, has her own design business in Charleville; and twenty-year-old Jenna is studying animal science at the University of Western Sydney. At the same time, Nell and David are still working hard on OBE Beef to bring it to even more tables around the world, as well as in Australia. They've added another couple of properties to their portfolio too: Murnpeowie Station on the Strzelecki Track in 1998, and another in Goondiwindi in 2006, bringing their holdings of land in the Channel Country to more than 30000 square kilometres, the size of a small country like Belgium or Taiwan. That brings its challenges. The properties require more than 4000 kilometres of fencing alone and, one year, along the whole 1200-kilometre span of their land they had not a single drop of rain.

While Nell and David remain devoted to each other – and in 2004 returned to Rome's Trevi Fountain to relive their first school-days meeting – both also manage to pour enormous amounts of energy into keeping Birdsville (population now 105) on the map. The hotel has recently undergone a fresh renovation, with the old eighteen rooms refurbished and nine new rooms added to increase the amount of accommodation available in the town. It's retained an extremely welcoming Outback atmosphere, and continues to be frequented regularly by locals as well as tourists, many of them four-wheel-drivers stopping off after completing the Birdsville Track. 'Nell's helped build it up into even more of an icon,' says Robyn Davies. 'It's now something incredibly special in the middle of a really dry, unforgiving landscape. Whatever she decides to do, she gives it a really good go.'

Increasingly visitors to Birdsville are persuaded to stay a while too, dropping by the museum, art gallery, historic cemetery and the local billabong, home to hundreds of native birds and rare waddy trees. Most take the opportunity to drive out of town to the Big Red, which intrepid four-wheel-drive enthusiasts love to try to conquer. The town offers plenty of twenty-first-century comforts too, like cappuccino from two coffee shops and a variety of meals from five food outlets. The hotel also serves a full menu of meals and good coffee in a very relaxed atmosphere.

That's a tradition Nell is determined to preserve. Although the partnership has now put the hotel on the market, feeling it's time for someone else to take up the challenge, they've turned down a number of good offers from over-eager entrepreneurs who want to fill the place with poker machines and cash in on one of the world's most isolated oases. Instead, they're holding out for a buyer they believe will care for the essential qualities of the gracious stone building with its high ceilings and eclectic collection of memorabilia on its walls: army insignia on one from all the units that have passed through over the years, and broad-brimmed hats on another from anyone who's stayed in town more than a year. Tourists wishing to take photos have to put a gold coin in the charity jar on the bar, and the hotel itself – with the look of a beautiful old-style Outback pub yet with the comfort of a city bar – prides itself on its quality meals and shady verandahs where people stand and gaze out towards the surrounding deserts.

'It's a very important feature of the town, and we're in no hurry to part with it,' says Nell, who in 1999 was named the Diamantina Shire Council's Citizen of the Year in recognition of her contribution to the community. 'We want to make sure it continues to be cared for as an iconic part of Australian history, and a living slice of the Outback.'

The town itself appears to be flourishing with the amount of care Nell and others are investing in it too. On the edge of the scattered collection of buildings is a large dirt field, neatly mapped out into twenty subdivisions for new houses – the first land to be made available in 110 years. Telstra's new mobile technology soon to be rolled out across the Outback may support a proper Next G mobile phone network in the area as well; an astonishing advance when you consider that the telephone only arrived in Birdsville in 1989. Green electricity for the town is supplied by one of the few low-temperature geothermal power stations in the world, deriving its energy from the near-boiling water taken out from the Great

Artesian Basin that also provides the water supply. Meanwhile, there are plans to seal the road to the north towards Bedourie and Mount Isa within the next five years, and possibly to the east some- time later, thanks to David's tireless lobbying of government.

Even the recent outbreak of equine flu failed to dampen enthusiasm for the Birdsville Races. In 2007, for the first time in their 125-year history, the event was held with no horses present. Instead, racing from elsewhere was beamed in, while competitors ran around the dusty course on hobby horses and dragged wheelie bins to the finish to compete for a $100 prize, in place of the usual $120000.

'Birdsville is a very special place,' smiles Nell, who's now work- ing on her next pet project of seeing a golf course built in town, with sand greens and trees to indicate fairways. 'I think there's a little bit of bush in everyone, whether they live in a city or the country. Although in the Outback you have to fight a lot harder for services and recognition, whereas in the city you already have them, you get so much more freedom in the Outback. That's always absolutely beautiful, and well worth fighting for.

'When people talk about the Outback, some think of isola- tion, drought, dust, hot summers, flies, nothingness . . . Others of us think wide-open spaces, deep-blue sky, amazing sunsets, river floods, birds, wildlife, rain, peace. If you told me tomorrow I had to leave Birdsville, I couldn't tell you where I'd go. I'm happy right here. It's a very special place, and it has a very special future.'

4

A Land of Plenty

Mitjili Gibson Napanangka, *Lake Mackay, Western Australia*

A tiny Aboriginal woman with a shock of white hair under a bright orange and blue headscarf strides across the vast dry salt beds of Lake Mackay, in the wilds of the Western Desert of Western Australia. The dazzling crust of bleached salt crunches beneath her bare feet, the sun pounds down from a cloudless sky, and a million bush flies hover like a thick cloud around her. She seems to notice neither the blistering heat nor the constant buzz in her ears.

'This is where I grew up,' she's saying in one of the two Aboriginal languages in which she's fluent, Pintupi and Warlpiri. 'We walked around here even when we were young. I became a mother of children here.'

It's hard to imagine life being possible on these blindingly white flat, featureless plains that stretch off as far as the eye can see.

71

But it was, and Mitjili Gibson Napanangka, a sprightly, cheery descendant of the age-old desert peoples of this area with an irrepressible spring in her step, a mischievous smile and a stubborn glint in her eye, is all the proof anyone could need. For the first twenty-five years of her life, she lived here, on her ancestral lands, in the traditional way.

Growing up, she was taught to hunt and was told the legends about her country and the Dreaming stories associated with Lake Mackay, a sacred site for her social groups, the Napanangkas and Napangardis. 'Out bush, we didn't have houses,' she explains. 'Single men and woman were in separate camps. Our grandmothers would teach us in the women's camp. We would wash, swimming naked. If a man snuck up to spy on us, we would chase him away.' As she entered her teens, she learnt the strict social protocols required of women from her mother and sisters, and then became one of two wives to her late husband, whose name is now taboo. And while most people would view her homeland as a bleak wilderness in an area bounded by the Gibson, Tanami and Great Sandy deserts, in the furthest remoteness of Western Australia, close to the Northern Territory border, she certainly doesn't.

'To us, it looks like a barren desert, devoid of any food or comfort,' says Jessie Bartlett Nungarrayi, Mitjili's 21-year-old granddaughter, of those traditional Pintupi homelands, 700 kilometres west of Alice Springs and 1200 kilometres east of Port Hedland. 'But you go out there with her now, and within hours she'll have caught goannas to eat and other wild foods, located water and made shelter. To us, it looks like nothing. To her, it's a land of plenty, offering a real feast.'

*

As a descendant of Australia's very first Outback peoples, Mitjili has managed to hurdle a huge gulf between civilisations. Firstly, she proved she could survive some of the harshest terrain the country has to offer, hunting and gathering not only for herself but for her husband, his second wife and their four children. Secondly, she's now shown she can also thrive as a comparatively newly urbanised woman, even while making regular forays back into the bush.

For these days, Mitjili (now aged around seventy according to her family's reckoning, or eighty, if her official government-allocated birthday is to be believed) has become a woman freshly revered for her Outback skills. She's in huge demand to catch animals for natural history documentaries and feature films, as well as helping out biologists, zoologists and botanists, and teaching others bushcrafts.

Ethno-biologist Dr Rachel Paltridge, who's worked with Mitjili for over fifteen years, says she's constantly amazed by the old lady's agility and daring. 'If she sees a bilby hole, she goes down into it headfirst, often several metres into the ground,' she says. 'Her daughter Cindy usually holds onto her ankles to make sure she doesn't disappear completely. She just has no fear at all. There could be Western brown snakes down there – anything – but it doesn't seem to make any difference to her. Or she'll be there, digging a hole for another wild animal and a six-foot snake will slither out. But it doesn't bother her. It's incredible to watch.'

Although she's a tiny woman, albeit now a little plumper than in her bush days, Mitjili frequently amazes onlookers much bigger, stronger and fitter than herself. With a finger on one hand splayed from the time it was chewed by an angry desert possum, she's quite at home anywhere in the deserts of the west. Her keen eyes and persistence mean it's rare that she ever returns without a good catch of live specimens for the scientists or film-makers, or a bounty of fresh bush tucker for the family. 'Bush tucker is the best-tasting food,' says Mitjili, smiling.

Her tracking skills are unsurpassed, and she's frequently called upon to make modern use of them, looking for endangered species for conservationists too. She seems to know instinctively where she might be able to find even the rarest of animals. 'You see her looking at cracks in the earth, and tiny things that none of us would notice,' says award-winning documentary film-maker Beck Cole. 'Then she'll dig a hole to catch an animal – and these aren't small holes. They're huge. The degree of fitness she has is extraordinary.'

Back when she lived in the traditional way, those hunting skills were crucial to survival, of course, and Mitjili was renowned as an immensely gifted tracker and hunter, possessing a deadly aim with a digging stick she'd fashion herself from desert hardwood, and a stealth of movement that would take her prey by complete surprise. Lizards were her people's main source of protein, supplemented by berries, roots, seeds and flowers. In order to maintain an adequate supply of food, it's been reported that the average Pintupi family habitually roamed over an area of around 5000 square kilometres a year.

Managing to survive quite comfortably on her own wits, Mitjili and her small family lived as a semi-nomadic group, never needing to stray into white man's territory further east, over into the Northern Territory. There were few reasons for Europeans to come to them, either. With their lands centred around the 1300-square kilometre Lake Mackay, straddling the Western Australia–Northern Territory border and surrounded by red sand hills dotted with pale spinifex and mulga trees, there was never much to attract visitors. There was some prospecting for gold, but only the hardiest of men attempted it. For the desert was always extremely arid too, the lake rarely containing water except in uncommon times of heavy rainfall – and even then it was undrinkable. The harshness of these conditions generally protected her people from outsiders and, overall, it left the Pintupi as one of the last indigenous groups on earth to encounter Europeans.

Indeed, in 1984, nine Pintupi people caused an international sensation when they were discovered in the Gibson Desert, still living their traditional lifestyle, never having met white Australians before. Travelling naked but for belts woven from their own hair, and carrying long wooden spears and a few implements hand-carved from stone, they were instantly labelled 'the lost tribe', and celebrated as one of the last indigenous people in the world to still be living as they'd done for the past 40 000–60 000 years.

For Mitjili, her first formal encounter with Europeans came in 1957 when a member of an expedition into Central Australia, led by anthropologist and ornithologist Donald Thomson, happened upon her small party north of Lake Mackay, or Wilkinkarra, as it's known to local people. She'd heard about Europeans before from some of her relatives who'd visited a remote Catholic mission station at Balgo in Western Australia's East Kimberley, and she'd seen their tracks and spied cattlemen from afar. But when she first saw this party coming close, she hid herself and her young child in a crack in the rocks. She was probably aged around eighteen.

'Some whitefellas came,' she recounts. 'We saw them come

across the plain in cars. We hid in the soakage but they came and found us here. They said, "Come to the water". We went to a place called Lappi Lappi and they took photos of us. It was good without white people, but they gave us food.'

Those photos still exist today, showing Mitjili as a young woman, looking shyly at the camera, holding her little son Lyle, around two, in her arms. With dusty short black hair, she's obviously pregnant with her second child and completely naked except for a scarf that Thomson insisted she tie around her like a loincloth. She's standing tall against a background of sharp rocky ground and rough spinifex. In another, she's standing stiffly to attention, her digging stick in her hand, at the Lappi Lappi rockpool. Lyle is trying to hide behind a boulder in the background, while two other women drink from the pool, bending down to lap at the water. Their digging sticks are held against the rocks below to steady them, but upside down, so their sharp points wouldn't pierce the ground below and wake the legendary sleeping rainbow serpent.

Many of the Pintupi were afraid of Europeans, assuming that because they were generally so fleshy and overweight, they were cannibals. In the 1930s, this fear was further fed by a prospector called Sam Hazlett, who'd been looking for surface minerals scattered across Pintupi country. Called Kungki by the local people, Hazlett had apparently once offered a party a wedge of bacon fat. It was just as they'd imagined human tissue might look, so they immediately leapt to the conclusion that he too was a cannibal. As a result, they felt Europeans generally were to be feared, but were often eventually won over by the quantities of sweet treats that were given to them, like treacle, sugar and jam. When successive severe droughts hit in the late 1950s and early 1960s, they were particularly susceptible to expeditions and patrols who were actively encouraging them to leave the Outback to live in settlements closer to town with a guaranteed supply of regular food. The tragedy was that, once they'd left the desert in search of European foodstuffs, it nearly always meant the end of their traditional lifestyle forever. 'They left,' said one white Australian onlooker at the time, 'because they were hungry. They didn't know they could not go back.'

Like the rest of her community, Mitjili was eventually persuaded by a native patrol officer to move her family away from Lake Mackay, so she walked due east until reaching Mount Doreen cattle station, and from there to the Aboriginal reserve at Yuendumu, 350 kilometres due east of Lake Mackay, set up by the federal government as a rations camp. There, despite her incredibly specialised knowledge of the land and her formidable bushcraft skills, she was allocated one of the most menial jobs possible – picking up rubbish as part of a clean-up gang. 'But she made the best of it,' says her white Australian son-in-law, Peter Bartlett. 'She's always had an incredible work ethic, and everything was very new to her there.'

Darwin-born Peter had gone to Yuendumu to work with language experts to produce bilingual books for the local school, and had met Cindy, Mitjili's daughter. The pair became good friends and, in 1987, partners. The couple's daughter, Jessie, says Peter's first meeting with her grandmother has become part of family folklore. 'He was a whitefella learning Aboriginal languages and was very nervous of meeting his prospective mother-in-law for the first time,' she recounts. 'And there she was, this diminutive little old lady with a cheeky grin. He was a bit apprehensive, but soon relaxed. They got on great right from the start. There were no cross-cultural hang-ups with Mitjili and my father. She has always been gregarious and while sometimes they would argue, they'd always end up having a good laugh.'

Those early days in a major community weren't particularly happy for Mitjili, however. It was mostly made up of Walpiri people and Mitjili, as a Pintupi, felt marginalised and isolated. Alcohol was being regularly brought into the community too, and drunkenness and violence were rapidly becoming acute problems. In addition, Pintupi people were always restless and Mitjili found it terribly difficult to settle anywhere, so used was she to roaming free across the lands. As a result, she moved out, travelling 150 kilometres back west to Emu Bore, much closer to her desert country, and then to a newly developing community called Nyirripi. Here, she once again began supplementing her diet with subsistence food gathering.

'We never had a house, just humpies made out of sheets of corrugated iron,' says Cindy. 'They could be moved to fresh ground every time someone passed away.' Peter, then working as the outstation coordinator, visited regularly from Yuendumu.

A few years later, Cindy, now forty, and Peter, fifty-three, settled in Alice Springs to be closer to a school for their five children. Mitjili finally agreed to come and stay with them. 'So she lives with us now, but she still frequently goes off hunting for goanna,' says Jessie. 'We can't stop her. She says goanna still tastes better than beef. And she's such a stubborn and contrary lady. If she wants to go out hunting, then she'll go out hunting. We always say, "Let's stick together, as it's so easy to get lost out there". But you can never tell her what to do.

'You try, and then she'll do the complete opposite. She has a mind of her own. You'll be hunting and saying, "Let's go this way", and she'll go off on a tangent, and end up somewhere else. It's hard to keep up with her.'

Nowadays, Mitjili has been rightfully recognised as a 'Queen of the Desert' and, while living most of the time in Alice with Cindy and Peter's family and several great-grandchildren, near her only other surviving child, Lyle, she still regularly returns to her old haunts on official expeditions. Her life, together with those of her tribal people, was recently the subject of a major exhibition and book, *Colliding Worlds: First Contact in the Western Desert, 1932–1984*, exploring the journey of one of the last Aboriginal groups to make contact with Europeans. Developed by Museum Victoria and the National Aboriginal Cultural Institute, Tandanya, it opened in Melbourne and then toured the country.

The demand for Mitjili's skills as a tracker and hunter continues to grow from film-makers around the world, as well as from scientists, fascinated by the great western deserts' fragile ecosystems and the myriad fauna and flora they support. The cameras from a number of those films have often been turned on her too, making her the star. She's appeared in numerous documentaries, both Australian and international, the latest being a French film, *The Last of the Great Trackers*.

For another documentary, *The Lore of Love*, written and directed by Beck Cole for the Central Australian Aboriginal Media Association (CAAMA), she was taken back to her old stamping grounds around Lake Mackay. There, together with her late husband's co-wife Nancy Gibson Napanangka, she instructed granddaughter Jessie, then eighteen, and Jessie's skin sister Lizzie Spencer Nungarrayi, on the old ways, about becoming a woman and on the rules of love, as she was once taught herself by her older female relatives.

In the half-hour film, Mitjili confesses how jealous the two co-wives were of each other, and the pair demonstrates how traditional Aboriginal women used to fight with sticks over the attention of their husbands. She also shows the two younger girls how to paint themselves in white ochre to enhance their beauty, and how to dance and sing in the traditional desert way to please members of the opposite sex. As Mitjili reminisces, sings, dances and wanders through the ridged red sandhills and across the dry lake beds, it's hard to believe this woman is now in the twilight years of her life.

Beck is full of admiration for Mitjili. Her documentary team drove for three days through the desert, with no idea where they were going, totally dependent on Mitjili's directions. 'She hadn't been back to that area for so many years, but she knew exactly where we were all the time,' says Beck. 'She'd say there's a water-hole here, then guide us to the tiniest hole, totally hidden, but which turned out to be full of soakage water that had obviously been there since time began. She was incredible. We were looking around and there was nothing anywhere, not even a tree, but then she'd take us past some dunes and there'd be a small natural amphitheatre with wind breaks, shade and water – a beautiful little oasis that we'd never have been able to find. She was extraordinary.'

Another film starring Mitjili, *Nana*, has also proved a landmark production, winning the Crystal Bear for the Best Short Film at the 2008 Berlin International Film Festival and the Holding Redlich Best Short Film Award at the Inside Film 2007 awards. Cheered by the audience after its Australian premiere, which opened the 2007 Sydney Film Festival, the five-minute film went on to screen at festivals around the world, winning a number of other prizes for its maker, writer–director Warwick Thornton. 'I cast Mitjili in the lead role of *Nana* because she *owned* the role,' he says, having again just cast her in one of the country's first fully-indigenous feature films, *Samson and Delilah*. 'Mitjili is a nana – she can hunt, she can fight, she can paint. She's the quintessential Aboriginal nana growing old her own way, in her own time. I've worked with Mitjili on a number of films now and every time she's brought new insights to the script and character she plays. Her knowledge of bush life is second to none, and she always shares it with the cast and crew. Sometimes you can get lazy in your research and pre-production, but you find yourself saying, "It'll be all right, we've got Mitjili . . ."'

Nana is a warm, humorous film, showcasing the fun side of Mitjili, dancing, singing and playing the fool for her little skin-granddaughter, Kiara. But there's also a serious side: it shows Mitjili at an Aboriginal community that has outlawed the impor-tation of alcohol, attacking a couple of whitefellas who are trying to sneak in grog for sale at night. As she always has in the past, she still makes a formidable adversary today. She flogs the men hard with sticks, to the clear delight of the little girl looking on in both admiration and awe.

Three years ago, Mitjili suddenly revealed yet another talent. Her niece Dorothy Napangardi, who started painting in 1987 after a stint also picking up rubbish for the local council at Yuendumu when she came in from the desert, had been acclaimed as one of Australia's top artists. With Dorothy's exquisite canvasses selling all over the world and fetching as much as $129 000 for an individual piece at auction, Mitjili decided she'd like to have a try at painting.

Dorothy's agent Roslyn Premont, the owner of the art dealership Gallery Gondwana in both Alice Springs and Sydney, was unsure how she'd go, but agreed to provide canvasses and paint to see if she had talent. The results simply blew her away.

'They were absolutely extraordinary,' says Roslyn, who's been involved with Australian Aboriginal artists for twenty years now, nurturing and working with a small core group of artists from the Central and Western deserts, the birthplace of the world-recognised Western Desert Art Movement. 'The diversity of style in her work is amazing. The layering of meaning indicated almost a parallel existence. She painted stories of Dreaming and the story of her life, about seeing her father being speared. There was such an authenticity about them, they were just magical.'

Mitjili plainly enjoys painting and works as hard at it as she'd worked previously at everything else in her life. She now goes into the small studio above the gallery in Alice Springs every day to paint. 'She likes to work,' says Cindy. 'If she's at home, she'll often be up at dawn sweeping the yard. With painting, she seems to treat it as a job, and turns up early every morning to start.'

Very quickly, Mitjili had amassed a body of work and the art world was buzzing with news of a major new Aboriginal artist about to burst onto the scene. But first, Roslyn took every single one of Mitjili's paintings and hung them all around another studio, then led the elderly woman in. Her eyes immediately lit up to see them all together, and she sang and danced before each picture in turn, reliving every moment they'd portrayed so far in her life. Everyone in the gallery watching felt tears well in their eyes.

'It was like one big reminisce and, with such an amazing life, it was a wonderful moment to share in,' says Roslyn. 'She ran around the paintings and sang and danced, it really made everyone's spines tingle. That day, she transformed all our lives.'

Mitjili's official debut into the art world was no less memorable. Even as her paintings were being hung at the biennial Melbourne Art Fair in 2006, many sold. Before the show was a few days old, every one of her works had been snapped up, many by Australia's major art dealers. *Sydney Morning Herald* art critic John McDonald wrote that Mitjili showed 'extraordinary talent', and that her work was 'extremely good'. Sydney art dealer Martin Brown described her paintings as 'new, fresh and adventurous – and, not least, joyously coloured'. The head of the Aboriginal art department for the auction house Lawson Menzies, Adrian Newstead, praised Mitjili as one of the most exciting new indigenous artists to emerge in recent years, with the layers she applied to her paintings giving them a depth and ethereal quality, 'as though the creation ancestors are flying over the land'.

Later solo shows have proved just as successful, with larger works now selling for up to $40 000, of which Mitjili receives the same proportion – the price minus commission and cataloguing expenses – as any European artist, and spends the proceeds in pretty much the same way, on housing, food, education and living expenses for her extended family. 'Her work is never repetitive; virtually every dot is different,' says Roslyn. 'You really never know what's going to come out. She's a major talent.'

Today, Mitjili is happily painting at the studio, sitting on a massive canvas, daubing it with yellow, red and purple. She's dressed in a bright-green T-shirt and green skirt, but is spattered with paint. Her black handbag, off to one side, is similarly daubed with paint, while she also has a splotch of purple on the toe of one sock. An attendant rushes to help her wipe it off, and Mitjili switches her attention to the purple collection of dots she's just smudged. Her concentration is unwavering. A bowl of stew sits, cold and untouched, against one wall.

Her son-in-law Peter is sitting nearby, looking on. 'She is an amazing woman,' he says. 'She lived all those years in one of the most harsh stretches of Outback Australia, and yet she's managed to also make a success of living in Alice. When she's out in the country, she's the real queen of that country, but then she brings that all into her work.'

It sometimes creates dilemmas for her family. At the moment, Jessie is torn between moving away from Alice Springs to go to university to take a biology or teaching degree, and staying close to continue to learn from her grandmother. 'To have someone extraordinary like her in your life makes it more difficult choosing which path to take in life,' says Jessie. 'I want to go off to university, but I also don't want to miss any of the time I might have left with my grandmother, learning traditional knowledge from her, and taking part in the inter-generational transfer of our stories. It makes it very hard.' She doesn't want to miss sharing the times when Mitjili goes back into the desert to hunt goannas and wander under the wide open skies as generations of her people have done before her. 'They are very special times,' says Jessie.

Yet, as a measure of Mitjili's versatility, she still manages to forge strong bonds with people who've always lived an urban life. Peter's mother, for instance, Billie, a cultured and well-dressed woman who used to live in Sydney's wealthy North Shore suburb of Mosman, has moved to Alice and become one of Mitjili's very best friends.

The first time Mitjili and Billie met, against all expectations, they hit it off immediately. Despite neither speaking the other's language, somehow they understood each other, and it became a common sight to see the two older women – one tall, stately and dressed immaculately; the other much shorter and dressed in the brightest rainbow of colours – walking down Todd Street in Alice Springs, hand in hand.

'They've developed a really interesting relationship over the years,' says Jessie. 'You have this urbane, middle-class lady who, when she gets sick, ends up being cared for by Mitjili, with all her traditional healing techniques and bush medicine. They're complete opposites, yet their relationship works somehow. They share five grandchildren, and Billie now has a skin name too. It's wonderful to see. Mitjili just never stops surprising us.'

5

The Sweet, Sly Work of Song

Sara Storer, *near Wemen, Victoria*

'Hands up any single men in the audience!' yells country music sensation Sara Storer at a packed-out gig in the open beer garden of a pub in a small town outside Dubbo, New South Wales. 'Here!' shouts a gruff voice back. 'I'm single!'

Sara peers through the crowd from the makeshift stage. 'Are you tall, dark and handsome?' she asks the man, who's promptly revealed to be rather short, squat and overweight. 'Well, that doesn't matter,' she responds immediately, 'how's your bank account?'

Her audience roars with laughter, but her admirer is undaunted. 'I saw you sing at Gympie,' he calls back, of the night when the woman billed as country music's equivalent of the pop industry's Delta Goodrem sang before 40 000 people at the annual muster. Sara smiles. 'Oh yes, I remember you,' she says, quick as a flash. 'But when you're dancing, could you keep your clothes on tonight please?'

The crowd bursts into spontaneous applause. It's clear they love this bona fide country girl from the tough mallee district of Victoria, the self-taught singer-songwriter who's now won more Golden Guitars than any other woman in Australian country music. For not only does Sara Storer sing like an angel and pen her own songs – on everything about her beloved Outback from drought to drovers, to farmers' solitude and suicide – she also wears her heart unashamedly on her sleeve.

Quite apart from all those jokes about dates with wimpy city slickers who get stressed from being late for their yoga classes and how she's on the hunt for a good (bush) man, it's her ongoing love affair with the land that gets the most airplay. 'My connection is all about my family and my upbringing in the country,' says Sara, who burst into the public consciousness with a record haul of seven Golden Guitars at the 2004 Tamworth Country Music Festival. 'It's a genuine love of the land and the people who live there. I just believe the earth looks after us so well, we have to treat it with care and pay something back.

'For the first time, I think everyone's becoming much more aware of the country. Drought is now affecting people in the cities too, with the cost of food, so they're beginning to take notice. And if my music starts a conversation about the land, and makes people think about it more, then that's a wonderful thing. I couldn't ask for more.'

Tell the rain to stop falling
Tell the banks to stop calling

Tell the politicians where they can put their plans
Tell the day to hold on longer
Tell our sons we can't be bothered
And then tell these hands to give up on the land
Tell these hands
(From 'Tell These Hands' by Sara Storer)

Sara Storer comes from a long line of women who've given up their successful city-based careers to follow their men onto the land – and some of the roughest land in Australia to boot.

Her grandfather, Lindah Storer, was a pioneer in the harsh mallee country of Victoria's north-west, the hottest and driest region of the State, and the last to be settled. Despised as useless scrub by the first Europeans to arrive, the land was covered in drought-resistant eucalypt that proved hugely difficult to uproot and destroy, with the soil underneath sandy and often salty. 'Mallee is one of the most barren regions in the world', wrote explorer Thomas Mitchell contemptuously in 1836. 'There were tufts of a prickly bush, which tortured the horses and tore to rags the men's clothes about their ankles.' He wasn't alone in his scorn. Explorer William Lockhart Morton, who followed in 1861, was similarly dismissive, saying 'a more worthless sand-desert country, in its natural state, cannot be imagined. There is plenty of vegetation, but it is useless.' Thirty-five years later, another expedition leader, David Carnegie, labelled it 'a vast howling wilderness of high spinifex-clad ridges . . . ghastly desolation and hopeless dreariness.' In the earlier twentieth century, *The Bulletin* followed suit. 'Nobody knows who made the mallee,' it reported, 'but the Devil is strongly suspected.'

The early settlers, however, weren't to be deterred, and the invention of the stump-jump plough in 1876, which hopped over the hardy mallee roots that remained in the ground, allowed farmers to prepare large areas of the land for crop growing. After every harvest, they burned the thick stubble and new shoots. 'Mallee King' Edward Lascelles pushed the area further forward still by persuading the State Government to run a railway link there to help the farmers, swearing that it had a good future as a wheat bowl. It was men like Lindah who then benefited most, helping turn it, eventually, into the State's major producer of wheat and barley. 'My pop bought a team of bullocks to help him clear his land,' says Sara. 'So he knew every inch of that land, and poured so much love and care into it.'

When he met his wife-to-be, Olive Taylor, on a holiday in Brisbane – she was a well-known fashion designer there – he hoped she'd share his enthusiasm. He brought his new bride to the mallee in February 1934 and, arriving at dusk, she was charmed by the silvery vision of the moonlight shining on the quivering canopies of mallee shoots. The next morning, when she woke up and looked out at the desolation, she wept. 'She was a real career woman and was torn between marrying Pop and becoming a mallee wife, or continuing on with fashion,' says Sara. 'She had a name for herself in the thirties, and would have probably gone on to be somebody important. It would have been so hard to give that all up. I think she thought, at first, it was romantic. But then she cried, though she said she only ever cried once, and then told herself, That's it! I'm a mallee farmer's wife now . . . And Pop was lovely, he used to spoil her a lot.'

The pair had a son first, Sara's dad Lindsay, then two daughters.

Lindsay inherited the 5000-hectare wheat and sheep farm, just outside the tiny settlement of Wemen, south of the Murray River, 36 kilometres away from the nearest town, Robinvale, and 100 kilometres south-east of Mildura. His bride Fay had grown up in the country but had moved to Melbourne to become a nurse. Her career too was flourishing, and she'd just finished a midwifery course when she met Lindsay. 'She also had to decide between her career or being a farmer's wife,' says Sara. 'And she chose the farm life. I think she just loves it. She loves being home, and really appreciates the fresh air, and not having neighbours peering over your backyard. It's very healthy for the soul.'

Lindsay and Fay, in turn, had six children: Doug, now forty-one; Jodie, forty; Greg, thirty-seven; twins Ben and Sara, thirty-four; and Kate, thirty-two. All still live in the country, except Sara, whose career has forced her to move to the New South Wales' Central Coast to be closer to where her music is produced, and to provide a convenient base for touring. She doesn't feel that's home, however. She's never been a coastal person, doesn't like to be in big towns, and longs to be back in the bush, with its tight-knit sense of community. The question then arises: Is she likely to be the third generation of Storer women to give up their careers to go back on the land?

She pauses for a long time before responding. 'Do you know what?' she says finally and slowly, choosing her words carefully. 'I probably could. If there was a good reason for it, if I got the opportunity, then I think I might. There is something so special about living that lifestyle. What could be better, really, than living out in the country, with all that fresh air and sunshine? It's the smartest lifestyle that anyone could ever come up with.'

Sara arrived as a complete surprise to her parents, who hadn't known they were expecting twins, and she grew up quiet and shy. Her older twin Ben did most of the talking for her, something she felt very comfortable with. She was most relaxed messing around with her three brothers and two sisters in a rural backyard that ran for kilometres, playing in the billabong that came up to their chests, swimming and yabbying, and calling in for a soft drink and lollies from their nan – their grandfather had died when Sara was six years old – who lived in a house just a kilometre away from their own.

Indoors, Sara spent most of her time with her ear pressed to the radio, singing along to the music. It helped too that everyone in the family was musical: her mum played the piano and her dad loved the piano accordian and sang a little, instilling in his daughter a real appreciation for performers like Willie Nelson and John Williamson. 'As soon as my ears were able to hear music, I guess I was listening to it,' says Sara. 'We're a very musical family and there was always music in the house.' The whole family these days occasionally jams together, just for a laugh, as the Bullagreen Mountain Breakdown Band.

Sara's first real performance was in the Sunday school Christmas concert at the age of seven. She was singing 'Greensleeves' but was so nervous she sang two words, then her voice faltered and died completely. She reacted like any good stage star: 'I sat down and started bawling in front of everyone,' she says. 'Someone said, "Give her a clap!" – and I've had counselling ever since,' she laughs. 'Now, I just can't believe that I can get up and sing in front of crowds. It was quite a nerve-racking experience, and it still can be.'

Her eldest brother Doug remembers their childhood well. 'She was always buggerising around doing something, being funny and singing and playing around with a guitar,' he says. 'But I remember it wasn't until about seven years ago that we all got together at Christmas and she sang. It was the first time I'd heard her properly perform. I thought, Gee, that wasn't too bad! It's unreal what she's achieved in the last few years. I think we're both surprised by her success. I'm probably a bit biased, but I find I can put on one of her CDs at the beginning of a long car journey and by the time I get to where I'm going, I'm still listening. I can't listen to anyone else's music like that for so long.'

It was obvious from the start that Sara would never make a farmer. The family joke was that she didn't even know where the back paddock was. Her siblings still laugh about the time she was asked, at age fifteen, to take smoko down to one of them driving the tractor and ended up on the next-door farm because, even after all those years, she still hadn't known the colour of the family tractor. 'They always used to say, "That's dopey old Sar",' laughs Sara. 'But the thing is, I'm just not handy. I would have been hopeless as a jillaroo. I was scared of the horses, the sheep and the cows, and I would cry if they got too close to me. I always thought the cows were going to rush me and run over me because they're so big. I wasn't much of a farmer's daughter, but I still loved it.

'The three boys did everything and loved it and, as a girl, I got mostly house duties, which suited me. But we did have to go and help out now and then if the boys were busy mustering or in the shearing shed. We'd whinge and whine, with me the worst of the lot. I'd be saying, "Ugh! There's all these yucky things out here!" so that Dad might think it wasn't worth having me there. He'd always

93

end up yelling at me anyhow: "Get back in the ute!" because I didn't know what I was doing, I was so hopeless. But I still loved just *being* in the country. I had an extremely lucky childhood with great parents and a close family made up of all different sorts of personalities.'

Her mum Fay agrees that no one was under any illusion that Sara would end up a farmer. 'She was more of an *observer* of farm life,' she laughs. 'She loved the lifestyle and being part of the community, but she was a storyteller more than anything, with a natural ear for music.'

Sara did well at school in Robinvale and, with a fondness for children, went on to the University of Melbourne to take a degree in early childhood teaching. She didn't enjoy university at all, however, felt she didn't fit in, and loathed studying. She made some friends, but found few people with the same taste in music. She'd go home for the holidays and cry when it was time to go back again. Her mum encouraged her not to give up so, at the end of each break, she'd grit her teeth and set back off for the big city, all the time daydreaming about heading instead to the wide open spaces of the Northern Territory and finding adventure. 'It sounded exciting – and faraway – a little bit risky,' she says. 'I thought that I wanted to give it a go, which is probably not really like me at all.' By the time her course ended, her tutors were all set to fail her but, terrified by the idea of having to spend another year there, she pleaded desperately, and successfully, for them to change their mind, and then headed straight for the Outback.

It was 1994, and Sara had decided to take a year out before starting teaching. Her travels took her to the remote little town of

Camooweal, just over the Queensland border from the Northern Territory, 200 kilometres north-west of Mount Isa. Out of money, she was offered a job in a Shell truckstop roadhouse, flipping burgers. Much to her surprise, she absolutely loved it – not for the work, but for the array of colourfully eccentric characters she met there. As well as the constant stream of truck drivers, station workers and tourists, there were also the people hanging around the area itself, often on the margin of mainsteam society.

One of her favourites was Harry, an old retired buffalo shooter, who lived in a donga (a portable cabin) out the back of the roadhouse, and was paid to look after the gardens. Often, in the evenings, Sara would sit with him and play cards, listening to his tales of life in the old days while he sipped from his daily glass of Lambrusco. 'Harry inspired me,' says Sara, simply. 'He was such an amazing man. Of course, I've always loved music and I've always loved songs, but after getting to know him, I thought I'd have a go at writing a song about him. I wanted to give him something. I knew a few chords on the guitar, I wrote some lyrics and put my own melody down. It was an amazing buzz.

'I sussed a few things out, asking him what kind of gun he'd use if he was sitting riding a horse, for example, because I had no idea. It turned out to be a .308. I should, in retrospect, have asked him more questions because in the final song I used the word "stampede" which I thought was the word for a cattle rush, but which turned out to be the American term. We just use the word "rush". That was actually very embarrassing. Then, when I sang it to him as my gift, he got quite teary. I thought, This is really cool, this songwriting. It felt good. So I just kept writing.'

After nine months in Camooweal, Sara finally decided it was

time to move on. The teaching job she eventually took in 1995 was in Kalkaringi, a faraway Aboriginal settlement 500 kilometres south-west of Katherine. Again, she relished the experience. While she taught her class, mostly made up of Aboriginal kids, they in turn taught her about their ways. 'I'd bring a glitter pen into class, and they thought that was fascinating,' smiles Sara. 'Then they would dig in the sand and find a frog, and *I'd* find *that* fascinating!

'I made some great friends there. As I'd grown up on a farm where all the money goes back into it, and as long as you had a nice cosy bed not much else mattered, Kalkaringi wasn't too much of a culture shock for me. There's a big level of trust you have to build in communities; it takes a lot of listening. Many residents still followed their culture, laws, ceremonies and traditions, and the majority of kids were lovely, even the naughty ones. I think a lot of outsiders who go to places like that want to change the world, and that's the wrong approach. You've just got to go there, fit in and do your job, which for me was to educate the children.'

Sara stayed there two years, then taught in Katherine for a year, then spent another two back at Kalkaringi. 'She was a natural teacher,' says her former boss Donna Westaway. 'She'd have the whole class eating out of her hand. She was terrible with the paperwork but was always so natural and open with the kids – they loved her.' The feeling was mutual, and Sara found it hard to tear herself away. She loved the wide-eyed innocence of the children, some of whom had never seen a shower before, or visited a city like Darwin. 'It was hard to tell them about where I came from, four days away by car, when they'd been nowhere themselves,' says Sara. 'They were just in their own little world, and I thought there was something precious and sacred about that. I loved the way Aboriginal people related to the land. There's a connection between the spirit of a person and the spirit of the land. Aboriginals are clever in understanding that connection and I think people who live on the land have that similar connection.'

In all the years Sara spent there, she continued to sing and write songs, playing at station parties, rodeo sing-songs and to the kids in the community. Then, during one of the school holidays, Donna insisted on entering her in a talent quest in Adelaide River, 800 kilometres away. Sara dragged her feet so much, Donna was forced to ask for an extension to the entry period and made her fill in the forms in front of her. 'She was pretty modest about her singing,' says Donna. 'She's such a dag, and she's such a procrastinator. But she often said she'd love one day to go to the Golden Guitars, and I'm from Tamworth originally, where my parents used to drag me along to so many shows, and I knew she was a lot better than many of the acts I'd seen.' In that quest, Sara sang her first song, 'Buffalo Bill', inspired by Harry. She felt she performed terribly – shades of those old Sunday-school nerves again – but, to her shock, she won the Encouragement Award. The prize was a two-week stay at the Country Music Association of Australia's College of Country Music in Tamworth.

There, early one evening when she'd already gone to bed, she was woken and asked to play in front of Garth Porter, the multi-award-winning country music producer and former keyboard player with Sherbet, who counted Lee Kernaghan and Gina Jeffreys among his line-up of credited artists. Sara wasn't sure, but her fellow students were, and insisted on dragging her out of bed to play a song for him. 'I thought I'd better go,' she laughs. 'I was so nervous, but forced myself to do it. I was still in my pyjamas, but thought, What the heck!'

Garth was blown away by both Sara's songs and her voice – if not her outfit – and signed her up immediately. Two weeks after the course finished she went to Sydney, where they recorded a few songs. 'We'll see what happens,' Garth told her. 'I'm taking these to the ABC, but don't get your hopes up. They might get who you are – or they might not. But we should give it a go.'

Two weeks later, in the middle of taking a class back in Kalka-ringi, one of the teacher's aides came in to interrupt Sara. There was a call waiting for her in the staffroom, she said. It was a woman from the ABC.

After Sara took the call, she stood stunned in the middle of the room. Executives at ABC Music had loved her songs, her voice, her fresh approach. And now they wanted her to make an album with them. She raced into the principal's office. 'They want me to make an album!' she gasped. 'What do I do? I don't know what to do!' The principal was in no doubt. 'Do it!' he said calmly. 'This is a wonderful opportunity for you. Don't miss it.'

Two weeks later, Sara was travelling south to Sydney, staying in Garth's studio and sleeping on his couch while she recorded her first album, *Chasing Buffalo*. Released in September 2000, it gave her three number-one singles in the Australian country charts, with her old favourite 'Buffalo Bill', and 'Roller Coaster' and 'Man Trap'. Performing live, however, proved just as traumatic as it ever had. Her first big concert was for 200 people, with Troy Cassar-Daley and John Williamson in the audience . . . and she forgot to plug in her guitar. 'But I was myself,' she says. 'And that was the easiest way for me to win people over – to just be myself.' It soon began to reap her huge dividends. At the 2001 Tamworth Country Music Festival, she scored five Golden Guitar Award nominations and won one as Best New Talent.

'I think I was just really lucky,' says Sara. 'Friends had been saying my songs were great, but I didn't know what to do with them. I was living in the middle of nowhere, I didn't know anyone in the music industry or how to go about a career in music. Then everything just seemed to fall into my lap. The competition Donna entered me in . . . meeting Garth Porter . . . the record deal . . . I didn't have to do anything but grab the opportunities. I think I owe it all to that six years living in remote Australia, gaining experience, meeting those characters. I'm really grateful for that time in my life.'

Since then, it's been a real roller-coaster ride. She began singing all around the country, supporting big acts like Troy Cassar-Daley and Beccy Cole, then her next album, *Beautiful Circle*, released in November 2002, became a huge hit. The single, 'Raining on the Plains', which she'd written with her brother Doug and Garth Porter, and performed with her all-time country music hero John Williamson, won national airplay, and former radio host John Laws loved it so much he played it every day on his show. That exposure and success meant she could finally start making plans to headline her own tour.

Then came the greatest breakthrough of all: Sara's astonishing seven Golden Guitar wins in 2004, smashing the record set by Lee Kernaghan in 1999 when he took out five. 'That just blew me away,' she says. 'I was sitting there with my brother Doug and

I was so nervous when they went to announce the winners. Then we won the first Golden Guitar and I thought, That's great – I can relax now. It would have looked terrible to have so many nominations and not win anything. And then there was the next one and the next . . . It was a little bit embarassing. I started worrying that I might look like I was hogging them, and thought people might say I didn't deserve them. I was handing out my Golden Guitars to everyone to hold them, and had quite a bit of trouble finding them again for the photo at the end of the night. It didn't feel real.'

But it was, and Sara found herself performing before packed-out audiences on a five-month tour of Australia, which had been booked just before her Tamworth triumph, with extra shows hastily tacked on, and selling 6000 CDs in just two weeks.

'I've been so lucky,' says Sara again, shaking her head in wonderment. 'Everyone's been so good to me. The great thing about country music is that people want to help you get on. It's been hard, the last four years, but now my music has given me so much.'

Some might say luck is much less important than true talent, but Sara won't have a bar of that. 'I'm not a great singer or anything,' she says, 'it's just that my voice suits my songs. And I'm pretty basic on the guitar too.' She doesn't have much confidence in her looks either. With shoulder-length dark hair streaked with red, pale skin and startling blue-green eyes, she frets about her teeth being too crooked for a photo (they're not), and eyes she describes as 'the colour of sewage' (they're not either). Often, Sara appears awkward and ill-at-ease on stage as well, a persona that contrasts dramatically with the showy professionalism of many of her contemporaries.

Yet that obvious shyness and simple, unaffected modesty is

something that's further endeared her to fans of her music everywhere. Even over in the UK, they rave about her. The industry's prestigious British magazine *Country Music People*, as well as giving *Beautiful Circle* a five-star review, said, 'as we lament the death of Slim Dusty, here is evidence that authentic, yet contemporary, Australian bush country has not died with his passing'. It's praise that humbles Sara, who grew up listening to Slim's music. But she was soon in the company of another Australian legend, this time Paul Kelly, with whom she toured Australia following the release of her third album, *Firefly*, in 2005. That was followed up the next year by a performance for the Queen and prime minister John Howard during the Melbourne Commonwealth Games.

'It gives me goosebumps when I think how well she's done, and how she's now the most awarded female country artist in history,' says her old mate Donna. 'After such a short time, she's at the top of the game. I don't think she realises how successful she is. She's not a great self-marketer, she still doesn't have enough confidence, but she writes from experience and paints such a vivid picture for people of the land, with such conviction, people just fall in love with her and her music.'

The autobiographical feel of many of her songs is certainly one of the reasons Sara has done so well, winning fans from both the country and the city. Her earliest hit single, 'Tell These Hands', a story of rural hardship, was written after the family's farm was flooded. By the time of its release, the farm was drought-stricken. Other songs praise the virtues of Outback men as boyfriends, husbands and lovers; the joy of rain; the misery of drought; the pride of workers on the land; the facelessness of the increasing corporatisation of farming; and the warmth of close community.

Now used to performing in front of audiences in the city and the country, Sara often has to stop herself, mid-chat between songs, to remind herself where she is. 'Most of my songs are stories but in the city you sometimes have to explain what you're singing about. One time in the country, I found myself explaining what a rouseabout is. I had to stop and say, "Now, I think you know what sheep are, don't you?"

'But I'm proud that people in the city seem to like my music and my stories as much as those in the country. It's such a great thing to wake up every day, to be writing songs and music and doing the things I love. I just feel I should maybe have done more to deserve it – like working as a volunteer at St Vinnies for ten years. But I think I've been more successful writing my own songs than I ever could have been singing covers. People feel like they know you. And I like singing about the land. Sometimes people can make country and Outback people out to be dull and backward when I think they're the smartest people of the lot, living such a wonderful lifestyle. They're also having to be cleverer, coming up with better ways of farming because of drought and land erosion and climate change.

'Farmers have such hard times – it's extremely unfair. I'm interested in the strength that keeps them going. Life is very much in the lap of the gods for those in the Outback. I don't think others understand how precious they are, or what they do.'

Sara Storer is up on stage in Sydney, sharing the limelight with mates Gina Jeffreys and Beccy Cole, in a three-person show the trio invented called *The Songbirds*. Gina, the veteran country star, and Beccy, smart, sassy and self-assured, are a complete contrast in style with Sara, who still looks self-conscious, demure and a little wide-eyed, like a startled mallee rabbit caught in the spotlight. She talks slowly but is deceptively sharp, taking soft pot shots at Beccy whom she laughingly accuses of being backstage putting on another layer of make-up. When a woman in the crowd shouts out her appreciation, 'Good on ya!', Sara shoots back immediately, 'Thanks, sis!' You can feel the audience warm to Sara's guileless charm, the gentle humour and the distinctive Australian accent that comes through even more strikingly in her songs, when so many of her colleagues slip into the usual American twang that characterises so much country music around the world.

It's those kind of qualities that have so impressed fellow singer-songwriter Paul Kelly. 'Sara's songs are grounded in real stories,' he says. 'You know she's paid attention, heard the bush waking up in the morning, listened to the worries thrashed out at the kitchen table, smelt dry summer wheat up close, dreamed of faraway places in a bedroom with a window on a big sky, driven miles on dirt and bitumen and fallen in and out of love. She's found her own way to sing the stories that are all around her and then inside her bubbling out. She doesn't copy over-emotive, fake-sincere twangy country singers from overseas. She's found her own restraint and steel and lets her songs do their sweet, sly work.'

That's something country music legend John Williamson loves her for too. 'The first time I saw Sara perform it brought tears to my eyes,' he says. 'At last I was hearing the true voice of an Aussie country girl, with no sign of a twang from Nashville. If she sticks to her guns and is not swayed into the international trap of losing her identity, in my book she will grow to be a legend in Australia. We need women like Sara for the growth of Aussie culture; to encourage young Aussie women to be proud of who they are.'

These days, however, Sara's music is becoming more wide-ranging, with songs about friends and broken romances – like her own recently ended relationship – just as much as on Outback themes. With also a change of record company to EMI Music, there are increasing comparisons being made with more main-stream singers like Missy Higgins and The Waifs. Indeed, the latter's Josh Cunningham worked with Sara on her latest album, *Silver Skies*, which came out in November 2007, and in January 2008 she supported American singer Suzanne Vega during her Australian tour.

She's come a long way from those early days when she'd often be so nervous her voice would quiver mid-song, although she still occasionally sings the wrong verse, or starts in the wrong place. 'But, in the end, if you're able to laugh at yourself, the crowd doesn't seem to mind,' she says. 'If you're prepared to admit you've made a mistake, you can get away with anything.'

On stage now, alone, Sara's voice grows soft when she introduces the lead single from *Silver Skies*, 'Land Cries Out', a sad and moving tale of rural suicide. 'The rate of suicide is terrible among Australian farmers,' Sara says to the hushed venue. 'The drought has pushed many over the edge. And the land misses any farmer who dies; no one will love the land more than a farmer who has had it passed down through the generations.' As she sings about the tragedy in her sweet, husky voice, no one stirs until the last word. Then there's thunderous applause.

Afterwards, she confesses the song means a great deal to her. She was shattered when she was told of a friend who'd ended his life for reasons no one may ever fully know or understand, she says, but the drought was always there as a dark shadow. 'Everyone's suffering at the moment because of drought and financial pressures and some people can't cope,' she says quietly. 'There are a number of cases you hear of or know about. People worry they're going to have to leave the land. Things are so tough at the moment, and then not having much money means you can't just nick into town because of fuel prices, or have dinner with your friends and talk it over, which is healthy. Instead, people tend to sit in silence and suffer. They become depressed, and the suicide rate goes up.

'I'd been talking with my mum and I got all emotional about the subject and then wrote the song. I didn't write it with this intention, but if I get up on stage and sing it, someone might be sitting there and turn to their partner and talk about it, or come up to me after the show and talk about it. Maybe it'll start a conversation that could save someone's life.'

Her mum Fay thinks that's an enormous contribution to the Outback. Singing about the issues that affect those on the land, the hardships and the triumphs, enables rural communities to realise they're not alone. 'It's very comforting to know there are others in the same situation,' she says. 'And it does remind city people what's going on in the country.'

Sara agrees wholeheartedly. 'Music can bring people together in that way,' she says. 'It can make you talk, it can make you laugh, it can make you cry. But whichever it does, it is a great release for people. It can make country people realise that they're not alone and make people in the cities understand more what they're going through. That's so important, particularly at a time when life can be so tough for people in the Outback. Whatever the future brings, my heart is still there with them.'

6

Giving It a Go

MAREE STOCKMAN, *Lake Cargelligo, New South Wales*

When the police turned up late one evening at her front door, Maree Stockman instantly knew something was wrong. The news couldn't have been more terrible: a light plane carrying her husband, her only son and her father-in-law had vanished off the radar, and no one could be contacted. The search had begun, but had so far found nothing. Everyone was hoping for the best but feared the very worst.

Ten excruciatingly long days of alternating desperate hope and utter despair followed, before the wreckage, and the bodies, were finally found. Maree was devastated, but knew she had to hold herself together for the sake of her three young daughters. So she coped with the crushing grief the only way she knew how: by getting on with caring for the girls, and working to keep the family's farm going in the heart of red mallee country near Lake Cargelligo, in western New South Wales.

As the day of the funeral approached, everyone expected housewife Maree to start on the heartbreaking task of putting the 3000-hectare wheat, barley, oats and sheep property up for sale, and moving into town with her children. It seemed the only viable option. But no one had reckoned on Maree's quiet courage, stoicism and growing determination to hold onto the farm her husband, Mick, and her father, Allen, had made their lives' work. 'I didn't really spend too much time thinking about it,' says Maree. 'I dealt with the grief by getting on with the work, and from there just thought I would carry on and give it a go.

'I felt the kids had been through enough change in their lives, losing both their father and their brother. They were happy on the farm, and I wanted to keep their lives as normal as possible. I wanted to stay too. I felt that if I went to town that would be the end of me. Mick had worked so hard and started something worthwhile, but hadn't seen much reward for his efforts, and the farm had been in my family before that. I wanted to finish his work. I didn't know what would happen – I didn't know much about farming, and I thought I might make a mess of it – but I decided to try.'

On the morning of the funeral, just after Easter 1987, Maree, thirty-six, dressed with a heavy heart and helped daughters, Linda, thirteen, Mandy, five, and two-year-old Karyn, get ready to say farewell to their father, aged just forty-one, eleven-year-old brother Darryl, grandfather Ross and close family friend, Peter McDonnell, who'd piloted the plane. Everyone from the neighbourhood turned out to pay their respects to a family who'd long been an integral part of the small community's tightly-woven social fabric. Maree had arrived in the area as a five-year-old when her parents had leased a neighbouring farm, and then bought the current property, Forest Lodge, in 1960. Her husband Mick had been a bulldozer driver before their marriage and moving onto the farm. He'd adapted surprisingly easily to the life, quickly earning the respect and admiration of all the farmers in the district with his strong work ethic and eagerness to help everyone else out. He used his 'dozer skills to clean up paddocks and build dams for many of his neighbours, and created a sportsground at the local school.

A few days after the service, Maree heard a commotion in the paddocks, and raced out. A noisy convoy of twenty tractors had arrived. As a mark of appreciation for Mick's life and a gesture of goodwill to Maree and her plucky resolve to keep going on the farm, all the farmers of the neighbourhood had decided to pitch in and sow the next season's crops for her. As the machinery wove up and down the red dirt, there were few dry eyes in the neighbourhood.

The challenge of working the farm was huge for a single mum with three young daughters, who'd never played much of a role on the land before. Maree was also a shy, self-effacing woman without much natural confidence, who found it hard to ask for help. With only the experience of tending her vegetable patch and fruit trees in the backyard and helping her dad out, she now faced growing up to 800 hectares of crops each year on the property at Gubbata, north-west of West Wyalong, an hour from Griffith, while also running a flock of 3800 Merino breeding sheep. 'I didn't really believe that I could do it,' she says. 'But I thought I'd try. And if it failed, it was my own fault and no one else's.'

The learning curve was so steep, Maree felt she might fall off at any moment. Mick had started a pasture-upgrading program, planting clovers to replace the skeleton weed and saffron thistle, and Maree tried to learn as much as she could, asking neighbours for advice, researching as much as she was able and following Mick's old plans on what he'd been trying to achieve. It was often extremely painful. 'It took a lot of patience,' she says now, smiling. 'I sort of knew what had to be done but I didn't quite know how to do it. I had a casual worker, Fred Mancy, with me, who'd worked with Mick before, and we had to figure it all out. Fred was five-foot nothing and when I said we'd have to do a job, he'd take a deep breath and say, "Okay . . ." Later, I had many macho-type men who'd simply say, "No, I don't know how to do that". But, with Fred, I followed Mick's markings and tried to copy what he'd already done, not daring to change a thing.'

Good friend and neighbour Master Farmer John Daunt was taken aback at first by Maree's decision to keep on the farm, then amazed by her determination to keep going. He vowed to give her as much help as he could. 'Everyone thought she'd sell up and move, but she just didn't.' Instead, he says, she approached some of the best farmers in the district to pick their brains about the management of crops and stock, to work out a future program. She examined others' pastures, then took a good hard look at her own. And she asked agronomists for expert advice and went along to field days with John, trying hard to distill from them everything that could possibly prove useful to her own situation.

As things started to go well, Maree's confidence grew. She hired contract fencers to make sure her entire property was properly fenced, and finished installing watering points to give all her paddocks access to water, rather than only those with dams. The neighbours then formed a working bee to lay 3.5 kilometres of poly pipes to keep troughs constantly filled for the animals. 'She became more prepared to try things, and she had good results,' says John. 'Her average wool yield went up from 5 kilograms per head to 7.5 kilograms, and then 8 kilograms. Her lambing percentages increased enormously. Her neighbours were always supportive but after a while, when they saw the success she was having, they were even keener to help. Without doubt, she's developed into one of the best and most progressive farmers in the district.'

At the same time, however, Maree was also trying hard to cope with her grief. Soon after the funeral, a plaque was unveiled in honour of Mick and Darryl at the local Naradhan Public School, where Mick had also served as president of the Parents and Citizens' Association. Around sixty people from the district crowded around the little ceremony to pay tribute to Maree's lost husband and son, watched two native trees being planted in their memory and saw Mick's sportsground officially opened. When a tape was put on of Darryl playing the recorder at the school's annual concert the year before, Maree struggled to keep her composure.

But what kept her going was the need to be there for her daughters. While her dad often called round to help, it was particularly difficult trying to work full-time on the farm and still keep enough of herself for them. She found she had to compromise every step of the way. She'd often work a full backbreaking day outside, sowing or harvesting, while Linda and Mandy were at school and Karyn was with a generous neighbour, would return home for tea with them and then, when they were safely tucked up in bed, go back out into the paddock at night to do another complete shift.

'When you've done five hours at night, you actually do five hours' work,' she says. 'During the day, there are too many interruptions. You have to refuel, or change points or change paddocks – always something. And I am a bit of a night person. I can work at night no problem. During harvest, I'd always work till the bins were full.'

At weekends and school holidays, the girls often came out with her too. They'd ride in the ute or the tractor, or play in the paddocks, chasing sheep. When the little ones grew tired, Maree would simply lay them down on the floor of whatever vehicle she was working in, so they could go to sleep and she could continue on.

Slowly, all her efforts began to bear fruit. There were two years of good rain, and the harvests were a triumph. Maree began to relax. Maybe she would be able to make a go of it, and do her late husband proud. But then disaster struck again.

Maree was out working alone one night in the paddock, driving a harvester to collect the last boxful after another long shift. The rain had affected the crops and wet straw kept clogging up the header comb. She was keen to be finished and impatient to free up the machinery. On the last round, rather than disengaging the machine and freeing the blockage by hand, she seized the drive belt with both hands and pulled on it hard. To her relief, the blockage freed. A split second later, however, she saw that her hands were covered in blood. The belt pulley had severed eight of her fingers.

The heat from the belt had almost sealed some of the wounds, and Maree was able to drag herself back into the harvester cab and raise the house on the two-way radio. Her elderly house-keeper raced down into the paddock to find her. 'I asked her to take me to hospital, but she was very upset and not in a state to drive that far,' says Maree. 'So I went to the nearest neighbour and he drove me to Ungarie, which has the closest hospital. From there, they took me to Wagga by ambulance and then flew me to Melbourne. By the time I arrived, it was twelve hours after the accident, and then I had another twelve hours of microsurgery to sew four of the fingers back on. Three didn't take; they couldn't get the blood flowing through them again. It was my own silly fault, putting my hands somewhere you're not supposed to.' Maree had been left with just two thumbs and the little finger on her right hand.

When they heard the news, Maree's neighbours were devastated. Here had been a young woman whose life had already been destroyed once, but she was courageously making a go of everything – against all the odds. And, now, to be dealt another such cruel blow . . . 'We were horrified when we heard,' says John Daunt.

Maree, however, was philosophical. The visitors to her bedside kept saying she'd never manage, that she'd have to give up the farm and move to town this time, but she refused to listen. 'I just put my mind in neutral and thought I'd see what happened when I got home. The worst thing was, I felt I'd failed my family.'

When Maree left hospital, she went to stay with her parents for a few weeks, then went home. It was just before Christmas 1988, so the children were all on school holidays. They helped her manage, and she started believing that everything, possibly, would be all right. Then, when they went back to school and the housekeeper quit, Maree was suddenly left alone for the first time.

'That first day I didn't know what I was going to eat for lunch,' she says. 'I couldn't handle a knife or fork because my hands wouldn't bend. I had nothing in the house I could eat without cutting. I couldn't cut a slice of cheese or meat at all. So that was a bit of a quick awakening. I thought, I'll have to get organised. I *have* to make this work.'

Her eldest daughter Linda, then fifteen, was stunned by her mother's willpower. 'Her determination just shone through,' she says. 'She was back writing, holding her pen in the V between her thumb and the palm of her hand, even before she'd left hospital. She seemed to say that this accident wouldn't stop her doing anything, and then she set about proving it. She's got such a stubborn streak in her. If she wants to do something, she'll manage one way or another.'

Under doctors' orders to go to the physiotherapist to try to get some feeling back into her hands, Maree realised it was going to be a battle just to get there. 'I didn't feel inclined to impose on anyone to keep driving me, so I knew I had to drive myself,' she says. 'If I could do that, life wouldn't be a problem. If I couldn't, I'd have had it with the farm.' So Maree practised for hours, alone, in a paddock, using the palms of her hands on the wheel to drive. 'Once I could drive again, I knew things would be pretty much the same.'

While Maree smiles at the thought of past difficulties and makes light continually of her situation, insisting that she really is no one special, onlookers shake their heads in disbelief. 'She's an absolutely incredible lady,' says John Ridley, chairman of the New South Wales Farmers Association's grains committee. 'She was thrown into adversity of the most extreme kind and coped with it exceptionally well. It's one thing having the heartbreak she endured, but then to fill the shoes of your husband on the farm at the time, and to go on to do it as well as she's done. Then there was the harvest when she had the dreadful accident with the header. But that didn't stop her. She just kept going.'

Maree simply shrugs and her hazel eyes dance with amusement at the difficulties *others* face with her. She recently won a prize, only to discover it involved a manicure. As soon as the organisers realised what they'd done, it quickly became a pedicure. She pushes a curl of her soft brunette hair, now tinged with grey, out of her eyes, and chuckles at the memory. 'And there's still some things I can't do,' she offers. 'I can't sew that well any more, and I can't do fiddly things. But I found I could type on the computer with my two thumbs, although I'm a bit slow. So I can do most things. Sometimes it requires a bit more patience, and takes longer, but most of the time that doesn't matter.

'And when it first happened, the neighbours rallied round again to help me. They helped bring in the remainder of the harvest, and brought me so much food. My poor neighbours! They were wonderful . . . all over again.'

A true battler, it is perhaps no surprise that Maree comes from tough Outback farming stock. Her father Allen Allison, originally from Forbes, had faced his own struggles with the land. He bought Forest Lodge as a undeveloped area made up of seven undersized blocks subdivided from former Crown land, given out to returned soldiers after World War II. Many, however, drifted into debt as the Depression hit, prices fell and the 400-hectare plots turned out to be too small to be economically viable. As a result, few were able to clear or do much with the land at all. So when Allen and his wife Elsie bought the blocks in 1960, he worked hard to try to clear the thick mallee scrub, and turn the venture into a going concern.

Maree, born in Forbes, the eldest of three sisters, loved growing up on the property, riding horses and bikes, building cubbyhouses, tending the animals, doing her own thing in the safe, empty landscape and daydreaming about one day becoming a farmer's wife. When Maree was eighteen, her mum's sister from Tamworth came to visit over Christmas and brought the son of a family friend with her. Later, Maree went for a few weeks' holiday to stay with her aunt, and again met up with Mick Stockman, who was home visiting his family. A young man with a real appetite for hard work and a mischevious sense of fun, he constantly made Maree laugh. He had travelled all over Australia driving 'dozers. 'He seemed to have been everywhere, and knew a lot about nature, trees, plants and animals,' says Maree. 'Mick had a big sense of humour and was always laughing. He had so many stories. I liked everything about him.' Mick went back to work in the Northern Territory, clearing a beef road at Borraloola on the Gulf of Carpentaria, and Maree took a job at the Wagga Wagga Research Institute.

The pair started writing to each other, and gradually the letters multiplied from one a week to three, then four. Mick came to visit her in August 1970 and, after a few moments of awkwardness, meeting up again almost as strangers after exchanging so many intimate thoughts by letter, they soon hit it off once more. He returned to the Northern Territory, promising he'd be back by the end of September to see Maree again, but the job continued on

ABOVE: Gayle Shann with her faithful helper Tuffy, on her property near Moranbah in Queensland (*Jimmy Thomson*)

LEFT: Gayle participating in a campdrafting event in 2000, before her accident (*Sue Jones*)

ABOVE: Molly Clark's isolated homestead is a mere speck against the vast plains of the Simpson Desert *(Sue Williams)*

INSET: Molly at her homestead Old Andado, in the Northern Territory *(Jimmy Thomson)*

Top: The Old Andado homestead, more than 330 kilometres south-east of Alice Springs, remains largely the same as when it was built in the 1920s (*Sue Williams*)

Bottom: The interior of the homestead is still filled with the necessities of daily life through the ages, with the kettles taking pride of place (*Jimmy Thomson*)

INSET: Nell Brook gathers wild flowers at her home in Birdsville, in the south-western corner of Queensland (*Karen Brook*)
SPREAD: Birdsville is a tiny town way out back of nowhere (*Sue Williams*)

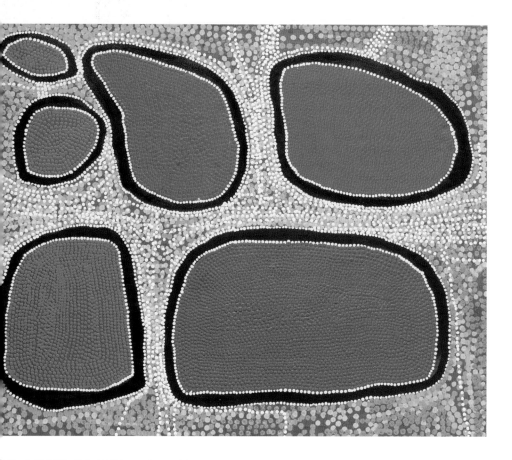

Opposite Top Left: Mitjili Napanangka photographed in 1957, holding her son Lyle (*D. F. Thomson, courtesy of Mrs D. M. Thomson and Museum Victoria*)

Opposite Top Right: Mitjili Gibson Napanangka at Lake Mackay, Western Australia, in 2007 (*Warwick Thornton*)

Opposite Bottom: Mitjili with Lyle (hiding) at the Lappi Lappi rockhole with friends in 1957 (*D. F. Thomson, courtesy of Mrs D. M. Thomson and Museum Victoria*)

Top: Mitjili's artwork today (*Photograph courtesy Gallery Gondwana*)

Left: Country music singer Sara Storer hails from near Wemen in Victoria (*Ian Jennings, reprinted with kind permission of EMI Music*)

ABOVE: Maree Stockman with her beloved big machinery at Lake Cargelligo, New South Wales (*Jimmy Thomson*)
BELOW: Drover Susan Cutler surveys her herd as she drives them through the long paddock near her home, close to Thallon in Queensland (*Photos reproduced by kind permission of The 7.30 Report, ABC TV*)

and on. In the end, impatient to be with her, he quit and travelled back down to Gubbata to help with her family's harvest.

Maree's dad liked the young man straightaway, and they often worked side by side. People looking at the two men – both tall and dark – regularly assumed they were brothers, but their personalities were quite different. 'When they worked together it could be a disaster,' says Maree. 'Mick was very particular and had to have everything done just right. Dad was a bit more casual. It wasn't a good mix.'

When Maree turned twenty, the couple became engaged. With Maree's next sister, Gayle, eighteen, getting engaged soon after, the foursome had a double wedding at Easter in April 1971. 'Mum and Dad thought it was terriby convenient,' laughs Maree.

For the next two years, the newlyweds travelled around Queensland, Mick taking on bulldozer jobs, usually clearing land and pulling up scrub, with Maree sitting in their caravan parked nearby each day waiting for him to come home. She'd spend her days knitting, sewing, cooking and writing letters. It was a hard life, but she was in love, and everything was so new it was exciting. 'I enjoyed the travel,' she says. 'I liked to see the country and visit the stations we were working on. But they were long days for me, in a caravan out in the scrub all day on my own. Sometimes it got a bit lonely, but I suppose I'm sort of used to being alone.'

In 1973, Maree fell pregnant and her parents said the pair should come back home. They also had a house in West Wyalong, 80 kilometres away, so they suggested Maree and Mick settle on Forest Lodge, and work for them on the farm, with Allen travelling in from town every day.

'It was nice being home again, and this is a good place to live,' says Maree, still in the same house. 'Mick took to farming like a duck to water. He liked the outdoor jobs, and growing good crops gave him a great sense of achievement. Life was busy. We had a big vegie garden and a flower garden, and I helped out on the farm when I was needed.'

She didn't have too much spare time for that, however. After Linda was born, Darryl came along two years later. Five years on, Mandy arrived, on Maree's thirtieth birthday, then Karyn three years after that.

The farm was ticking along nicely. 'They weren't especially good years, but then they weren't especially bad,' she says. 'The farm was going reasonably well, but it was always a bit of a struggle because we didn't have a lot of money when we first started. We couldn't afford everything we wanted, but we built it up gradually. All the money we had, we were pouring into the farm.' Mick had been continuing to improve the land, then started planting better pastures. On a trip over to Western Australia in 1978, they visited similar mallee country and marvelled to see natural clovers growing tall and strong, so they started experimenting with clovers and lucerne too. The land had always been poor quality for farming but, with the right fertilisers, varieties and rotations, Mick discovered that their crops of wheat, oats and barley could really improve. They also bought their own breeding ewes.

Gradually, the couple were establishing themselves. When they'd first moved onto the farm, they'd worked for Maree's father, then they bought some machinery and share-farmed. Later, they leased the farm and, in 1983, bought it. Maree did all the books and sourced equipment Mick needed, as well as running errands, going into town for spare parts, cooking, cleaning and looking after the children. She helped out in the paddocks a little at harvest time, but while she once drove the old tractor for her dad as a kid, she now wasn't allowed near the newer, bigger farm machinery they'd bought. But she was happy. Being a good farmer's wife and a mother were all she had ever wanted.

So when Mick organised that fateful Easter 1987 for a friend to fly him over to Wauchope, near the coast at Port Macquarie, to pick up some parts and his dad decided to come along for the ride, with Darryl and Linda vying for the one seat left, Maree didn't give it another thought. On the afternoon of April 23, she kissed them all farewell, and never saw them again.

After the crash, then the loss of her fingers, Maree Stockman's life gradually settled down into the quiet routines of the country. When Mick's five-year plan ran out, she simply devised the next one on her own. There were a few good years of rain and marvellous harvests in the early 1990s, enabling her to buy better farm machinery. She relished her newfound competence and skills and loved driving the big vehicles, with the header her favourite, despite its previous terrible toll on her life. 'I still love big farm machinery,' she says. 'If I had to lose my fingers, better to have lost them like this than just an accident in the kitchen or something.' She loved nothing more than to see the girls off to school in the morning, then climb into a big machine to work all day on the land on her own. 'I'd just jump in the tractor or header, close the door, turn the wireless on and have peace all day,' she says. 'You're free to think and plan and do whatever you like, with no interruptions. After being a housewife with four children, it was absolute heaven.'

The crops grew better and better with the advances in fertilisers and more effective rotations, and Maree diversified into other crops as her confidence grew. In 1994, she was one of the first in the district to try her hand at growing canola and, while it was too dry to flourish that year, the crop showed enough potential for her to persevere with it again in a better year. She also tried lupins and lentils, experimented with new seeding methods and used canola as a 'break' crop to reduce disease in later high protein wheat, oat and barley harvests.

At first, she envied the men who'd been farmers all their lives, with so much experience to draw on. But she came to realise that farming was changing so rapidly, they were all pretty much in the same boat. It gave her even more courage to try new methods and products. 'I have this view that if you change before it's forced on you, then you won't be afraid to try something different when you have to,' she says. 'Now I've tried a few different things, I'm not afraid to change. I know I can cope with sticking my neck out.' Against all the odds, this quiet achiever soon became a leading light in the community – an active member of the Kikoira branch of the New South Wales Farmers Association, the local Stockcare and TopCrop groups and the Rural Lands Protection Board.

'She's certainly a very smart and capable woman, who's achieved a great deal in a comparatively short time,' says Hanley Armstrong, the manager of the Condobolin Rural Lands Protection Board. 'She's pretty courageous. She's played a role on our Board for ten years now, and makes a real contribution to the community.'

Along the way, Maree steadily earned the admiration of those around her. 'Everyone really respects her,' says John Daunt. 'She had difficulties – lost a lot of workmen along the way as they didn't like taking orders from a woman – but she always managed. We started thinking of her as one of us. She'd join us for a beer around the barbeque, where we'd all be talking farming, and she'd be there, taking it all in and offering an opinion. The other ladies would sit around together with their cups of tea talking about the kids at school.'

With the increased cash flow, Maree renovated the timber and fibro farmhouse that had been her home for so long, cladding it with brick to make it more solid and warm in the winter, and changing the rooms around to make it more modern. Good harvests in 2000 and 2001 were followed by rising prices for wool and sheep and, by then, Maree had become so successful, she even bought another 1000-hectare property, Pine Park, on the Lachlan River, to spread the risk.

Her daughters were all amazed that their quiet, self-effacing mum had become such an indomitable presence on the local farming scene. 'Mum floored everyone in the first place when she decided to stay on the farm,' says Linda. 'We kids thought we'd have another year or two there . . . great! We thought sooner or later it would end and we'd move into town. But we never did. And it's amazing when you think that mum had left school, then basically got married and been a housewife with kids. So to do what she's done since . . . she's incredible.'

However, the last eight years of drought have been a real set-back. 'I tried so hard to have reserves set aside for when the girls decided to settle down, but the drought has eroded every cent and, just when we want to expand, there's no money,' says Maree.

The property has deep dams – a happy legacy from her 'dozer driver father and husband – and hasn't, as a result, had real water problems. But the drought hit the crops hard and the normal harvest of 5000 tonnes fell to 250 tonnes in 2002, and then to a miniscule five tonnes in 2007. 'It used to be that 70 per cent of the income came from cropping and 30 per cent from the sheep,' says Maree. 'But during the last seven years, it's probably been the reverse. The sheep are carrying us through at the moment, that's why we are putting more effort into them.' Her achievement of high lambing percentages have won praise from sheep classers but, with pastures slowly drying into dust, relying more heavily on sheep is still not an easy option and numbers have been successively cut from a peak of 5500 to about 1200 by the end of 2007.

Additional fodder needed to be bought in, even though she had a good store of oats in the silo three years ago – the oats had already been bought by a miller and she honoured their contract. She also started drought-lotting the sheep in 2006, locking them in a confined area and feeding them a maintenance ration to prevent irreversible dust and wind erosion on bare paddocks. 'It's a time-consuming job feeding them all the time, but there's been no alternative,' says Maree. 'The most rain we've had in one fall is just 15 millimetres. It's never been as bad as this. We're getting some little showers, but we haven't had an inch of rain at any one time for the whole year. We desperately need more rain. There's no subsoil moisture, and the ground is badly cracked; extremely rare for a sandy-loam soil. But we always hope it'll get better, that's why we keep planting the crops.'

That lack of natural feed also brought other problems. With the sheep on a grain diet for so long, many started falling sick. The vets all scratched their heads in bewilderment. Finally, they pronounced that the sheep were suffering from a lack of mineral and trace elements they would normally get from green grass. Maree sighs in bemusement. 'You think you're feeding them so well,' she says. 'And look at the country now. Where would you find a single blade of grass? But when some grass did eventually come, we turned them out into the paddock again, and they were fine.'

Yet the drought's greatest blow is a far more personal one. For years, it's been a source of enormous pride to Maree that all three of her daughters wanted to stay on the land, something now unusual for farming families, but probably a result of Maree involving her children every step of the way in running the property. 'Farmers tend to keep their kids, when they're young, far away from the working areas of the farms now, secluded from what goes on, and then complain because they're not interested in the farm,' says Maree. 'My kids were with me all the time, so they really know all about it.' Her two eldest would love nothing more than to come back to live with their husbands on Forest Lodge and Pine Park but, with the drought hitting so hard, the properties can't be developed further and, at this point, can't support them.

That's a real tragedy, since it was always Maree's fervent wish to have Linda and husband Greg Thomas build a house on Pine Park and make it their own; and for Mandy and husband Will Johnstone-Kerr to take over the other cottage on Forest Lodge. Both daughters are now wonderfully qualified to take on an active role in the further progress of the farms. Linda, now thirty-four, graduated from Charles Sturt University with a Bachelor of Applied Science (Agriculture), has worked as a header contractor, farmhand and rouseabout, spent time with the Department of Agriculture as a soils officer and with the farmer research group Central West Farming Systems. She's particularly interested in cropping. Mandy, twenty-six, on the other hand, is more absorbed in livestock; she has been helping Maree with the sheep side of the operation, and taken over the breeding of goats after graduating from the University of New England with a degree in agricultural science. Karyn, twenty-three, wants to stay on the land too, but has a diploma in childcare and currently works as director of after-school care at a local school, and is also working in special-needs care three days a week.

Instead, the drought has meant that the older daughters' husbands have had to seek work elsewhere, at Barrick's Gold Mine at Cowal, 32 kilometres north of West Wyalong, so at least they can be earning in the meantime. As a result, Linda and Greg, who is from the land too, now have a one-year-old daughter and another child on the way, and rent a house in West Wyalong, closer to the mine. 'We just have to wait and be patient,' says Linda. 'If there's anything I've learnt from Mum, it's that you have to roll with the punches. At the end of the day, you find the good, the positives, in everything, however hard. We do have big plans, but this gives us a chance to sort ourselves out as a family before we take the next step. It'll help us in the long run.' Mandy's Will, a mechanic by trade, and who changed his surname to Stockman to keep the family name going, travels daily to the mine, a round trip of 200 kilometres, so Mandy can stay working on the farm. Happily, Karyn is set to marry a neighbour's son, Jordan Hoskinson, so they'll hopefully live on the farm next door.

'The mines are really carrying this district through the drought,' says Maree. 'If they weren't there, the young men would have to go a long way away for work, and probably never come back. It's sort of good in a way – it's a job that pays them well – but they don't really like it so, as soon as they can, they'll come back to farming. I'm really looking forward to that day.'

Maree, now fifty-six, has certainly had far more than her fair share of bad luck in her life, but she's never been bitter. She doesn't even think of it that way. 'No, I'm not that kind of person,' she says, smiling gently. 'I think towards the future, I try to forget about the past.'

And, of course, there have always been the positives alongside the tragedies. Her neighbours, for example, have been so wonderful to her, their kindness is something she'll always treasure. 'How do you thank them enough? You can never really do that.' There's also been the satisfaction of not only keeping the farm going, but turning it into an extremely efficient, effective operation. For someone who felt she'd too often been dismissed as 'just a housewife', her triumph has been enormously fulfilling.

As well as taking pleasure in her current achievements, there's always the promise of the future to savour. Karyn, for instance, has just postponed her wedding after discovering that her fiancé Jordan is actually the nephew of the man her dad sold his old black Dodge car to when he first came to Gubbata to live. They recently uncovered it in an old shed on the farm where he lives, and she's now hard at work renovating it to be her wedding car. It's all set to be a very special day.

Then there's always the hope that the drought will break, and Maree will finally have all her family back home. And at a time when young people are leaving the rural areas of Australia for the cities in their droves, that will again be no mean feat. 'I really think it's what you project onto children,' says Maree. 'If you're telling them that farming is a hard life they're going to believe it. But if you enjoy what you do and it really is a wonderful life – no deadlines, no bosses, not having to harass people to make money – then they'll absorb that and feel the same way.'

Linda agrees. 'Mum really has been inspirational for us all. She's been a great role model, an incredible woman. You look at her and think you can do anything in the world. But she doesn't think she's special at all, or that she's done anything special, when she really has.'

Maree modestly begs to differ. 'I just don't tend to dwell on the hardships,' she says. 'I value the past, but if a disaster happens, I believe in picking yourself up and getting on with life. I always look ahead and try to think what I can do to improve the situation. If you dwell on the bad, that can ruin your life. Things happen, but you have to continue moving forward. That's what Outback life is all about.'

7

Gone a-Droving

SUSAN CUTLER, *near Thallon, Queensland*

When Susan Cutler takes to the highways and byways of rural Australia, passers-by often stop to stare. She doesn't quite fit the traditional image of the rugged, rough and tough drover of Australian bushlore, defying some of the globe's harshest elements to herd stock in search of food and water.

For a start, she's a woman. And for seconds, she likes to run an all-female droving team, in what's become an historic world-first. 'Well, why not?' she laughs.

'We do get a lot of people driving up to us and then giving us a second look, but I just find girls are a lot better with stock. They've got soft hearts, they care about the animals, they're good horsepeople, and they think about what they're doing. It's good to be part of an all-women team. I had two boys last year and they drove me mad. And they were both boys off the land!'

Droving would be a tough life for anyone, let alone a woman, but Susan says it's now second nature. The only thing she finds hard is when the stock suffers – through drought, extreme temperatures, or accidents with thoughtless drivers who fail to slow down.

There have been times when she's sat and wept. 'Oh yes, sometimes life can be very disappointing,' she says, biting her lip. 'When stock have enough to drink and eat, and they're full and they lie down, they look lovely. But when you see them poor, their hips sticking out and the skin hanging off, you think, Oh my God! Why does this happen? I then get very upset, especially if I lose some. It's not a nice feeling.

'We took cattle on the road for someone about seven years ago. I took six poddies, good weaners, and I brought only two home. The others were victims of the drought. That was a big loss. I did cry that time.'

Susan Cutler was born the third of five sisters on a property in Collarenebri between Moree and Walgett in north-west New South Wales. The family kept sheep and cattle, a few pigs for pocket money and grew all their own vegetables. As a result, Susan learnt how to do everything that needed doing around the place. The freedom of being on the land meant plenty of fun, but drought years brought hard times and punishing hard work.

All the children went to the local school, then Susan went to board at the New England Girls School in Armidale for eighteen months. She only liked the practical subjects, however, and the next time she went back after leaving it was to do what she far preferred: shoeing the schools' horses.

In 1978, at nineteen, Susan married a station hand, became Susan Grime, and had two children in quick succession, Katie and Joseph. The couple split up soon afterwards, and Susan reverted to her maiden name, resolving to raise her kids on her own. Not long after, her parents' own marriage broke down, and her mother Patricia left home. As a result, Susan decided to stay with the kids at her dad, Bill's, property, to help him out. They worked long and hard, but eventually the crushing toll of successive bad droughts forced him to sell up. 'It's always been her dream ever since to buy the property to bring it back into the family,' says close friend Shirley Lang. 'It's her dearest wish.' But at that time, there wasn't much room for dreaming in Susan's life. She had two young children to support, and was determined to do the best she could by them.

Susan had become an expert in crutching sheep but in those days women weren't allowed into the shearing sheds to work. By pure dint of her determination and skill with stock, she was eventually admitted, inspiring awe in her fellow – male – workers with her speed, efficiency and indomitable work ethic. 'She worked so hard, they ended up *having* to give her a go,' says daughter Katie, now twenty-eight. 'And once she was in, that was it. They wouldn't let her go. What she's achieved and what she's put up with, and put back into women's rights – I'm so proud of her. She's always worked so hard to look after her family.'

Every day at the sheds, the workers were given a sheep to kill for their meals. As a youngster, Joseph never understood why the men would ask him where his mum was, making sure she was elsewhere, before they butchered the chosen sheep of the day. It was only years later that he found out. 'One of the blokes confessed that none of them wanted to kill a sheep in front of Mum because they all knew she could kill them far quicker and cleaner than any of them,' says Joseph. 'They were big blokes, but they were ashamed. They said she could work as hard and as well as any man they knew.'

Other jobs included driving a school bus in Lightning Ridge, working with horses and cattle, and managing properties far and wide across Australia, including in the middle of the Simpson Desert. One time, she even took the children droving, when they were just six and seven, with 5000 sheep. Both rode their own horses, just as Susan had once done with her own father. 'It just came naturally,' says Susan, now forty-nine. 'I had them on the road for six months, walking sheep and looking after them.' There were always plenty of adventures along the way. One day, the children rode into a mud dam they thought was dry. When Susan caught sight of them sinking into the mud and silt, she had to sprint in to their rescue.

Friends and family were constantly amazed at Susan's energy levels. She could work hard physically all day, go droving at night and still find the enthusiasm to play polocrosse and compete in showjumping and one-day eventing. She became a champion campdrafter too, with dozens of ribbons, awards and several silver trophies. Just eight months after Joseph was born, the 22-year-old travelled more than 700 kilometres to take part in Australia's first Iron Stockman event, held on Queensland's Gold Coast on Australia Day, 1981.

It was one of the toughest endurance events ever staged, with race entrants having to light a fire, boil a billy, saddle a horse, ride over an obstacle course – wading through a large pool of mud along the way – dig a post hole, sink a fence post, chop down a tree, lug a bale of hay, drink a hot beer and eat a cold pie . . . all within the hour. Twenty-eight competitors entered but just twelve finished, with Susan the only female to cross the line. Her time: fifty minutes. 'I really enjoyed myself,' she says. 'It was definitely worth the long trip.'

She went the extra yards as a mother as well. The little family was exceedingly close and did everything together. 'They've always been my mates,' says Susan of her children, with pride. That served them well through the difficult times. At eighteen, Katie was raced to hospital with a huge tumour on an ovary. 'I was very, very sick for a long time, and they didn't know if I was going to get better,' says Katie. 'Mum nearly had a heart attack. I ended up spending six months in and out of hospital before I improved.' She eventually made a complete recovery and, now married to Clinton Hughes, has a daughter of her own, one-year-old Grace, and is expecting another child.

For five years, from 1986, Susan tried her hand at a whole new career: training racehorses. Her adored father Bill had a licence up to his death from cancer in 1995, and his daughter had enormous success with champions like Top Memories, Cowboy's Teacher and Trudi's Affair. She's also bred and trained her own dogs, which have won her many awards in dog trials.

But for the past ten years, Susan has turned to droving more or less full-time, a return to her first love, with the joys of the open road, healthy, well-fed cattle and the silver stars in a clear dark night her biggest thrills. 'I enjoy it tremendously,' she says. 'It's a good life. People come and help you and you have a lot of fun. When your animals are all nice and big and fat and round, I can't think of a better way to earn a living.'

*

It's just after dawn, and Susan's two young female helpers already have the billy on a roaring fire, browning chops on the grill. They slept the night in the truck, taking turns to watch the 1000-strong herd of cattle drowse in the enclosure on their six-month march northwards through the heart of southern Queensland. Susan, short, nuggety and with a glint of determination in her eye, has already been out on a four-wheel quad bike to count heads, making sure all are present and correct. After a hasty breakfast, she yells, snaps her whip on the ground and the three move assuredly through the mob, urging them out of the enclosure and onwards on their journey.

Susan swaps back to her horse to gallop after a couple of stray beasts, runs a hand through her short dark hair and settles back into her saddle for the long ride ahead, her twenty-odd kelpies, kelpie-crosses, cattle dogs and border collies keeping all the cattle in check. They race around, barking whenever they want an animal to get back in line. 'She has incredible skill with dogs,' says son Joseph. 'Someone can give her a bad-tempered mongrel and she'll turn it into a $1000 dog. You watch her work with them, and she stands there, not saying anything. She just moves her head a fraction and all the dogs understand. It's amazing to see.'

Sometimes, she'll work with thirty dogs at a time while droving, because the girls have their own dogs too. 'We don't have any shortage of dogs, and we need every dog, because in the middle of summertime they can't run as long in the heat,' she says briskly. 'Cattle will learn. If you haven't got your dog with you, they can be very naughty, but if you've got your dog, they'll behave themselves.'

She digs her heels into her horse's flanks and, with little more than a flick of the wrist and a tilt of the head, her helpers seem to understand instinctively what she wants them to do, and rush to their tasks. The cattle all amble on, stopping to feed on patches of green where they can find them. Once, it was mostly sheep that were driven but now, with the number of sheep in Australia shrinking to under 92 000 000 – the lowest figure since 1925 – and the price of wool so low, the demand is now mostly for droving cattle.

Those cattle are currently in good condition. Susan looks out at her charges, noting their shiny coats with satisfaction. 'It's a nice sight, isn't it?' she asks. 'Yes, it's a good job. It pays decent money and you've got no one to hassle you. You're doing your own thing, especially if you've got reliable staff. I've been lucky; I've always had good staff. You need them when you spend so long on the road. I spent all of last year on the road.'

It's a peaceful, timeless sight, this quiet meander through the scrub along the network of old stock routes that crisscross the Outback of rural Australia. You can well understand what inspired Banjo Paterson in the late 1880s to write his acclaimed poem 'Clancy of the Overflow', when an office worker stuck in the city longs, nostalgically, for a life like the drover Clancy:

> *In my wild erratic fancy visions come to me of Clancy*
> *Gone a-droving 'down the Cooper' where the Western drovers go;*
> *As the stock are slowly stringing, Clancy rides behind them*
> *   singing,*
> *For the drover's life has pleasures that the townsfolk never know.*
>
> *And the bush hath friends to meet him, and their kindly voices*
> *   greet him*

In the murmur of the breezes and the river on its bars,
And he sees the vision splendid of the sunlit plains extended,
And at night the wond'rous glory of the everlasting stars.

Some nights, Susan camps in her truck, which is set up with a stove, fridge and a portable shower, fed with water brought in big containers. 'We have a generator, so in the summertime we can put a fan on – we are modern-day drovers, we do like a few little luxuries!' Some nights though, she'll unroll a swag on the ground and sleep out under the stars.

'That's the best,' she says. 'It is so nice being out in the open all the time. The stars are absolutely magnificent at night. I think you have to be born and bred to this life; it wouldn't be for everyone. Some people wouldn't go droving for love or money. But we don't go without much.'

What about a comfortable bed? A nice bathroom? A good restaurant meal? Susan looks nonplussed. 'We sleep pretty well out here,' she laughs. 'All that fresh air. And look, we don't need a bathroom. We have our own little toilet we take with us.' She produces a little half-moon contraption from the back of the truck, unfolds it to reveal a plastic toilet seat and throws it down by a tree to show me. 'That's comfort!'

'And I'm a good cook. We have a camp oven and I cook stews, curries, scones . . . everything. I do a lot of cooking for other functions too; when we go back home for events, I cook for 600 people at a time. I have eight or nine camp ovens.' She climbs back into the truck and emerges with a collection of simple cast-iron pots that sit on coals or a fire on the ground and constitute the iconic

Australian 'camp oven'. 'I'm always the cook. You can make beautiful damper in them. You just have a few coals on the ground, and you're all set.'

At the heart of the lifestyle, however, is a love of the great outdoors and of animals. Susan's been riding horses for as long as she could walk, and there's nothing as relaxing, or as grounding, she says, as caring for a mob of cattle or a flock of sheep.

'I've been born and bred around animals, and I love being with them. I'll feed them before I feed myself. Animals should be fed before you come inside and when you come inside, it's your time then. But it's fantastic being around them. They come up and nuzzle you and look at you – that's the horses and dogs, and even the cattle or the sheep. They all have different personalities. You get the real quiet ones, or ones that'll come up and talk to you. Some are lovely, and some you want to kill! Most are happy to cruise along, but some just want to take off, which can make things tough.

'You've got to watch what you're doing all the time. You've got to make sure you've got all your cattle or sheep, you've got to count them, you've got to know which is the leader, who's the tail, and if he disappears, you've got to go and find him. At the same time, you have to know your leaders aren't going to walk away and leave the rest. You've got to have your wits about you all the time.'

Apart from drought and natural hazards, the biggest problems are usually presented by other humans. Motorists can provide real danger, especially when they're driving too fast along unmade roads, or assume animals will instinctively know how to get out of their way quickly. One Christmas, a car ploughed into a group of cattle Susan had managed to fatten up after taking them on when they'd been close to starvation. For the ones with two broken legs, she had to seek out someone with a rifle to shoot them – she gave hers back when the gun laws were tightened following the Port Arthur massacre in 1996. 'That was heartbreaking,' she says sadly. Inexperienced drovers can also be an issue. Some of the young men don't seem to have a clue; they need to be told every single thing to do which can be difficult and time-consuming. 'Boys today are different to what men used to be,' she says. 'Sometimes I think they're too . . . How should I put this? Too *spoilt*.'

On the other hand, many of the passers-by can be delightful, presenting the drovers with cold drinks, a piece of fruit, the latest newspaper. A number of them take photos, and Susan's picture is proudly displayed as a slice of 'real Australia' on walls as far apart as Japan, Ireland and the US. 'They're all fascinated by our life-style,' says Susan. 'They love to hear a yarn too. You can string a good yarn along for a while . . .'

Sometimes, families ask if they can come along for a ride, and they'll join them for a couple of days here and there, camping out alongside the drovers and sitting around the camp fire at night, listening, spellbound, to the myriad tales of life on the road. Then there are a few beers, a sing-song, a few more beers, the laughs, and a few more beers . . . At times it can be hard to shake off the visitors. But when they do finally leave, Susan's invariably relieved for the team to be back on their own once more.

'It's nice to get back in your own pattern again. For this life, you must be able to enjoy your own company. You've got to be able to live with yourself. Not everyone can do that.'

*

The very best times as a drover are when there's been rain and food is plentiful en route. One memorable trip, Susan's cattle put on a kilogram a day on the move. The very worst times are when the rains simply fail to come and the grass is shrivelled and offers little moisture and no real nourishment. Then, plumes of dust from the parched earth rise up and coat the cattle or sheep, and they're either restless and moody, or dispirited and quiet.

Sadly, that's the time when there's the most droving work – when owners can't feed their animals on their own property and send them on to the long paddock in the hope of feed along the way. 'If your stock is in a paddock, and only live in one place, they don't go fossicking,' says Susan. 'But if you move every day, they learn to look for something, and your stock will find something to eat.

'You'll occasionally lose some. You'll have deaths with cattle hit by eagles or those that have eaten toxic weeds. They are just natural losses. But most of the time you don't lose any. The mob before last, we had them for five months and we never lost one of them. They were good cattle and they were good times.

'But this other mob we had – around 900 of them at the end of 2006 – we'd been on the road six months, we had Christmas on the road, and it just got drier and drier, and it hasn't rained since. This is the worst drought for a long time, and the price of grain has sky-rocketed. Every other time, everyone had a bit of grain and stuff put away, but this time it's just gone on and on. Nearly every dollar we've been making has been going on horse feed and the calves. By the end, we had nowhere to go; there was nothing to eat anywhere. We ended up sending the cattle home. One bloke has sold all his stock since then, and others have probably lost some. It hasn't rained for them. I just feel sorry for the people who own the stock.'

It's at those times that droving can be the most stressful. Usually, the permit demands you move 10 kilometres a day to make sure the stock route isn't eaten out by cattle or sheep allowed to graze too long on the way. A go-slow permit allows a slower pace of 5 kilometres a day, or 10 kilometres every two days. A slower pace can earn a large fine, and inspectors drop in regularly to make sure nothing's awry. But when feed is poor and with each bullock valued at $800–$900, everyone becomes anxious about losing them. The team may feel down and tempers can fray. The need for good, reliable staff at these critical moments is paramount. Whingers need not apply.

The equine flu outbreak of 2007 also hit hard, and the temporary restrictions placed on the movement of horses severely limited droving. Then, Susan had to turn down many jobs, like moving cattle from a big mulga block when feed ran out as she'd have needed horses to traverse the terrain; bikes just wouldn't have got through. To tide her over any lean droving times, she'd also bought a fine white stallion, Officer, to earn extra money servicing mares. But all his bookings were suddenly cancelled too.

'She's had some really hard times in her life, and she's a tough bird and a bit rough around the edges,' says friend Shirley. 'But she's so kind-hearted. She's always there for other people. She's never managed to get her dad's place back for her kids, but she'll never give up.'

For the down times serve only to make the fun times even more treasured. At Christmas 2006, Susan and her helpers were joined on the road by four generations of her family: mum Patricia; sister Robyn and family; son Joseph, now twenty-seven, doing his apprenticeship as a boilermaker in St George, 400 kilometres west of Brisbane; daughter Katie and her baby Grace. Planning a nice picnic halfway between Moree and Warialda, they ended up shivering on the coldest summer's day any of them could ever remember. Yet they still had a great time. With Grace being sat on a horse from the age of five months, squealing with excitement, it won't be too long before she has a pony of her own.

Another time, they were joined by Susan's partner of the last ten years, Bernie Southern, and his son Mick. They were seeing the New Year in with a bit of a party and, after a few drinks, all finally went to bed. Mick climbed onto the truck roof to sleep. In the early hours of the morning, there was a loud thud. 'What's that?' Susan asked Bernie, alarmed. Mick coughed, then replied in a small voice, 'I've just fallen off the truck.' In the pitch black of night, he'd decided to go for a pee and stepped clean off the roof to go crashing into the ground below.

'He was lucky not to have broken his neck,' chuckles Susan, who's had a few falls from horses while droving from time to time, but hasn't broken a bone for a while. 'You've got to have a sense of humour on the road. You can't take things too seriously. You make your own fun.'

Sometimes that's not so hard to do. Strange folk turn up from time to time. One young man was left to look after the sheep at night while Bernie went into town. When he returned at dawn, the man was nowhere to be found and the sheep were scattered all over the hills. It turned out the man was scared of the dark, and had scuttled to town straight after Bernie, too terrified to stay alone. 'The poor bugger, he was so frightened,' says Bernie. 'When he eventually returned, I told him not to worry, and it only took us a few days to get them together again. I felt a bit sorry for him. Poor fella.'

If Susan has the choice, she'll always choose to go out with her girls, her 'A team' comprising her friend Tammy Hughes, twenty-five, and her niece Trudi Picton, eighteen, who's about to study animal husbandry at university. 'I love going droving with Susan; she teaches you so much about the land and the animals,' says Trudi. 'She takes such good care of us all. She likes a laugh too, and she has a very good heart. There's nothing like being on the open road with her.'

Apart from girls being gentler with the stock, there's also the convenience of being around women. 'If you want to have a piddle, you can duck around the back,' smiles Susan. 'Or if you want a shower, you can, without having men all around you. It's so much easier. But the main thing is that if an animal is down, the girls will get it up and pat it on the head and make sure it's all right.'

For the last three years, when Susan's not droving, she's lived in a sheep-shearing shed with Bernie in the middle of a field on a property owned by his brother, near Thallon in central Queensland, 80 kilometres south of St George by the New South Wales border. It's pretty basic accommodation but Susan sees nothing wrong with it. 'It's a waste of time having a nice house because we're never there,' she grins. 'It's very quiet here, and we know all our neighbours. Young fella up the road comes down for a bit of a yarn sometimes. We would know everyone who drives past.'

In the summertime, it has natural ventilation – the tin roof doesn't quite meet the wooden walls – but in wintertime the bed takes pride of place in the middle of the shed, so the pair can huddle under the doona. There's a makeshift shower in one corner, and a toilet in another. Throughout there are plenty of fridges for beer and the odd slaughtered bullock which, unsurprisingly, takes up quite a deal of room. Pride of place around the walls are a selection of ribbons, rosettes and trophies for horse racing, campdrafting and stockhorses. There are also sashes from Susan's two second places, in 2004 and 2005, in the Australian Ladies Championship Poly Saddle Buckjump from the Warwick Show and Rodeo, an event where riders have to cling on to a bucking horse for a hair-raising eight seconds. 'I've forbidden her to do it any more,' says Katie. 'It's ridiculous. The winners each time were eighteen and nineteen-year-olds, and she's now forty-nine! She still loves doing that stuff.'

There's a small TV to watch the news and the odd episode of *McLeod's Daughters*. For a woman who's actually the real thing, however, it's a series that doesn't hold much sway. 'Eat your heart out!' she laughs. 'People like us can see so many things wrong with it, it can sometimes look a bit silly. One of the episodes with a big wild brumby . . . Anyone with any experience could see it was an old horse, and it certainly wasn't wild!' Preferred viewing are TV series like 1989's western *Lonesome Dove* with Robert Duvall and Tommy Lee Jones, and that old favourite romance on the land, the 1939 movie *Gone With the Wind*.

For despite Susan's weathered exterior, she's a softie inside. 'Mum's always been an extraordinary woman,' says her son Joseph. 'She's the strongest woman anyone could ever know, having spent her life working from place to place to place; a real battler; someone who'll never give up. But she's also very soft at heart. If anything's wrong with her kids, she'll get upset pretty quick, and she'll do anything for her animals. A cow might die and everyone'll say the calf will die too, but she'll spend every bloody minute with it, caring for it, making sure it'll survive. She might only have $100 left, but she'll spend it all on feed for her horses and her dogs.'

One of the steers Susan befriended on a long drove, she asked someone else to feed for a month before they reached their destination. 'They all have personalities,' she explains, a little shame-faced. 'I used to pat him, and he'd come straight up to us. I wouldn't have liked to have spent more time with him before he was to be killed. People think I'm tough, but I put on a good front.'

Yet whatever the future holds, Susan is certain there'll always be a place for droving. People favoured trucks for a while to transport their animals to market and to the slaughteryards, but the price of diesel these days mitigates against any economies. Droving is actually a much cheaper option. 'In addition, you can walk a mob from A to B and B to A, and your stock will get there in better condition,' says Susan. 'On a truck, they get knocked around a fair bit. You can get good truckies and bad truckies. A good truckie will load them right. Then you get the other truckies that try to get too many in the one pen and they're all congested. As soon as you put them on a truck, as well, they start to panic and poop a lot more than when they walk, and they lose a lot of weight.

'So I think there will always be a job for a drover. They've been trying to close the stock routes but I don't think they ever will. Too many people use them. It's part of our Australian Outback tradition.'

8

The Blossoming of the Mulga

LYNNIE PLATE, *Oodnadatta, South Australia*

This bloody town's a bloody cuss,
No bloody trams, no bloody bus,
And no one cares for bloody us
In Oodna-bloody-datta.

Just bloody heat and bloody flies,
The bloody sweat runs in your eyes,
And if it rains, what a surprise!
In Oodna-bloody-datta.
Anon

Oodnadatta was little more than just another hick town in the middle of the South Australian Outback when 22-year-old Lynnie Trevillian arrived with her boyfriend, a friend, two Aboriginal stockmen and a motley assortment of wild camels and donkeys. Only two months into their planned epic overland trek from Alice Springs to Gulgong in New South Wales, the town provided a handy pitstop. Everyone was flagging after walking around 700 kilometres in 45 degrees Celsius across some of the harshest desert in Australia. The group's homemade saddles had quickly given the camels sore backs that rendered them unrideable, and tensions within the group were flaring.

Desert-bound Oodnadatta, officially the hottest place in the country, with only a few houses and outlying pastoral stations, a tiny population of around 300 – half of whom were Aboriginal – and a single hotel, seemed at first to offer scant promise of respite. By day, as a railway stop on the old Ghan line, the solitary main dirt road of the town could be busy. By night, it was often like a Wild West movie when stockmen and rail fettlers from the maintenance gangs came into town on benders, with the nerve-jangling smashing of bottles outside the pub, loud arguments and fights.

Yet as Lynnie and boyfriend Adam Plate stayed on, she became more and more entranced. It was 1975, she was totally relaxed about life and time, and full of idealism about small-town Australia and the fond vision of bucolic bliss it conjured up. 'I found it a fantastic place,' she says today. 'You leave Port Augusta and suddenly there's no trees, just some hills and low scrub. It's so open and free. I loved it.'

The couple decided to stay a while and see if they could perhaps open their own businesses: Adam with a mechanic repair shop and herself with a little café to offer locals and tourists alike a pleasant place to go for a cup of tea. There had been increasingly fearful speculation about the possible closure of the railway station and the building of a new line from Adelaide to Alice Springs completely bypassing the town, but Lynnie thought nothing of it. No sooner had the couple started on their entreprises, however, than the latest edition of the *Coober Pedy Times* newspaper arrived with grim tidings.

The new Ghan railway line was indeed to be built, and would this time travel far to the west, along the route of the Stuart Highway. The headline on the front page pulled no punches. 'Oodnadatta to die!' it screamed. For a moment, Lynnie was floored. But then her chin went up and a spark flashed in her pale-blue eyes. 'It was a challenge,' she says. 'It was one of the greatest challenges of our lives.'

More than 1000 kilometres north of Adelaide, 670 kilometres south of Alice Springs and nearly 200 kilometres north-east of Coober Pedy, Oodnadatta lies in the dead heart of the great desert plains of South Australia. With a name popularly believed to be an adaptation of the Aboriginal word 'utnadata' meaning 'blossom of the mulga', those vast, scorched gibber plains come alive in springtime with wild flowers, but look utterly barren the rest of the year.

The site of the present-day Oodnadatta had been used for tens of thousands of years by the local Arabana people as a stopping-off point on their trading route between the natural springs from Marree to the south-east, at the start of the Birdsville Track, and

Marla to the north-west. Later, when camels and their Afghan keepers were imported in 1838, they used the same track, dropping into communities all the way along, providing an important first means of communication and supplies. The tiny settlement of Oodnadatta really came into its own, however, after explorer John McDouall Stuart mapped the region in 1859 as part of the proposal for an overland telegraph line stretching 3200 kilometres from Port Augusta to Darwin, thence to Java, through China and India to Europe, to open up Australia's heartland and link the country with the rest of the world. That line, one of the great engineering feats of the nineteenth century, passed directly through Oodnadatta, and was completed in 1872.

The availability of regular communications across an area previously regarded as *terra incognita* meant millions of hectares of land were quickly taken up with pastoral leases. It then became only natural that the ambitious plans for a railway to link the south with the north should pass along the same route, so a construction camp for the mid-section was set up at Oodnadatta. In 1890, at about the same time as the discovery of a good supply of quality artesian water, the site of that camp was proclaimed a government township. The railway station was opened shortly afterwards in 1891, remaining the northernmost point of the railway until 1929, when the line was extended to Alice Springs.

By the time Lynnie Trevillian arrived in the mid-1970s, the town had settled into an easy rhythm. The population was mostly stable, there was a hospital, a police station and a school, and the local Transcontinental Hotel still had high hopes of living up to its ambitious name. 'I liked the place immediately,' says the bubbly blonde. 'It had a certain charm. We were hippies then, looking for the meaning of life, and there was a real appeal about a place where you could do anything, be anyone, and no one seemed to care. As well, it helped that there was always plenty of casual work around that paid good money.'

Canberra-born Lynnie and Sydneysider Adam were in no hurry to leave. They'd been working in Alice Springs for six months to earn enough money to continue on their BMW motorcycle trip around Australia and had been helping Greg McHugh, a friend planning to travel overland between Alice and Gulgong, the old New South Wales goldrush town north-west of Sydney, with a bunch of camels and donkeys. 'Greg had a dream of taking horses and camels from Central Australia to Gulgong where he had a property, to breed them,' says Lynnie.

'People living around there had one-acre plots, and in the 1970s a lot of them were a bit alternative and would put a donkey or a camel on their blocks, just to have as a pet. He thought he'd breed up all these donkeys and camels and sell them to people. He'd been working in the mines to get enough money together, and he'd got the permission of station owners to go out to their properties and round all the wild animals up. He was very ideal-istic, following a dream but, really, in retrospect, it sounds like a sure way to go broke!'

Back then, though, Lynnie and Adam were fascinated by his scheme and agreed to join him. Adam, together with two Aborigi-nal stockmen up for the adventure, Nugget and Jimmie, helped round up around fifty feral donkeys, six horses and six camels on their motorbikes, then camped with them just outside Alice Springs until they were ready to set off. The idea was that Lynnie, Adam and Greg would ride the camels or donkeys, with Nugget and Jimmie on the horses, but things soon started to go wrong. 'We set out in February, which is the hottest month of the year there,' says Lynnie. 'We ended up having to walk through bushfires and in really high temperatures, surrounded by flies. And the camels immediately got sore backs from the padded frames we made, so we had to walk most of the way. It was . . . challenging!'

Oodnadatta provided a welcome sanctuary from the endless walking under the burning sun and the arguments so, while Greg set off again after a few weeks, Lynnie and Adam decided to stay a while. Still hippies at heart, they bought a wagon with wooden wheels – which Adam soon replaced with rubber ones – and contacted a local station owner with a request that they be allowed to catch camels on his property. He was happy to let them, and also offered to help them break the animals in before they resumed their journey.

'But that never happened,' says Lynnie. 'We'd got the wagon, we'd fixed the wheels and we were on the way to doing it all. But somehow we just never left. You know how these things happen. And that was thirty years ago now.'

Instead, secretarial-college-trained Lynnie, the middle of three girls, took some work typing in the community welfare office. Adam, meanwhile, took on a variety of odd jobs, including driving camel-drawn carts on the world's largest cattle station, Anna Creek, 200 kilometres south of Oodnadatta, as the only whitefella in a camp of fifteen. Then, in 1978, Adam started a motorbike repair business while Lynnie began a part-time snack bar called the Tuckerbox. 'A traveller just couldn't buy a cup of tea easily in town at that time,' says Lynnie. 'Only beer, and I hated that boozy image of the Outback. We also saw a need for a soup kitchen to feed hungry kids who'd be waiting for their parents to leave the pub, hoping they'd have enough money left over for dinner.'

The Tuckerbox had the town's first jukebox and Adam, an ex-art school student and the grandson of Carl Plate, one of Australia's most outstanding abstract painters of the post-war period, painted a huge Rolling Stones-type lips and tongue over the entrance, so no one could miss it. 'It was a bit different for Oodnadatta but it was fantastic, and the town embraced it,' says Lynnie. 'They loved all that colour and our youth, I think. You really were allowed to do what you liked.'

The closure of the old Ghan railway was a huge blow to the town. Granted, the line went through some of the most desolate and flood-prone land in the country, and the tracks often suffered wash-outs that marooned passengers sometimes for several days at a time. But despite that unreliability and the financial crises the Central Australian Railway regularly weathered, it had become a very valuable service to the Outback – and a lifeline for Oodnadatta. Its last journey took place in October 1980, when it was replaced by the new Ghan, which travelled via Tarcoola and up along the Stuart Highway to the west of the old.

When the news of its imminent closure first hit and the dire warning delivered by the local newspaper that the end was nigh for Oodnadatta, Lynnie and Adam drove around on their motorbike, having a long, hard look at the town. They felt it was in a good spot to service the growing four-wheel-drive trade, and could easily be supplied from Adelaide by road. In addition, they felt the town was at the centre of a really rich area of the Outback, with numerous attractions to lure visitors. Its features simply weren't well enough known or signposted.

So the couple then set out on a mission: to put Oodnadatta on the map for the rest of Australia – and the world. The old well-worn 620-kilometre unsealed track from Marree to Marla they named 'the Oodnadatta Track', and Adam carefully mapped each point of interest and handpainted signs on 44-gallon drum lids to erect along the route. 'We had a real belief in the area for tourism,' says Lynnie. 'But in those days, everything was un-signposted, so you took your life in your hands if you went anywhere. If you were from the city like me, you'd end up following the most-used track and end up at a bore somewhere – silly things like that. So Adam started the signposting to make your average travellers feel safe, to reassure them that they were on the right route, and relax them enough to look beyond the edge of the road to what's out there, instead of being tense and gripping the steering wheel and wondering where on earth they might be.'

For there certainly is an embarrassment of riches both on and just off the Oodnadatta Track. Marree, of course, is also the start of the Birdsville Track across the Simpson Desert, and is close to the beginning of that other great Outback route, the Strzelecki Track to Innamincka. Following the line of natural springs, the first of which is Hergott Springs just north of Marree, there are reminders all along the way of those who have gone before, from the local Aboriginal people to the European explorers, from the camel men to the workers who put in the telegraph poles, laid the railway tracks and erected the 5300-kilometre dog fence, which crosses the Track 40 kilometres north of its start. There's also the massive white salt Lake Eyre to the west, whose basin covers more than a million-square kilometres and one-sixth of the continent, with a lookout on the track, the Stuart Creek railway bridge, the bubbling Mound Springs and the burnished red dunes of Irrapatana. Midway to Oodnadatta is the town of William Creek (population five), Anna Creek Station is nearby, as are various homestead ruins and more sandhills.

Oodnadatta, of course, has plenty to see of its own, including graves of pioneers and Afghan cameleers, the old Ghan railway station building, a bush nursing hospital and an Aboriginal school. Off the Track to the south-west is the painted desert, a mountainous area streaked with reds, pinks, mauves and purples from different-coloured sands and rocks, and to the north-east is Dalhousie Springs, which offers 37-degrees Celcius hot ponds for bathing and swimming. Further along the track there are numerous bores, stations, creeks and a white-crusted landscape that could well be the moon, before one finally reaches the other end at Marla, and the road north to Uluru and south to Coober Pedy. 'Many people on the coast believe the Outback is just endlessly bland,' says Lynnie. 'But the Oodnadatta Track has constant variety. You live here with the feeling of being absolutely surrounded by contrast.'

In 1978, Lynnie and Adam's first child was born, a son called Jack. Three years later, they married and had their second child, a daughter, Alice. The next year, in 1982, the couple shifted shop to the main street and changed their business name to Oodnadatta Traders. With Adam looking after vehicle repairs to the side, the adjoining shop steadily grew to include the café, store and accommodation out the back, consisting of a camp site, caravan park and demountable rooms.

In order to stand out, and as a bit of a joke, Adam started to spray everything pink. An old 1969 Dodge Phoenix that Lynnie had been given by her dad was parked out the front of the store and became pink. The building became pink. The garbage bins became pink, and all the seats around. Even the scales, tractor and vehicle wheels became pink, and Lynnie gave everyone pink aprons and started wearing the colour every day herself – including a pink T-shirt, a pink headband to hold back her curly, shoulder-length hair, and bright-pink lipstick.

It then seemed a natural progression to call the place the Pink Roadhouse. 'It's just to make people smile and relax when they arrive,' says Lynnie. 'It's a very happy colour. The only problem is that everything has to be repainted every two years as it fades so much in the sun.' That didn't put them off, however. Even the special Oodnadatta burgers served up by the roadhouse are liber-ally topped with beetroot to give them a pink colour.

The Pink Roadhouse at Oodnadatta has today become an Outback landmark and a beacon for weary travellers. Thousands of people now drive the Oodnadatta Track every year, and the town itself has managed not only to survive but to flourish on all the tourists passing through. After a bitter legal battle with the government-financed store in town, the roadhouse was allowed to add fuel to the range of services offered. It now has a toll-free number for anyone planning to drive the Track to call and check road conditions before they set out, as well as a range of free maps, driving tips and guides to all the sights. While also serving as the local post office and bank agency, not to mention looking after the airport and running a transport busines, the road-house has very successfully managed to brand itself 'Your mates in the bush', and keep up its trademark friendly, laid-back approach, while sharing business, quite happily, with the Aboriginal-owned Transcontinental Hotel.

Yet there have been a fair few struggles along the way. With no experience of running a business and so little communication with the outside world, everything was trial and error. 'You ended up having to learn to do absolutely everything yourself,' says daughter Alice. 'When you did something right, great! But when you did it wrong, it could often be disastrous.' Also, with two more children coming along – Tilly, born in 1984, and then a surprise souvenir from a beach holiday, Ruby, in 1990 – it was tough trying to cope with the demands of a growing business alongside the demands of a growing family, especially in the middle of nowhere.

'Raising children and running the business while having Adam away on the road so much doing our own carting from Adelaide, that was hard,' says Lynnie. 'We never had much and were always struggling. We worked hard and long, and it was always difficult without extended-family support.' There were times when she sorely missed her mum, her older sister Kay and her identical twin, Annie. 'Sometimes you just want family to babysit your kids and give you a break. But they're a long, long way away. And in a place like this, your doctor is the flying doctor, which is strange having a doctor who doesn't even live here.'

The isolation per se, on the other hand, never worried her. 'You never get the chance to be lonely in a place like this!' she laughs, taking an order for food while at the same time serving someone else wanting stamps. 'If anyone ever imagined you could be bored or have nothing to do . . . they'd be so wrong. I don't know how many people come through here, but it's thousands every year. To survive, you just need to be a doer and have dreams and a bit of energy to make them happen.' With the right attitude, even the physical challenges can be turned into fun. The year the rains came – usually the district only receives 150 ml of rain per annum – the town was so badly flooded, the family took a delivery of canoes. If they'd have been so inclined, they could have paddled all the way to Lake Eyre. The canoes were pink, of course.

Visitors, in turn, often come back again, as they've enjoyed the experience of both the Track and the roadhouse so much. 'People come in every day just to say hello,' Lynnie smiles. 'They might say, "Remember me? I was here ten years ago driving a blue Kombi". I reply, "How lovely". They don't realise that thousands of blue Kombis have passed through here in the interim. But I'm blessed in liking people. I enjoy talking to them and I get a lot out of that.'

Friends are often amazed at how much trouble Lynnie will take to help people. One day, a man arrived during the school holidays, when the roadhouse was at its most frenzied, with 200 people passing through at the same time, demanding fuel, meals and information about the roads ahead. He stopped Lynnie as she was running from counter to counter and asked her if she remembered a staff member who'd worked for her a few years before.

'He told her that this young man had suffered a broken romance and had just committed suicide,' says local station owner Janet Williams, who has known Lynnie for nearly thirty years. 'She immediately dropped everything, ran into the house and found all her photographs of this young man. She then gave them to the visitor and said "Take these back to his mother. She will want to have these photos". She's such a caring person. A neighbour of mine calls her "the Outback Angel". She'll go to great lengths to help anyone. She'll even make you a cake and send it out on the mail run when she knows it's your birthday. Sweet things like that mean a lot to women out here, surrounded by bushie men.'

Lynnie has always put back into the town. One year she assisted in upgrading the Railway Museum with a series of photographs chronicling the town's history. Another time, Adam took on the twice-weekly 600-kilometre mail run to all the stations in the district, then managed to turn it into a one-day tourist adventure, carrying visitors as passengers. The facilities the couple makes available for the annual 'Bronco Branding' event in July means that every year they now have between 400 and 500 people camping out around the bronco yards for the occasion, with a full house for the racing Oodnadatta Cup in May too. 'She works so bloody hard for that community,' says her twin Annie Trevillian, an acclaimed textile designer who also lectures at the Australian National University in Canberra. 'I keep telling her to slow down, but she never does.'

Even holidays are commandeered to help the cause of giving Oodnadatta an ever-higher profile. Regularly, the whole family stops off every 20 kilometres on their camping trips to check Track signs and keep them in good repair. Lynnie also routinely writes in the local newspaper, now called the *Coober Pedy Regional Times*, helps teenagers with their community radio station, collects oral histories of local characters and agitates for the town to receive more financial aid from the government.

At issue is the way many remote Outback communities in South Australia are looked after by the Outback Areas Community Development Trust, rather than community members having a voice in their own local governments. The money distributed by the Trust is often said to be too little for essentials like streetlighting, the maintenance of services and the upgrading of roads. It's supposed to be supplemented by local fundraising, but many

argue there's no way the demands of modern living can be satis-
factorily met within such a system. 'Communities' services are
expected to be supported by volunteers, but the era of the volunteer has largely gone in the city and in country towns,' says
Lynnie, who admires how well kept a similarly-sized town like
Birdsville looks. 'Everyone works so hard, people don't have much
spare time to do other things, especially if you have a family. And
how can you raise funds in a town that today has a population of
around 180 people, all of whom are low-income earners? So raising funds for things is very difficult. I'm non-political and I don't
like conflict and confrontation, but it's very hard to just walk away
from an issue like this.'

Lynnie has made many allies in her fight to keep the town going.
She's always had great relations with the Aboriginal community,
who now make up 90 per cent of the population. She's done some
work for a hostel in town for children of remotely located parents
and those facing difficulties, and, in the early 1980s, even took a
busload of Aboriginal people from Oodnadatta to Sydney, just for
the experience. In addition, when her kids were young, they all
went to the nearby Aboriginal school, which was bilingual, so they
grew up speaking the local Antikirinya language. 'They learnt all
the good, positive parts of Aboriginal culture and went out hunting with the kids and were taught lots of skills,' says Lynnie. 'They
were often the only white kids there and they loved the music, the
feeling of community, and really appreciated the experience.'

It wasn't until they were ten or twelve that the children were
sent to Adelaide's Pembroke boarding school. 'I think by that age
they wanted to play sports in a team with everyone the same sex,
the same age and the same height, rather than all different ages

and genders and sizes, and with someone's grandma in there helping to make up the numbers . . . Yes, Aboriginal culture is so different from my culture, and their work ethics are different. But I've been able to work with the local community in all different ways, and we've learnt so much from each other.'

The Aboriginal community in Oodnadatta is very stable, and one of the reasons for that is Lynnie, says her friend Janet. 'Other people come in to help but they're only there for the short term. She's been here for thirty years and is so connected. She's seen many Aboriginal people through ups and downs. If someone dies, she's the first on the doorstep with flowers, food and a hug. And other people might not notice an elderly Aboriginal woman in the roadhouse when it's busy, but she'll always stop and have a chat and maybe compliment her on her clothes. She'll always make sure to stock in the shop the kind of colourful dresses they'll like.'

Lynnie once brought twin Annie to Oodnadatta to run a fabric printing workshop in the tiny town hall, which proved a huge hit with the Aboriginal community, pastoral families and cameleers alike. The fact that some had to travel 200 kilometres to get there, plus the challenges of working with paper mesh screens in heat so fierce the ink promptly dried, didn't dampen anyone's enthusiasm. 'She's always been such a caring person,' says Annie. 'When we were small, we all went for our certificate to swim a width of the local pool. Our eldest sister, Kay, got hers, and Lynnie hers, but I couldn't do it. I wasn't upset but Lynnie was. She cried for me. She's always been able to talk to people, make friends and take on their pain.'

As a result, Lynnie soon forged a reputation for caring about absolutely everyone at Oodnadatta, whether residents or visitors. There were always people staying in the family's own house and, one Christmas, a German couple who'd just crossed the desert – and nearly died in the process – were amazed to be invited to stay for a couple of weeks, even while Lynnie and her brood went away for the holidays. 'They couldn't believe Mum had trusted them, and they were completely overwhelmed,' says Alice. 'Our house was always open to so many people – pastors, stockmen, tourists and backpackers alike – and we were taught as kids to be open and non-judgemental, and to embrace our surroundings.

'Mum always created an environment for everybody that was very kind, gentle and supportive. People always seemed to be comfortable in her company and to trust her implicitly. We used to laugh about how she'd meet someone for five minutes when she was refuelling their plane, helicopter or just serving them in the shop, and they'd immediately tell her their deepest, darkest secrets. She'd know exactly who had marriage problems, who was suffering with depression or who'd just lost a son in an accident. We never knew how she did it. I think she was always just so positive and generous.'

But it was in 1999, just when Lynnie and Adam had decided that maybe, after twenty-five years, it was finally time to move on from Oodnadatta and do something new, that fate intervened, and in the cruellest way imaginable.

The Plate's eldest child Jack was just twenty when he fell asleep at the wheel of his car and crashed into another vehicle, killing himself and two young women in the other car instantly.

Naturally, the tragedy was absolutely devastating for the family. One day, still consumed by grief, Lynnie walked into the house to find Adam lying weeping on the couch as he gazed at one whole wall of the lounge covered with photographs of their uni student son. Lynnie just crumpled. As her own tears streamed down her face, she told her husband, 'If you can't handle Jack dying, then I'm just going to have to die too. I can't survive.' He turned to her and replied softly, 'I just have to go through this. I'm sad, but I'll be all right tomorrow. I'm not fighting it. I'm letting it be. I just have to be here.'

Lynnie's voice cracks and her eyes again fill with tears as she remembers. 'But I felt that was really wise and it helped me a great deal, because when I do get sad, I know it's not permanent – although it feels as though it is. It's just fortunate that men and women grieve so differently. Life would be so very cruel if you were both struck by grief at the same time. When I was down, Adam was able to help me, and when Adam was down, I could help him. I wouldn't be here now if Adam didn't nurture me, and me him at times. But I don't think I ever felt normal in the following five years; not able to cope with life, to laugh and to cry . . . You're never the same; nothing's ever the same.'

Immediately, all thoughts of moving away were shelved as the close-knit family fought to come to terms with their grief in the house where Jack had grown up, and where there were so many memories of him. The community of Oodnadatta pulled around them too. The local Aboriginals knew death intimately, since it's such a common visitor among their people, so they helped comfort Lynnie. More than 500 people attended Jack's funeral in Adelaide, many travelling more than 1000 kilometres to do so. 'It really showed how much support we have from the community,' says Alice. 'But it was very hard. Mum cried every day for at least a year.'

Jack's death near Port Pirie as he was travelling to visit a friend had come at a particularly difficult time personally for Lynnie, too. She'd just been through a bout of thyroid cancer when the accident happened and, three months before that, she'd had to endure the death of her mum. Lynnie was suffering panic attacks, so Annie came to stay with her for three weeks. 'I felt that if I glued myself to her I could help her through her pain,' says her twin sadly. Then Adam's mother came for three months to look after her. 'Oh! I felt so miserable,' Lynnie says of that time. 'I went to work every day and just sat there.'

Only once was she able to smile through the tears. She and Annie went together to visit the crash site on the Stuart Highway, collected some branches of a bush from the site and read the tributes. Both found it complete agony. Then they decided to recite the Lord's Prayer together, but towards the end couldn't agree on the right words. 'We looked at each other and finally we laughed,' recalls Annie.

Lynnie had some telephone counselling, and the flying doctor also came to talk her through the pain. 'He said that I'd just had three whammies – three big things – and some people go through life and don't even have one,' says Lynnie. 'I'd never thought of that; I thought everyone must, but maybe not. Every time the doctor came to town for the first two years I went to see him for counselling. Now he complains he never sees me, but I know he means it in a nice way.

'I suppose I've always tried to be a positive force for the

community, but when I wasn't positive, when I was really sad, they supported me.'

Now, for the first time since Jack's death, Lynnie Plate is bubbling over with ideas, plans and projects. The landmark Pink Roadhouse is still going strong, with a pink Volvo stationwagon now replacing the Dodge out front, and Ooodnadatta has received a real shot in the arm (as has much of South Australia) from the resources boom. Suddenly, there are more jobs for the townspeople, more money and, as a result, more optimism. The mining industry is also training many more local Aboriginal people, giving them real trades and skills that will serve them well into the future. 'There's such a positive feeling here now,' Lynnie confirms.

As for herself, she has a new venture in mind: writing a history of her family and Oodnadatta around the Pink Roadhouse. She's always kept mountains of scrapbooks, photographs, diaries, newspapers and leaflets from the community, and now files them carefully, ready to trawl them for material.

The decision to organise them came after a night-time road accident nineteen years ago when Lynnie's car rolled over five times, with herself, Adam, Alice and Tilly inside. Alice, then aged eight, was knocked out cold and the car came to rest with her lying, unconscious, pinned to the ground by the tray of the car. Lynnie and Adam couldn't find her in the blackness and when she failed to answer their calls, they feared for a few terrible minutes that she might be dead. However, she finally came to and called back. Adam, with three bruised ribs, managed to lift the car so she could crawl out. He then walked to the nearest station to raise the alarm, and the group was taken out by the Flying Doctors.

'None of us had any broken bones; we were lucky, but it made me realise I had to put my life in order,' grimaces Lynnie. 'And that's been wonderful. Our youngest, Ruby, who's now sixteen, said she didn't really remember Jack, but now she's able to look at all the photos and letters he wrote to her, and cards they made for each other. It's now made their relationship so much more real . . . and meaningful.'

In late September 2007, Lynnie was involved in another car accident, this time with Ruby driving. The ute fishtailed on the dirt track to Alice Springs, slid off the road and rolled over, crushing Lynnie in the passenger seat. After treatment in hospital for a damaged vertebrae and a badly bruised arm, she spent a month in Adelaide recuperating. It brought back terrible memories, not only of the accident she'd had before, but the crash that caused Jack's death. At the same time, however, it showed how much she is treasured by the Oodnadatta community. 'There were so many flowers sent to her hospital room, I had to ask people to stop sending them,' says Alice, now twenty-six, and a presenter of ABC Radio's Northern Territory Country Hour program. 'And a ridiculous number of people came to see her. One of the cards someone sent described her as, "One of the Outback's most treasured people". I think that's true. She's so warm and loving, people really respond to her. And while she's had a lot of troubles in her life, she's never bitter or resentful. She has this saying, "Breathe in pain, breathe out love". I think, in turn, people just love her for it.'

One day, Lynnie and her family might leave Oodnadatta to go somewhere new, but she's not in any real rush. The city doesn't beckon, either. Lynnie reckons she really couldn't cope. 'I find it so stressful,' she says, in between serving a customer breakfast, switching on the petrol pumps for a car in the forecourt and getting ready to go out and refuel a visiting aircraft. 'It's all those cars, traffic lights, noises and queueing up in the supermarket. I can't manage that.'

Yet Lynnie's urban vision fires her with the same dream: of opening up the Outback to cityslickers who don't know it and are perhaps a little afraid of it. 'I want to encourage people to come out here and feel confident enough to enjoy it, because it is wonderful,' she smiles, finally sitting down during a lull in the flood of customers. 'It would be awful to miss out on this.

'And mine is not an extraordinary life; it's just an ordinary life lived in an extraordinary place. In a place like this, you can still follow your dreams, and I just hope I can be a little bit inspirational for people who haven't ventured out of the comfort zone of the city. That would be enough. I'd be happy with that.'

9

File Snakes in the Billabong

MANDY MUIR, *Kakadu, Northern Territory*

Up until the week before, the little English boy had never even been outside London. Now he's kneeling on the ground beside a deep-blue billabong scattered with lilies in the heart of Kakadu's spectacular wonderland, intently studying a dead file snake Mandy Muir is showing him.

He's listening to her talk about how the non-venomous snake lives, the local way of killing it and what it tastes like as a staple in a traditional bush tucker diet. His eyes grow rounder by the moment and then he gingerly touches the snake's 80-centimetre ridged scales. 'Mandy,' he suddenly says, looking up into her face, 'can I come and live with you here?' She smiles. Another satisfied customer.

It's been four years since Mandy set up her own Aboriginal cultural tourism company at her home by Jim Jim Creek in the shady monsoonal rainforest along the South Alligator River in the 20 000-square kilometre Kakadu National Park. When she first began, many people told her she didn't stand a chance of succeeding. Others predicted she wouldn't last the year.

But the number of visitors from both overseas and within Australia has increased steadily. Fifty came by that first year to see the sights and listen to the area's Dreamtime stories as they walked along the billabong 80 kilometres downstream from the Jim Jim Falls, as well as to learn about Aboriginal art and traditional weaving. Last year, that number had rocketed to an annual 786 in the small groups Mandy limits in order to keep the experience as intimate and meaningful as possible. And she's now also considering another tourism venture on her land, as well as expanding her arts centre and helping to set up a similar indigenous project in the Tiwi Islands, the ancestral homelands of her husband.

Early on, there were days when Mandy found the struggle to keep going almost overwhelming, and other times when she became terribly disheartened by the naysayers. Yet she never gave up and she's now reaping the rewards. 'I see cultural tourism as being a real way forward for Aboriginal people in areas like Kakadu,' she says. 'It's going to be a good thing for all indigenous people – and for other Australians too.'

As well as her business becoming an inspiring story of economic success, she's also playing a major role in making sure Aboriginal people have a real and valuable say in the future of Australia's last great wilderness. At the same time, she's helping ensure Kakadu will be here for many later generations to enjoy, with environmentally sustainable ventures that underline the importance of the area and demonstrate how it should be treasured. And, in the process, she's managing to connect a huge number of white Australians with black Australians, and their heritage.

As an Aboriginal woman setting up her own business in Kakadu, Mandy Muir reckons she's grown just about the thickest skin of any human in the area. 'I've got this really thick layer, I've got like buffalo skin,' she laughs. 'I've had that many knockers and so many knives in my back, I've got this thick skin now, as thick as the biggest pig out here, I reckon.

'But do you know what made me so determined? All the knockers, all the people who didn't think that I would get there. I don't like to say we are even totally there just yet, but someone said to me if you stay in business for over five years you can consider yourself really successful. We're not far off!'

It's never easy for women in business, and for black women in particular, it can be even tougher. But Mandy's worked hard at it. She started off with a small enterprise in silk-screen printing in the park's main town Jabiru ten years ago, then took a variety of jobs from park ranger to providing commentary on trips along the picturesque Yellow Waters. She combined those practical experiences with a long period of studying tourism potential and talking to other entrepreneurs in the field. As a result, Mandy, now thirty-eight, has become a real leader in the industry, with her operation a template for other indigenous businesses.

'She's a really remarkable woman,' says John Morse, the former managing director of the Australian Tourism Commission and the mastermind behind the global-tourism strategy for the Sydney 2000 Olympics, who recently developed a new tourism vision for

Kakadu National Park. 'Before she set up, she commissioned an Environmental Impact Statement, did all the tourism accreditation courses and then wrote manuals for her business and all the people who work for her.

'She told everyone that in the first two minutes of meeting anyone they should make eye contact. Most Aboriginal people are very shy, and wouldn't do that naturally. But she's made sure they do, which is so smart. She's such a good businesswoman and has an extraordinary ability to move between cultures, yet still retains a strong Aboriginal identity and style.'

That's certainly evident in everything Mandy does. With past studies of tourism in Kakadu finding that many visitors are really looking for some kind of contact with, and experience of, Aboriginal culture, she's helping provide a service that's critical to the long-term prospects for tourism in the region. Murdudjurl Cultural Tours, which she operates from her family's property at Patonga homestead approximately 65 kilometres south of Jabiru, offers a variety of activities for tourists, from around Australia and internationally, and most are eagerly sampled.

'I spend two hours with visitors four days a week,' says Mandy. 'They arrive here on our community and I have a small arts centre, which used to be our school where we look at a slide show, then we go for a walk down the billabong. We have a look around, talk about plants and their uses and how we've always lived in the country. Then we come back and do some weaving activities, using some of the pandanus palms. Our land is our life, so when people come to our home, we want them to experience how we feel about it too.'

Everything is carefully prepared and extremely well presented.

Fellow tourism operator Rick Murray, of Savannah Guides and Middlestar Consultants, says its simple content yet sophisticated delivery often takes visitors by surprise. The computerised slide show, for instance, is unexpected, as too are the words beneath the pictures – all in the local Gundjeihmi language. Mandy reads those, so everyone can hear them spoken, then translates. 'It's quite mesmerising to watch and listen to,' says Rick. 'It gives everyone a real taste of life here.'

Mandy talks freely about the lifestyle of the indigenous community in the area, about hunting, for instance, and the way her family often go out together to catch file snakes, which are usually to be found in darker, murkier stretches of water. Waist-deep in water, everyone forages for them with their feet, keeping a keen eye out for crocodiles nearby. Having lived in the area for so many years, Mandy knows the nature of the various crocodiles around, is intimately acquainted with the warning signs, like bubbles, darker water coming to the surface and their strong smell, and knows they're often intimidated by groups of people staying together. Similarly, they'll frequently hunt together for long-necked turtles too, which burrow down usually around a foot deep in the mud, with miniscule breathing holes left in the surface the only clue to their presence. Any extra snakes or turtles might be kept in a tub so they can be eaten fresh another day, and Mandy will talk about the best way of cooking them: on the coals of an open fire.

Afterwards, the weaving is both an educative and entertaining experience. All the materials are lovingly laid out, from the green leaves of the pandanus to the roots of various plants and petals that yield dyes from the dried strands, now all the colours of the rainbow, to the final woven product. As everyone tries their hand at weaving, it's always accompanied by a great deal of laughter. Kakadu's tourism and visitor services manager Paul Styles says it's not intended to be a quick, overly polished, strictly choreographed event. 'It's all very relaxed and flexible, with the emphasis on the quality of the experience,' he says. 'When everyone's sitting around weaving, they're talking and exchanging experiences and ideas. That's its real value.'

A talented weaver, artist, screen-printer and photographer herself, Mandy's arts centre contains a wide variety of locals' work, and often people are actually working there, painting, printing and weaving. All of them can then talk about what they're doing and explain the kind of stories their pictures tell. Mandy is always keen to involve as many in her community as she can and, for those who mightn't be such talented painters or expert weavers, she organised, with the assistance of artist and Kakadu Community Development manager Caroline Rannersberger, a print-making training course at Charles Darwin University's School of Fine Arts.

'She quite quickly came to the realisation that it was hard to maintain a sufficient stock of handcrafted and handpainted items for sale, as they went so quickly and were so hard to produce in volume,' says Paul Styles. 'So the print-making enabled her to produce limited editions of the original articles. It was a very creative approach. It immediately enabled her to stay away from the easy, mass-produced souvenirs. It's yet another example of the way she's managed to grow her business very successfully, but still stay connected to culture and country.'

Her fourteen-year-old son Travis, or Bardayal (named after Mandy's great-grandfather National Treasure 'Lofty' Bardayal

Nadjamerrek, who's famed for his art both on rock and paper) often plays the didgeridoo. Many tourists describe listening, as they look over the paperbark-fringed waters and verdant green savannah teeming with wildlife, as utterly subliminal.

Mandy puts a thirty-person ceiling on the size of groups in order that they'll be all able to savour one-on-one contact. That way, everyone can ask questions and stand a good chance of getting an answer. She also likes to ask questions of her visitors too, to elicit some idea of who they are and what they'd like to take away from the experience. Past tourists have come from all around the world, with the Australians drawn from every walk of life. The TV show *The Great Outdoors* has filmed a segment, hosted by Di Smith, on her tour, and Sorrel Wilby from *Australian Geographic* also featured Mandy in a film about Kakadu for *The Best of Australia* series that went to air on the Nine Network in 2008.

'It's all about educating people about us, and I want everyone to go away with a good feeling,' says Mandy. 'Sometimes, if I have bush tucker, I cook up whatever's in season. Just in the last few months we've had our file snake and long-necked turtle seasons, and then we get quite a lot of them. Most visitors taste what I have to offer and some of them quite like it. But there are others who find it's a bit too much for their tummies! I keep the smaller turtles and snakes that we don't eat and release them down the river. We've had masses of file snakes, about forty to fifty, and fifty turtles coming through. When I release them down the river, that's something I talk to my visitors about. We like to think about our numbers for the following season. We always think about the future.'

Often there are fresh tracks from the deadly saltwater crocodiles to show visitors as well, since some of them have recently taken to walking up the creek channels towards Mandy's homestead looking for food in preparation for their mating season. 'That's usually only in the late evenings after all the visitors have gone, or in the early mornings before they arrive,' she says. 'It's quite safe because of the timing, and the fact that the billabong is a fair way away. But I'm showing them very fresh tracks, and the tourists get pretty excited about it . . .'

Mandy Muir has lived on her traditional lands at Jim Jim Creek in Kakadu National Park all her life. Her mother, Kakadu Traditional Owner and community leader Jesse Alderson, is from the Murumburr clan, and Mandy is also connected to the Wardaman of the Katherine region through her late craftsman and artist father. His mother, Mandy's grandmother Hilda Muir, along with one of her brothers, was taken from her loving family at the age of eight by government officials and brought up in the barbed-wire-fenced Kahlin compound with other stolen children. In 1995, Hilda was one of those chosen to present a writ to the High Court, asserting that the forced removals were illegal as well as morally corrupt. In 1997 the writ was rejected by the High Court. She later wrote an acclaimed book, *Very Big Journey*, about the horror of being wrenched from her family and the struggle to adapt to a new life.

In Kakadu, Mandy grew up in an old shack on the banks of a small spring that her maternal grandparents built at Spring Peak, around 80 kilometres south-west of Jabiru. With no electricity, it was a simple lifestyle with everyone going out daily for food, fishing for barramundi and black bream, hunting frill-necked lizards, bandicoots, wild pigs and sometimes the odd buffalo, and collecting yams and the edible plants growing along the estuaries. To a young child, surrounded by family and a strong community, it felt like paradise. And, indeed, in many ways it was.

In the very northern section of the Northern Territory, stretching east and south-east of Darwin, Kakadu is the largest national park in Australia, a wonderland of high stone plateaux looking down over vast savannah floodplains, lushly tangled rainforest and picturesque, secluded beaches along the Arafura Sea. Nearly sixty varieties of mammals have made their homes here, while the park is renowned for its deadly crocodiles, poisonous snakes, massive goannas and, more pleasantly, over 280 species of birds. It's also revered for some of the oldest artwork in the world, with stunning pictures kept in pristine condition often by the remoteness of their locations. Along with the surfeit of everything else, it also boasts more seasons than anywhere else in the world. Locals divide the year into six distinct seasons, ranging from the monsoonal season of torrential rain, gushing waterfalls and full rivers, to times when the area becomes so dry, it looks as though it's in drought.

Back then, everyone lived more or less in tune with nature, with a simple lifestyle determined by the seasons. It was during Mandy's childhood, however, that things began to change dramatically. 'My grandfather and grandmother went through the transition of when they used to use a throwing stick to kill buffalo, pig and magpie geese,' she says. 'Then some of the early explorers taught them how to use a sawn-off shotgun. A lot of our people worked in the buffalo industry and, because of their bush skills, when it came to learning how to use a gun they became very skilful and were constantly sought after for the work they did in that era.

'I still like to go out and shoot pig, magpie goose and the odd buffalo, which is an important connection to the past. But I can't imagine how the old people would have hunted in the early days. My grandfather used to go out into the floodplains and set up a platform on the edge of the swamps. The magpie geese would fly over, and he'd be camouflaged against a tree. Then he would throw one stick and kill one goose. One for one. If you missed, you'd be starving for the night. It was very hard.'

Most Europeans avoided this region of Arnhem Land for a long time, finding it too hot; the soaring escarpments, rivers and swamps too inhospitable; and the populations of mosquitoes and other insects too rapacious. Thus, most of the Aboriginal inhabitants continued with a traditional lifestyle uninterrupted, until the first proposal for a national park in part of the area was mooted in 1965. Uranium ore was discovered four years later, sparking a mêlée between the Federal and Northern Territory governments, Aboriginal activists, environmentalists and mining interests. In the end, the controversial Ranger uranium mine began producing uranium ore, or yellowcake, near Jabiru in 1980, becoming the world's second-largest operating uranium mine after one in Canada. That same year, Kakadu's wetlands were listed to be protected and conserved internationally, with UNESCO conferring World Heritage status on the area shortly afterwards, in 1981.

As a child, Mandy looked on as more and more strangers arrived. 'Before, we had very little visitation from the outside world,' she says. 'Only the locals used to come quite regularly. Then before I knew it, we got a lot of balanda – Europeans or whitefellas – coming through and talking to our family. That was when they first started negotiating about the mine and the national park. It was all done about the same time. From there, it picked up. Yes, I saw it all as a little girl. It's been very interesting.'

Yet it wasn't until the 1986 Paul Hogan movie *Crocodile Dundee* that Kakadu really started getting going as a tourist destination. The movie, filmed lovingly against the magnificent backdrop of Kakadu's waterways, and a series of commercials through the 1990s fronted by Daryl Somers telling everyone that if they never never go, they'll 'never never know', inspired both Australians (accounting for 49 per cent of the visitors) and people from overseas to flock to the park. By 1994, visitor numbers had increased five-fold, reaching 240 000 a year. Mandy, fluent in Gundjeihmi and Gunwinggu, yet speaking English perfectly also, had plenty of work within the tourism industry, becoming a trainee with one of the hotels, then driving boats and doing cultural talks. The then Kakadu park manager Christopher Haynes described her as 'exceptionally good' talent, an extroverted woman who related really well to other people.

In June 2000, she was also singled out to drive a boat through the Yellow Waters carrying her maternal grandmother, Minnie Alderson, a very traditional elder from the Marrin clan near Maningrida, who'd been selected to take part in the massive relay carrying the Olympic torch on its journey to Sydney. Minnie was handed the flame by legendary 'Kakadu Man' Big Bill Neidjie, and then set off with bare feet to run and climb into the boat. True to her tradition, she would not look directly into the faces of the many journalists, despite all their coaxing. 'It was a very proud moment for us,' says Mandy. 'My grandmother is a very shy person and Big Bill was very outspoken, which was an interesting combination! We tried to tell her she had to lift the torch up towards the media, but she held her head down the whole time. So when she finally raised the torch, the old man grabbed it and shoved it in their faces and smiled away. My grandmother had an idea that this was some sort of a significant event because there were so many people there, and everyone was so excited. It was the most cherished moment of my life, and one I will remember forever.'

By 2003, however, the tourism industry was in trouble. The number of visitors had dropped back down to 170 000, the same number as in 1987. Some people were suddenly labelling Kakadu as 'Kakadon't' and extolling the comparative virtues of nearby Litchfield Park and Adelaide River, both much smaller and more easily and quickly visited. Mandy decided to buck the trend, choosing that slump period to go into business for herself. 'I don't work too comfortably for other people and while I always did well, I decided I'd worked long enough in the tourism industry listening to some of the tos and the fros, the goods and the bads, and I felt I could make a real difference myself,' she says. 'I did a course with Aboriginal Tourism Australia, and then the tour company APT (otherwise known as Connections Safaris) called me to say they were interested, and we started from there.'

The next year, a report into the area and its alarming tourism decline was commissioned, jointly funded by both the Australian and Northern Territory governments, with John Morse appointed to head it. His 'A Shared Vision' report, released in 2005, said Kakadu's strengths included being home to the world's oldest living culture, the globe's greatest 'art gallery' and a number of successful Aboriginal enterprises. In addition, there was its world-heritage wilderness, wildlife and diversity. Among its weaknesses, on the other hand, was confusion by visitors about its attractions, the under-emphasis of culture, limited Aboriginal involvement, the lack of tourism planning and direction, and lack of brand definition and strategic promotion.

'Kakadu is about subtleties,' Morse reported. 'Sometimes you have to just sit, listen and reflect to understand Kakadu and what it's all about. One day, two days . . . it's just not enough to do it justice. People leave saying "Is that all?" – not knowing much more than when they arrived.'

As a result, a $2.8-million Northern Territory-funded 'Share Our Story' advertising and marketing campaign was launched extolling the attractions of the Top End across Australia and New Zealand, with a distinctly indigenous feel. The government also started increasing support for indigenous tourism operators in areas like accounting services. It was all perfect synchronicity for the kind of tourism Mandy was pioneering. As well as drawing up her own business model and making sure it both cared for country and helped develop her enterprise, she also leased out land 6 kilometres up the river to a major tour company to set up a safari camp for visitors, incorporating a stay there with participation on her cultural tour. Future projects could even include building cabins on the billabong.

'She always has so many ideas about expanding and doing different projects,' says Leigh Phillips-Brown, Mandy's business mentor with Aboriginal Tourism Australia's Respecting Our Culture program. 'She'd like to develop her art centre and might expand further into the sale of art in the future. But she's had to fight to get where she is. Growing up with Kakadu her backyard, it wasn't always managed in the way it is now. But she's come through, and she's now a real inspiration for others, while always remaining true to herself.'

That also means keeping her family involved and, to keep pace with all the visitors, from time-to-time her mum Jesse, now also a park ranger, helps her, as well as partner Tony Vigona from the Tiwi Islands, her brother, photographer and one-time *Neighbours* actor Ben Tyler and her children, Travis, when he's home from boarding school, and seventeen-year-old daughter Jessica (or Kapindi), who's studied tourism and has also done some park ranger and tourism work. 'Because it's been so busy, I've had to get them to help me this year,' says Mandy. 'I did the 786 pretty much all by myself, with just three people helping.' Over 2007, she worked on training family so they could become involved and take a greater part in the business in the future.

And sometimes, another close member of her family also comes to visit and helps out; someone Mandy had no idea existed until fairly recently.

Singer-songwriter Shellie Morris had been told for years that she had a double living up in the Top End. Adopted as a child and brought up in Sydney's southern suburbs, she always had a feeling that something was missing in her life. Trained as an opera singer, studying flute, piano and organ, as well as taking up gospel, then writing and singing her own folk-country-rock songs, Shellie became well known among fans as much for her soul-searching lyrics as for the beautiful soaring voice that some have described as a cross between Janis Joplin and Tracy Chapman.

One day, someone came into the office where she was working and said they'd just met her mirror image in Kakadu. It was the catalyst Shellie needed to decide finally to try to trace her birth family. She moved to Darwin, launched herself into the search and eventually came face-to-face with Mandy. For both of them, the meeting ten years ago was a shock. 'We look like twins,' says Mandy, who's four years younger than her long-lost older half-sister. 'She showed me photographs of herself growing up, and it was amazing. We both went through the same phases. We both played soccer, we had similar hairstyles at similar times . . .'

Shellie was similarly dumbfounded. 'We have the same laugh, the same voice, the same walk, the same face,' she says. 'We're identical in so many ways. It was wonderful to find her.' The pair shared a father but, sadly, he'd died the year before Shellie found the family. Mandy, who had been told a few years earlier she had a sister but who felt Australia was such a huge country, they'd never find each other, found the experience simply overwhelming. 'At first, I had mixed feelings,' she says, 'but then I got to know Shellie. I know she cries a lot because she thinks about our life, and what it might have been like if we'd have grown up together.'

The sisters are now extremely close, with Mandy teaching Shellie all about the Aboriginal life and community she'd missed out on for so long. Shellie's been an eager student and, in between performing across the country with the likes of Tiddas, Yothu Yindi and Jimmy Little, has run songwriting and music workshops in more than forty Aboriginal communities with the Fred Hollows Foundation, mentoring many youngsters. 'She's taught me all about bush life,' says Shellie, now forty-two. 'It's been a really good learning journey, she's been a great supporter and a great help. She's my mentor and my hero in so many ways. She's so loving and warm, and has taken me into her family and her community and made me feel a real part of them, and of the life out there.'

Many of Shellie's songs, released last year on her first album, *Waiting Road*, now deal not only with loneliness, but also about finding love. 'She sings stories about her life,' says Mandy. 'She writes a lot about the life she had, and sometimes that's very overwhelming. But now she comes and hangs out with me and other family members. She just loves it here.'

After those first years of trial and some errors, Mandy's today feeling happy and relaxed that she's got her business right, and its future prospects look extremely bright. The main secret, she feels, is having the right people advising her. 'When you work with people who don't have any faith in you, you're not going to succeed,' she says. 'You're not going to have faith in yourself.

'Some people do have a sort of stereotype towards women: the belief that women should be at home and not out there being powerful. But it is changing. I was on the Northern Land Council for several years, and there were only fifteen women out of eighty councillors. But now there are more all the time, and women are becoming more and more outspoken. There are some black men and women who really support women being powerful whereas previously it wasn't the case, because they know we can do it better now. That's good for all the strong women, black and white, out there.'

Mandy has also been the target, at times, of some white racism, with people surprised to find the business being run by an Aboriginal woman. 'But our culture and our language keep us strong,' she smiles.

Serving as a director of Kakadu Tourism and of Aboriginal

ABOVE: Mandy Muir has established a successful tourism enterprise at Kakadu National Park in the Northern Territory (*Michael Nelson, Parks Australia*)

BELOW: Alice Greenup, near Kingaroy, in Queensland (*Melissa McCord, reprinted with kind permission of the* Australian Women's Weekly)

Lynnie Plate on the main street of Oodnadatta in South Australia *(Jimmy Thomson)*

ABOVE: Lynnie in front of the Pink Roadhouse she established, which has become a mecca for 4WD travellers (*Jimmy Thomson*)

Above: Jane Fargher in front of the Prairie Hotel at Parachilna, South Australia (*Amy McNamara*)
Below: The Prairie has become an unlikely five-star landmark out back of beyond
(*Picture courtesy the South Australian Tourism Commission*)

ABOVE: Sandy Thorne at Lightning Ridge in New South Wales (*Tanya Marschke*)
BELOW: Sharon Oldfield at Cowarie in South Australia (*Jimmy Thomson*)
RIGHT: Sharon's station is one of the most remote in the country (*Sue Williams*)

Terry Underwood toasts the future of the Australian Outback at her family's property Riverer in the middle of nowhere in the Northern Territory (*John Underwood AM*)

Tourism Australia, there are many information exchanges Mandy's constantly taking up, and conferences she attends where she speaks about her tourism vision for Kakadu, and listens to others' from elsewhere. Early last year, she was chosen to represent Kakadu's indigenous tourist operators at the 2007 Aboriginal Australia Road Show that toured overseas, showcasing Aboriginal art trails, Dreamtime stories and ancient traditions. As part of that, she visited the UK, Italy, France, Germany and the Netherlands.

Her versatility constantly surprises John Morse, now also a member of Indigenous Tourism Australia, part of the national Tourism Australia. 'At home, she goes down to the billabong and walks around in the crocodile-infested waters, catching these really fat and ugly file snakes,' he says. 'She sticks their heads in her mouth and bites down on them, which breaks their spines and kills them. Then I was with her at the Australian Embassy in Paris and she was chatting with all the top journalists there from magazines like *Paris Match*. She made the transition look so easy.

'Another time, I went to her house and she said, "You're just in time for lunch!" "Great!" I said. "What's for lunch?" "It's there," she said, pointing to the corner. Lying on the ground was a 3-metre-long python, and an upside down emu. In some ways, she can be very traditional, but then you take her to a conference in Broome to see other tourism products, and she speaks in front of 400 people and comes across as a very far-sighted and successful businesswoman. She's very driven. Her ambition is to be the first traditional Aboriginal woman in Australia to own a four-wheel-drive Porsche! I think that's fantastic.'

Recently, Mandy was in Melbourne being introduced to a number of tourism bosses after talking to them about the marvels of Kakadu. One of them remarked on how strong her handshake was. Rick Murray, standing off to one side, smiled when he heard them. 'If only they'd known what she was doing with those hands just a few days before!' he laughs. 'She'd been swimming among the crocs to catch file snakes and then she'd been hunting for geese. She's a very skilled hunter, and it helps her keep her connections with a traditional lifestyle.'

There are times too when he's amused at how Mandy'll leave a message on her phone saying that she's gone hunting and will be back in a couple of days. He imagines the frustration of tourism chiefs overseas, but admires her for having such gall, and for keeping the faith so completely. 'They might be thinking, What a bloody unreliable mob! but, really, she's keeping her culture strong, so that it, together with cultural tourism, can prosper,' says Rick. 'She's very strong, and very determined.'

Of course, behind the scenes, moving between worlds must be difficult at times, but Mandy usually finds the laughter in each situation. The ten-year-old English boy who was so captivated by the file snakes and the Kakadu lifestyle later – much to Mandy's surprise and amusement – stripped naked and plunged into the billabong when no one was looking. As a result, she then had to jump in alongside him to check there weren't any crocodiles in the vicinity. Another time, on a trip to the Kosciuszko National Park in the Snowy Mountains, she had to keep reminding her son Travis that hunting animals there was forbidden. And, constantly, she's amused by the expressions on tourists' faces when they see her bite the head off a file snake. 'They meet me and find I'm educated and fluent in English, and then it's a shock to see that,' she grins. 'Sometimes, I laugh my own head off.'

But there can be difficulties combining running a thriving business with caring for and supporting her family as well as the huge obligations she shoulders on behalf of her wider community. That's something that's always struck Shellie, coming from outside, most forcibly.

'She has a lot of cultural commitments that she has to look after,' says Shellie. 'She has to worry about her clan or if anyone is sick or if there's a funeral. She has a lot of obligations. It's amazing that she's managed to achieve so much, yet still be such a strong part of the community's grassroots, and such a role model for younger women.'

While Mandy treasures time with her own community, she does feel sad occasionally at how much it's changed over the past thirty-eight years. When she grew up, she was surrounded by elders, aunties and uncles, with relatives from every age group. 'My children don't have so much of that,' she says. 'We had a lot of old people around us, always talking our language, passing down the knowledge. But the younger ones don't have very much of it anymore. My mother is considered one of the elders in the community now and she's only in her early sixties. That's the saddest thing about it. Before, the old people lived a long time, but with all the social problems and European settlement, the more we get used to eating European foods, the more damage it does to us.'

Into the future, tourism, and taking charge of various tourism ventures, offers great promise for the long-term security of Aboriginal people, Mandy believes. In Kakadu, the imminent end of the Ranger mine lease will mean the last of the income from mining royalties, but tourism presents a much safer, healthier and environmentally sustainable opportunity anyway. 'It's going to be the best thing for a lot of us,' says Mandy. 'The only concern I have is to make sure our people get a good deal out of it. We're so much smarter because we've made mistakes in the past; now we have a much better idea of what will be good for the future, for our kids, and for our environment.'

And so far, so good. In 2005, according to Tourism Australia figures, 829 000 international visitors – up by a third on the previous year – and 584 000 domestic travellers participated in Aboriginal tourism activities. Yet while a total of 16 per cent of all international visitors take part in Aboriginal tours, the equivalent figure for Australians is just 1 per cent. For Mandy, that represents a challenge. She's often surprised at how interested international holidaymakers are in indigenous culture in stark contrast to locals.

'Some of the Europeans come through, and they don't even speak English that well,' Mandy marvels. 'But it still works. We have a lot of fun when we get to the weaving part, as that's so interactive. They just enjoy it, regardless of how much they're able to understand. I'm never really sure why they would have so much interest in our culture, but maybe it's because they have their own culture behind them too. And having been over to Europe now, I realise why there's a lot of people driving themselves around here: their places are so crammed up, they must love our open spaces.

'It is terrible to say, but the Australians who visit often seem to know very little about us. That's why I see it as such a great thing, having Aussies coming in, especially with the stuff that's happening in the Territory at the moment. I think some just imagine drunkenness and social problems, which is sad. So when they visit they just get so surprised. We are so welcoming, and they walk out having learnt so much more. I always talk openly and honestly with my visitors. They're free to ask what they want, and I'm aware I'm probably one of the first Aboriginal people they've ever met. They're often completely surprised by the richness of the experience.'

John Morse has certainly seen that first-hand. He says visitors are usually a little reserved, skeptical and anxious about what they'll find on an Aboriginal tourism experience, but Mandy is invariably so warm, friendly and open, she simply charms them all. 'They all fall in love with her, you can see it happening,' he laughs. 'She's so creative and generous, like most Aboriginal people, and she *wants* all of Australia to embrace her culture.

'Many of us have lost touch with nature and ourselves, and Aboriginal culture gives us all a chance to reconnect with the earth and the rich heritage of the oldest existing culture in the world. There's so much potential there, and Mandy, with her tremendous personality and respect for country, is at the forefront of an incredible Outback tourism industry with so much promise for us all.'

10

Outback Love Affair

ALICE GREENUP, *near Kingaroy, Queensland*

The flames were licking closer and closer to the vehicle and Alice McKiggan, sitting alone in the passenger seat, started to get nervous. Her farmer friend had lit the other end of a 15-metre-long wood heap on an area of land he'd been clearing, and the fire was darting along its length far more quickly than she'd ever imagined it could – straight towards her.

At first, dyed-in-the-wool city girl Alice eyed the blaze warily in the rear-view mirror. Then she watched it roar much closer. Now she could see it right beside her, thick smoke billowing up and into the open windows of the Landcruiser. In the distance, she could hear increasingly frenzied shouts: 'Alice! Alice! Look out! Drive! Drive!'

Suddenly grasping the urgency of the situation, she slid over to the driver's side and turned on the ignition. The car bunny-hopped half a metre. She turned the key again, and it bucked once more. She repeated the process three times until she was safely out of harm's way. At that point, her friend came racing up beside her, wrenched open the door, pushed her out of the way, snatched the wheel, started the engine properly and drove well clear of the inferno.

He then stopped and looked at her with an expression of sheer incredulity. 'Oh, Alice!' he spluttered. 'You can't even bloody drive, can you?'

There were a hell of a lot of things Melburnian Alice McKiggan soon discovered she didn't know the first time she went to stay in the Outback. For example, she had no idea how important it was to skip smartly out of the way of a bull when it was heading for an open gate behind her. In fact, she couldn't even tell the difference between a bull and a cow, and didn't have any idea what a steer might be. When she marvelled out loud at the size of the turkey that must live in a 'turkey's nest' the first time she was shown one, having no idea it was the moniker for a type of country dam, every-one else fell about laughing. And not being able to drive . . . no one could quite believe it.

'Well, who *can't* drive in the country?' Alice says. 'They learn to drive from the age of eight! It hadn't even occurred to anyone I couldn't drive – until my friend nearly lost his Landcruiser as a result . . .'

But today, just seventeen years after falling for a farmer and abandoning city life to settle in the Outback, Alice is standing chatting to some of Australia's most successful cattle farmers.

A few moments later, she excuses herself, and takes a place at the front of the room to give a talk on new genetic theories to improve their yields, better ways to market their products, how to organise their assets to the best advantage, and the latest ideas on caring for their land. And, what's more, they're all listening intently.

For Alice has carved a place for herself as one of the leading lights in the country's beef industry, running some of the biggest field days in history, bringing in experts to speak and business consultants to lecture, and developing training sessions for producers in every area, on every topic. At the same time, she helps run a hugely successful cattle breeding station that receives hundreds of visitors every year to study its methods.

'She was always such a city girl, and so social – we were amazed when she went to the country,' says old school friend Merran Elliot. 'She had no idea about anything to do with the Outback. But she's a force to be reckoned with. Whatever Alice sets her mind to, she achieves. She was constantly striving and ambitious, and was always going to do well, in whatever field or whatever place she ended up. Even in the country.'

Yet it was a long, twisting route from the city to where she's eventually made such a mark. As a kid, growing up in Melbourne's picturesque seaside suburb of Brighton, the closest she ever came to the Outback was family camping holidays, albeit usually chosen purely for financial reasons. Her mum Jill, an office worker who'd migrated from England in 1952, had split from her Perth-born mathematician father Ian in 1976, four years after Alice's birth. The pair continued living close to each other so as not to disrupt Alice and her older brother Douglas's schooling. It reaped dividends: Alice won a prized scholarship to the area's most prestigious co-ed independent school, St Leonard's College. There, the successful completion of the International Baccalaureate Diploma allows students entry to universities in Australia and around the world, including Oxford, Cambridge, Harvard, Yale and the Sorbonne.

'I thought I'd like to study law in France at the Sorbonne, because that was the kind of stupid notion you get in your head when you're a teenager,' says Alice, now thirty-five. 'I also always thought I'd be the first female prime minister of Australia. I had those grand notions. People said by the time I'd be old enough to be prime minister, there'll have been heaps of female prime ministers. But at this rate, I still have all the time in the world . . .'

Headstrong from the first, Alice quit her degree in philosophy and French at the University of Melbourne after just eight weeks, and took a year off to travel around Europe. At the same time, a male friend of her brother's asked if she'd like to come travelling around Australia with him first. 'I thought, yes, it would be sensible to see Australia before I go to Europe, so I said I would,' smiles Alice. 'And the moral of this story is: I still haven't got to Europe!'

Setting off on the back of his big 1200cc Yamaha touring bike, she soon discovered her error of judgement. They saw plenty of scenery, sure enough, as they drove through Victoria and up through South Australia to Alice Springs – although often Alice would nod off on the back seat, or sit backwards and try to read a book over the pannier to beat the boredom – but she didn't quite meet his expectations of the ideal female travelling companion. 'Because I'd been to co-ed schools, I never saw any intent in guys other than friendship; I never thought of them romantically,' says Alice. 'I was very naïve. So when he'd said he was looking for a mate to go with, I thought he just wanted company. But in hindsight I think he might've wanted rather more than that. So we parted in Alice Springs.'

From there, Alice joined a gang of backpackers who were delivering a hire-van back to Darwin, for only the price of the fuel. She stayed a while, hitchhiking up on her own to Kakadu and around many of the other sights of the Northern Territory. Her only real setback was when she came across a man who had a bunch of Blue Heeler puppies with him, far too young to have been separated from their mother. One in particular was very sick and Alice took possession of it, while taking the man to task for his neglect. Covered in ticks and fleas, and half-dead from dehydration, the dog's presence suddenly made hitchhiking much trickier.

The pair made it over to the Queensland coast at Townsville, where Alice was contacted by a close former school friend who was down at Yeppoon, just north of Rockhampton, 700 kilometres along the coast. She was thrilled to hear from him, secretly believing he could be the love of her life. So with her puppy securely tucked under her arm, she phoned her parents to tell them she was now heading south. Her father had a friend in Mackay, roughly halfway to her destination, who owned a backpackers' hostel, so he asked Alice to call in and pass on his respects. She said she would, but she wasn't keen; she was now in a hurry to get to Yeppoon. She was even less enthusiastic when, hitchhiking once again, she was picked up by a truck driver who was going straight to Rockhampton. But reluctantly, she scrambled off at Mackay and went to the hostel to stay the night. Over breakfast the next morning, the hostel was abuzz with news of a good short-term job going as a governess on a nearby cattle property, with the owner dropping in to interview candidates shortly afterwards. Alice was still looking for a lift but, because she was there, agreed to a quick interview – what the hell! she thought – then later that day set off for Yeppoon.

When she finally arrived, she met up with her friend, the pair hugging each other in delight to see each other again. Pulling away from the embrace, he looked at her tenderly. 'Alice, I've something to tell you,' he said softly. 'Yes?' she replied, her heart beating hard inside her chest.

'I'm gay.'

It was 1990 and, now heartbroken and without a plan, eighteen-year-old Alice decided to go home to Melbourne to see her father who was in hospital having an operation to remove a tumour. He'd been suffering from cancer, a result of working for years as a scientist at Maralinga, in the remote western deserts of South Australia, where British nuclear testing in the 1950s caused massive contamination with deadly radioactive waste. The government paid all his medical bills in compensation, until eventually he was killed by the cancer in 2002. But back then, her dad's plea that she stop off in Mackay had left Alice with an offer of a four-month job, so leaving the puppy, Darwin, with her mum, she went back up and took the post as governess on the cattle station out west of Nebo to earn some money.

'It was a bit like Mary Poppins, being governess to two children in grades one and three,' says Alice. 'They'd been doing the syllabus by correspondence. I thought I'd just spend some time on the property, earn some money and stay away from men.' But as she was being shown around the station on the first day, she was introduced to a bunch of workers shoeing horses in the stables. 'Meet Alice – she'll be around,' said the head stockman's wife. Alice smiled at the group. Jackeroo Rick Greenup stepped forward, grinned and tipped his hat. Alice's knees went weak.

'He had this big country smile and the way he tipped his hat . . . I was a goner!' she recalls now. 'He just exuded something. It was quite tragic. To think I fell in love with the first guy to tip his hat at me . . .'

Rick, nineteen, had grown up on a property at Jandowae, near Dalby, west of Brisbane. After school, he'd headed to the remote Barkly Downs on the Barkly Tableland, east of Tennant Creek, a place of big skies, vast cattle stations and rugged Outback beauty, to indulge his passions for mad, fast cattle, and mad, fast horses. There, he honed his skills in stockmanship and horse-breaking until a bad accident with a horse forced him back home. Then he'd gone to work on the same property as Alice, Tierawoomba.

He liked her from the first, but was often startled at how little she knew of the country. 'She was a bit of a shocker, really,' he says. 'She thought that spurs were something worn in nightclubs as accessories, and she even thought hats were a fashion item, rather than as a necessity to keep the sun off. We were poles apart. If we hadn't met there, the only way we could have conceivably met was if she'd chained herself to a tree for Greenpeace . . . and I'd been driving a 'dozer straight at her.'

For Rick, in stark contrast, was the real Outback deal. He loved rodeos, risk-taking and the land. Soon, he also loved spending time with Alice. In her time off from work, she watched him in rodeos, helped him in his weekend job on another property and they went campdrafting together. In return, he taught her the difference between a cow and a bull, what a turkey's nest was, that there was slightly more to keeping a property than letting the cows out to eat grass, how to ride a horse and, after the Landcruiser incident, how to drive a car. The local policeman took her for the driving exam and she was so nervous, she stalled and ran up onto the kerb. But Rick was always encouraging. 'You're doing well,' he told her. 'That's how I was when I started to drive.' 'Yes,' she'd reply, 'but you were only eight years old!'

Since Alice knew nothing of life on a cattle station, she became the regular butt of practical jokes. One day, she witnessed her first bush kill when a steer was felled with a direct bullet to the brain. The three jackeroos cut its jugular and were starting to bleed it when its back leg kicked out with a violent twitch. 'Look out, Alice!' one of them yelled. 'It's still alive! Run, Alice, run!' Her heart pounding with fear, Alice leapt up on to the rails to escape the enraged beast. When she looked back, the three men were falling over with laughter, the dead steer still at their feet.

Another time, one of Rick's friends gave her some valuable advice on Outback culture. 'A girlfriend should know her place,' he said. 'First comes the mates, then the car, then his hat, dogs and horses, and last of all, the girlfriend. Get that right and you can stick around.' Alice was nonplussed. But gradually, she learnt about life on the land, and her love affair with the Outback began. 'Being out there on the property, I loved what I had seen,' she says. 'I loved the land. I loved being there.'

She was also falling more and more heavily for Rick. At the end of the term, she headed to the sandy beaches and sandstone cliffs of Newry Island, off Mackay, for a complete change of scene and another couple of months' work, arranging to meet Rick back at his parents' home for New Year's Eve. That Christmas Day 1990, Cyclone Joy struck with its 200-kilometres-an-hour winds and record rainfall, killing four people and leading to central Queensland's third largest flood in over one hundred years. Alice was stranded on the island with fifty day-trippers, unable to leave for another three days. Finally back on the mainland, she hitched a ride south, battling flooded highways and closed roads and persuading her driver to continue even as he protested it was far too dangerous. Rick would be waiting for her.

By the time Alice arrived in Jandowae, it was one in the morning, and she was soaked to the skin, bedraggled and totally worn out, clutching only a black plastic bin liner holding her remaining clothes. But, delighted with herself for her ingenuity in getting so far, she called Rick and asked him to pick her up, oblivious to the fact that it perhaps mightn't be the best time to make an entrance. He drove her back home and, as they went through the front door at 2 a.m. on December 30, a foreboding figure shuffled down the hallway in a pink dressing-gown. Taken aback, Rick turned. 'Meet my mum,' he announced. The woman scowled. 'So *you* must be Alice,' she said.

Alice worked hard to impress Rick's family, but it was a tough call. She still wasn't so good on the land and even indoors, things often went awry. 'I really love what you've done with the pasta, Alice,' Rick's little sister Sally said to her one mealtime. 'Especially the way it sticks to the roof of your mouth.'

When it finally came time to leave, Alice felt sure Rick's parents were overjoyed. 'I'm convinced they breathed a sigh of relief when I boarded a plane and returned to Victoria,' she says. 'However, Rick and I continued to write and visit each other on holidays. This city chick was hard to shake.' Others looking on viewed her with suspicion, labelling her a hectare hunter – someone after a family's land – or a buckle bunny – a rodeo groupie. 'But buckles and hectares didn't impress me because I didn't come from the land,' says Alice. 'I was actually in love with the twinkle in Rick's eyes and his drop-dead gorgeous smile. All the city guys I knew seemed to have so much emotional baggage; he didn't have any.'

Alice had, in the meantime, applied to go back to university, this time deciding to study at Monash University to become a vet on the land. While she was doing the first year of science, however, she discovered an agricultural science degree course, and opted for that instead. 'I loved that you could learn all about animals, work with animals, work with people, then you can work in rural areas in general or adult education. I just loved the diversity,' she says. All the time, Rick and Alice wrote to each other, meeting up in the holidays.

After the first year, Alice transferred to the University of Queensland but Rick went off to a property near Halls Creek in the Kimberleys of Western Australia to gain more experience of cattle work. 'For the first two years we had so little time together that, by the end of that period, I'd sort of met someone else. Rick was just a foggy memory. We were still writing to each other, of course, but you needed to read between the lines in his letters. He'd write about a new bore that had been sunk or the thousand head of cattle he was looking after but I'd be left wondering, Yes, yes, but does he *love* me? We hardly spoke on the phone because he was out at stock camps all the time, so I really couldn't even remember what he was like. There was only a sliver of anything left by then. This other bloke I'd met, I'd always told him there was someone else in the background and that I needed to see him to find out what I still felt. So I finally met up with Rick again when he came back to work for his family and within two days I thought, Ah yes, this is why . . . He just had that effect on me.'

For her twenty-first birthday, Rick presented Alice with a pocket knife and knife pouch. 'I thought, what does a city girl need with a knife pouch? It wasn't a proposal but I thought it was a pretty good sign. That's the sort of romantic guy Rick is.'

The couple decided to marry, but there were members of both families who weren't keen. Alice's mum had gradually come around to appreciating Rick's well-hidden depths, but her dad hadn't. He was worried that she would eventually tire of this man of so few words, and wouldn't adjust to living such a long distance from her beloved beach. Rick's grandfather George was even more blunt. 'You won't last,' he told Alice. 'You don't know what this world's about. City girls don't make it in the country.' Alice would steal away and cry.

But finally in 1995, when Alice was twenty-three and Rick twenty-four, they married, going to live in a homestead on Rick's family's property, even as the grandfather continued to cast doubt on their future. 'I hear you're looking for a job,' he told Alice one day. 'What the hell are you doing that for? You've got a job. Your job is looking after Rick.' Alice stiffened, but looked straight back into his eyes. There was no way she'd ever agree to be dependent on Rick or his family. Inwardly, she was seething, but outwardly, she simply smiled. 'Yes, I'll come and work for you,' she finally replied, sweetly, 'if you want to pay me $40 000 a year, that is.'

Alice soon found work in the beef industry for the Queensland Department of Primary Industries at Kingaroy, looking at beef production across the board, from pasture, genetics, nutrition and reproduction, all the way up to marketing. As the beef information officer, the only beef position in the State that had a finger in every single (beef) pie, it provided the perfect grounding as well as all the networks necessary to build a stellar career in the industry. She started contributing to educational publications and holding field days, organising experts to come in and speak to cattle farmers, and starting training programs for producers. Alice's bosses were keen for her to specialise in a single field, but she felt there was a real need for someone to have a good overview of everything happening. 'When I was finally forced to tell them what I was going to specialise in, I said, "Beef business integration", which was everything – and nothing.'

She impressed everyone around her in a very short time. Colleague Jackie Kyte, who worked in the department's administrative sector, says Alice was never afraid to admit she didn't know something, and then seek out the right person for advice. 'She had a very inquiring nature and was keen to learn,' she says. 'She was always focused, passionate and had great ideas. She was also very confident, and had the courage to try new and different things. She's a pretty amazing person.'

With the drought beginning to bite, even Rick's grandfather was forced to admit Alice's career was going well, and the extra income was sorely needed. Rick's mother Peggy started to grow very fond of her. 'I could see she was a free spirit who had never been repressed,' says Peggy. 'My father-in-law was from the old landed gentry and Alice challenged him, whereas none of the rest of us would dare to. He was part of the old farming family where he was in charge of the dollar. But she's from a generation that if you wanted a dollar, you went and earned it. She had always been independent, and always wants to be.'

It was still hard for Alice, though, trying to match up to everyone's expectations. 'At times I felt like I didn't fit in, like I was in a no-man's-land,' she says. 'I wasn't what everyone thought Rick's wife was supposed to be. I missed the variety of food you get in the city, I missed being able to see friends every day. But then, bit by bit, people no longer cared where I was from and, slowly, it didn't matter to me, either. That first year, I was still trying to get season tickets to the ballet in Brisbane; I guess I was attempting to live in both worlds. In retrospect that was probably because I was homesick, not having properly integrated, and I'd been watching peers getting promotions in the city and thinking that I just wasn't getting the same opportunities.'

Then, one day, all the pieces started slotting together. Alice was asked to do a few months' secondment in the department's Brisbane head office and she had a spell back in the city, in an apartment, living the corporate life, and eating whatever food she wanted. In the middle of it all, she had an epiphany. 'I suddenly thought, I don't want this,' she says. 'I realised I didn't want to live in a high-rise building in the city. I realised I had the perfect world out in the country. Up until then, the grass had always looked greener elsewhere but that time, when I came back, I came back 100 per cent.'

Attending conferences on the industry, Alice was determined to bring the knowledge she'd gleaned back into the local arena. As a result, she started holding Better Beef Forums, a series of workshops to train everyone in new techniques and keep them abreast of new developments. Soon, they attracted the attention of Meat & Livestock Australia (MLA), the producer-owned company that provides services to livestock producers, processors, exporters, food service operators and retailers. They asked Alice to run another seminar with them on marketing, looking at what was happening in world markets, and then invited her to organise a Meat Profit Day, a model for major one-day conferences on beef or sheep.

Back at home, Rick was still working for his father while his family toiled through the succession process but, impatient to get ahead for themselves, the couple decided to buy forty-five head of cattle as a start on their own business – even though they had nowhere to put them. A neighbour, Brian Jackson, offered them agistment on his 6475-hectare block, but after getting to know the pair, and charmed by their enthusiasm and vision for the future, he asked them if they'd actually like to buy his property – despite it never actually having been for sale. When they explained they had no money, Brian offered them vendor finance as well.

'Finally, they said they didn't have enough cattle to make it work, so Brian said they could buy his cattle too,' says Terry McCosker, the managing director of Resource Consulting Services, who got to know the couple after Rick did a course with them. 'They were basically kids with no experience in the big end of town and dealing with large loans. But Brian saw something in them that he wanted to help develop. Alice had done her agricultural science degree but was still always looking for knowledge and wanting to learn. She's very enthusiastic and when she sees an opportunity she has the guts to take it. Together, they've managed to make giant strides forward in a very short time.'

The couple cashed in all their shares, maxed out the loans on investment properties they'd bought, took the finance offered and borrowed money from their families in order to buy the nearby property. They bought a four-wheel bike and a trailer to check water and fencing with and to cart hay. That last purchase, on top of everything else, left them completely skint, with no money margin left at all for error. They signed for the property in August 2000, with dams and creeks dry, trees dying and cattle in poor condition. In September, October and November, it rained, leaving the grass green and abundant, the cattle healthy, and beef prices soaring.

From that promising start, they set about building up a beef enterprise on their new cattle breeding property, Cardowan. Alice started working part-time to be able to invest some of her hours in their own property, mustering, branding and breaking in horses, as well as running a weekend bed and breakfast to encourage city people to come out and enjoy the land. 'In 2000, their net worth was $205 000,' says McCosker. 'By 2002, it was $810 000. By 2005, it had tripled. They'd bought at exactly the right time, just before land prices went up. Some people might say that was luck, but I would say they actually created that luck. If they hadn't gone out and bought forty-five cattle, without anywhere to put them, none of that would have happened.'

Then Alice decided to take things a step further and go freelance, taking on the MLA Meat Profit Day, as well as the role of project coordinator for its Edge training programs. In 2003, she became the first city person to win one of the beef industry's highest honours: The Young Beef Achiever Award.

Soon after, disaster struck. Rick and Alice were mustering one hundred head of cattle when she was bucked out of the saddle, and her horse kicked her in the face and chest with its back legs. 'I really thought she was dead,' Rick says. 'I screamed at the top of my voice, "Alice! Alice! Are you there?" She didn't say anything; her eyes just rolled back. I thought she was gone and there was nothing I could do. But at the same time, I knew the only way I could help her was to leave her and try and get help. I just didn't know if she'd be alive when I got back.'

Rick raced home to raise the alarm, and returned to find Alice still lying motionless in the dirt, covered with blood and ants. She was choppered out with liver and brain damage, and broken ribs. Three times during the journey to hospital, Rick was convinced she'd died. 'I don't remember the accident,' says Alice now. 'I only remember regaining consciousness. I was scared because I couldn't move my head but I kind of knew once I could wiggle my toes, and knew who I was – although I couldn't name the prime minister – I'd be right. I was very bad in hospital, in heaps of pain and vomiting. It was really gruesome, and Rick was terrified. I was very scared for him but I knew I was all right, so I was never really scared myself. I'm still learning about brain injuries. I think I now have problems with face recognition; it's quite bad, actually. I thought, There goes my prime ministership, because I won't recognise voters and remember their names . . .'

*

Today, sitting at the scrubbed pine table in the light, airy open-plan kitchen of Cardowan, Alice, her pale brown hair pulled back in a rough ponytail, and her face clear and open, looks back at that time with a shudder. It took a year for her to completely recover, but then she was back in the saddle straightaway.

Rick, now thirty-six, was shocked at how determined she was to resume their old life, and how much she had clearly come to love the land. 'So many people can't handle the lifestyle, but people look at her now and assume she's always been on the land,' he says. 'That's how well she's adapted. She keeps the cattle business going, has a high profile in the beef industry now, and she's very, very clever. I'm so proud of her.'

Alice looks back with wonder at how far she's come, describing her future direction with an excitement that brings a real luminosity to her face and soft brown eyes, her words tumbling over each other in her eagerness to get them out. Since the accident, she's taken on the unpaid position of Chair of the Kingaroy Meat Profit Day, become a director of Beef Australia and a member of their conference, seminars and education committees. She's also begun annual field days on their property and is taking much more of an interest in managing the ecology of the land. With the Department of Primary Industries cutting back the number of their extension officers by two-thirds to just twenty-five State-wide, it means there's a real hunger for education that's just not being satisfied in the community. It keeps Alice extraordinarily busy.

'Her life is remarkably different to anything I could have expected for her,' says her mum, Jill, still caring for Alice's Blue Heeler, which has since chewed her way through thousands of dollars of upholstery. 'I think the isolation out there was a bit of a shock for her at first, but she's now an integral part of the community – and the industry. It was a huge transition from the city to the land, but she's always been very single-minded and determined.' Her mother-in-law Peggy is now another admirer. 'Alice is the kind of girl that you never tell, "You can't do that!" because she probably can,' she says. 'Yes, when she first came out here, she didn't know anything about the country. But I always knew if she wanted to learn, she would. And she certainly did. She was never frightened to push the boundaries.'

Even the accident had its upside. In retrospect, Alice says it resulted in helping concentrate her mind on what she should be doing, and it certainly brought her and Rick even closer. 'I don't think country guys are as upfront about their emotions as city guys,' she says. 'They don't express how they feel, and they can't tell us about it. I was constantly looking for reassurance from him, and I was probably insecure about how he felt for a long time. Even after we married, in all honesty, I was still looking for declarations of love, and it wasn't until I had the accident and I saw how worried Rick was that I thought, Oh! He really does love me!'

A year later, the couple had their first child, a blonde-mopped, blue-eyed little girl called Ruby, now three, and then a son, James, now one. Alice is busier than ever, helping run the station with its 2000 Santa Gertrudis cattle and eleven kelpie crosses, putting on open days, doing her voluntary work with field days and still taking every opportunity to introduce as much learning as possible to the bush.

'Six hundred people attended the 2003 Meat Profit Day,' she marvels. 'We had to close the doors in the end. It was awesome!

We also bring in inspirational people from all over the country for rural people to listen to. It's sometimes quite a shock when you realise how much time you put into all the voluntary work, but it's really needed. I very much believe if you can influence people's knowledge and aspirations, you can make a difference. You need to help people understand how to thrive rather than to just get by. There's a great future in the country and in this industry. If you can help just one person on their journey, it's electrifying.'

Alice revels in how much more interested country people are becoming in practices once considered way out of left field, like dowsing or divining for water and sonic booms causing rainfall, as well as being open to discussing more emotional topics like depression and work–life balance. She's keen to explore anything to improve life, and recently had a feng shui audit done on their property to work out how to increase their energy levels.

'I don't necessarily understand this stuff, but we've had some good visible results,' she says. 'So if it helps, all well and good. We had cattle dying in one paddock for no reason and I called the feng shui lady. She told me to map where the cattle were dying, and I then realised it had been in all the places we had drilled for water. I really believe there are energy lines running through the land and our day-to-day actions impact on these. There's a lot more we are learning about the interconnectedness of nature, land and humans. It's an exciting frontier that we are very open to exploring, especially if it helps alleviate our footprint on the earth.'

As a matter of course, however, the couple are still regularly forced to weather the tough times Outback living always offers. At the end of 2006, 156 stud and commercial bulls had to be culled after suffering brain damage from eating a ration containing toxic levels of sulphur, a substance routinely included in small quantities to make food less palatable, thereby moderating the amount animals eat. The ongoing drought has also cut water on the property to dire levels. But on the plus side, Alice and Rick recently acquired the nearby Eidsvold Station's breeding herd of 1900 females. 'We believe "once in a lifetime" opportunities come along every day, and we like to seize the ones that fit our vision,' says Alice. 'We are prepared to walk away from those situations that won't take us there, as there are plenty more opportunities waiting around the corner that will.'

As for her future, and that of her family, Alice is in no doubt at all that they're in exactly the right place. Once, she used to wonder what she'd do if anything happened to Rick. Now, she doesn't have to think twice: she'd stay here, in what's become her treasured home.

'To imagine going back to Melbourne now really sends shivers up my spine,' she laughs. 'The noise, the smell, the neighbours . . . I also think country Queensland is coming of age all the time, and there are heaps of people out here who like a good wine, good company, good food, just like in the city. There are some beautiful people here and at the end of the day, I love the land, nature and its people. If I could throw in a beach, I'd be in heaven, but a pool one day is on my shopping list!

'We've got so much in the country. There are so many career opportunities, beautiful homes, massive blocks . . . and with roads and transport improving all the time, the cities are not so far away. I'm really sure I'm doing what I'm meant to be doing, and in a place I'm meant to be.'

11

A New Benchmark in Outback Hospitality

JANE FARGHER, *Parachilna, South Australia*

Cutting through a dramatic gorge of glowing red cliffs guarded by giant gnarled gums, the dirt road twists and turns sharply as it snakes towards the tiny township of Parachilna, squatting on the vast plains of South Australia's Flinders Ranges. The first clue that the railhead (population seven) is close comes as a surprise: pictures of a kangaroo, emu and camel on a sign reading 'On Your Plate 3 km'. The next is just as blunt: 'Feral Grazing Ahead'.

But when the legendary local landmark, the historic stone Prairie Hotel, finally comes into sight, all becomes clear. Top of the menu is a feral antipasto – smoked roo, camel mettwurst, emu paté, goat cheese, chargrilled vegetables and bush tomato chutney served with warm Turkish bread – while the house signature dish, a feral grill, comprises roo fillet, emu pattie and camel sausage.

The owner of the hotel laughs to see her newest customers staring at the specials board, bemused by the choice. 'We wanted a point of difference,' explains Jane Fargher, grinning. 'Everyone sees it as a real novelty. Some people say they don't want to eat the Australian national emblems, but we have plenty of other food on the menu too.

'We do get a bit tired of the roadkill jokes, though: people assuming animals are knocked over on the road and then cooked up for dinner. We've had some tourists even reporting that they've seen a kangaroo lying dead by the side of the road, and offering to bring it in for us . . .'

Jane's smile barely falters, however. She became the butt of every joke seventeen years ago, when she and husband Ross bought a run-down old pub that only existed to sell beer to railway workers, and was way off any beaten track. But since then she's managed to turn it into an internationally-renowned beacon of good taste in the Outback, counting some of the world's top movie stars among its clientele and officially anointed one of the hippest hotels on the globe. She knows she's having the last laugh.

And with railway property close by offering extra rooms for budget travellers, a second stylish pub further south and even a houseboat for hire called the *Parachilna Sunset* up and afloat on the Murray, the woman who's built a formidable reputation as an Outback tourism trailblazer shows no sign of having too much on her plate, feral or otherwise.

*

How did a woman whose passion was for waterskiing, of all things, end up in one of the most barren stretches of Australia, close to the towering mountains of the Flinders Ranges and surrounded by great swathes of harsh semidesert with an acute lack of water?

It all started with a terrible accident. Growing up the second eldest of four children on a sheep and cropping property in the farming area of Coonalpyn, 150 kilometres south-east of Adelaide, Jane had no idea what she wanted to do with her life. With a tomboy reputation, the then Jane Goodall loved the freedom of country life, working outdoors with her dad, Glen, riding motor-bikes and horses. By the time she'd finished Year 12 at boarding school in Adelaide, she was still none the wiser about her future direction, but a friend had applied for a course in dental therapy and, thinking that sounded interesting, Jane applied too. She got in; sadly, her friend didn't.

After training as a dental therapist, Jane worked through the South Australian Health Commission and went to work in Nara-coorte, south-east of Adelaide and close to the Victorian border, then travelling north to the Riverlands so she could pursue her love of waterskiing.

Within the first two weeks of her move, however, she was out on the Murray River waterskiing when her right hand got caught in the rope, ripping off her thumb. She spent six months in and out of hospital, having reconstructive plastic surgery, but it was never as successful as the surgeons had hoped. Although her thumb was replaced, it didn't have the full feeling in it that she needed in order to work as a dental therapist. As a result, she started work-ing in administration in the Health Commission – and absolutely loathed it.

'It was pretty menial kind of work and I really do prefer variety, and being outdoors,' says Jane. 'So I decided to go overseas for a while, and took a part-time bar job in a pub to earn extra money. I ended up doing more hours than I did in my full-time job. I liked it. My work became my social life. You got to talk and interact with a lot of people, which I really enjoyed.'

When Jane went overseas in 1982 at the age of twenty-four, she travelled widely, visiting South Africa, Kenya, Sudan and Europe – Greece and its islands, Italy, France – and then back over to Morocco. The experience proved a revelation. 'I was on quite a budget but it was my time in Italy and France that taught me so much about food and hospitality,' she says. 'It made me aware of the differences in our cultures and the emphasis in parts of Europe that they placed on eating. In my family, meal times were more of a chore really: Eat up, get the dishes done and go off and play. My mother always said openly she didn't enjoy the domestic chores, preferring to work outdoors most of the time with my father and employing a girl to work in the house. But particularly in France, it was much more about grazing, with bread and brie and grapes, and going in with your bottle to buy cheap wine – it was that side of eating that I liked.'

After eleven months away, Jane's father fell ill with heart problems and she returned to Australia. At a loose end, she teamed up with Ross Fargher, an old friend she'd known from boarding school. Jane's elder sister Di had married his brother Ian and Ross had just finished at Longreach Pastoral College and, like her, was kicking around, wondering what to do next. The couple found they had a great deal in common, and gradually their relationship became more and more serious. Jane, however, was still fired with enthusiasm about European food and eating habits, and enrolled in a hospitality course in Adelaide. Three months in, Ross's parents, third-generation Flinders pastoralists, bought a new 870-square kilometre sheep property at Nilpena, 500 kilometres north of Adelaide and just 35 kilometres north of Parachilna, and asked him to manage it. It was 1984, and when Ross asked Jane to marry him and go up there with him, she quit college to move.

She'd only visited Nilpena Station once before, and was taken aback by the vast, flat ocean of endless red sand dunes, the forests of shrubs, the mountains that glowed purple in the distance against the setting sun and the stunning gorges. But she was also excited by its promise. 'It wasn't a hard decision to go at all, really,' says Jane, then twenty-seven. 'I liked my country background, and loved being outdoors doing station work. The rest of the Farghers lived in the ranges, but their new station was on the western side, on the desert plains. Eventually I grew to love those desert landscapes, but thought I'd probably never use my hospitality skills again.'

The pair worked hard together to make a go of their station, on the flats close by the ancient mountain range. Formed around 640 million years ago and first charted by explorer Matthew Flinders in 1802, the Flinders Ranges are 400 kilometres of spectacular rock formations, gum-lined creeks and magnificent viewing points. The first pioneering graziers had pushed through these ranges with their flocks in the 1860s, and the land was still wild and barren, with a fierce, stark beauty. Since then, many enterprises have failed, beaten back by the semidesert and the lack of water, with crumbling stone buildings dotted across the yawning expanses of land bearing testament to the bitter end of their former owners' hopes and dreams.

Jane and Ross were determined not to be among them, and quickly realising the area was much more suited to cattle than sheep, they converted the whole property, with a rating to carry 1500 beasts. But times were tough. Dry conditions were more the norm than a cyclical problem and, when it rained, the creeks would often flood out onto the desert pastures towards nearby Lake Torrens.

They soon had more mouths to feed, too. Son Lachlan was born in 1986, and his younger brother Edward arrived in 1988. Jane found her days divided between childcare and station work, but started becoming disillusioned with the way things were going on the land. The couple always seemed to be working so hard to get ahead but, at the mercy of fluctuating commodity prices, they felt they were making little progress.

Then Jane had an idea. Every time she drove south past the five-person settlement of Parachilna, she'd look at the old hotel there, sited just by the old Ghan railway line. Known as the 'Para Pub', it had once been a busy attraction in the days when Parachilna was a scheduled stop on the Great Northern Railway before the rail line was re-routed in 1980, taking with it the town's whole *raison d'etre*. Since then, the pub, built in 1906, had become extremely run-down, operating as little more than a shabby watering hole for railway workers and the decreasing population of the surrounding Outback.

'We just thought it had enormous potential,' says Jane. 'We've always liked a good time and a drink, and it wasn't happening there. Then we got into conversation one day with two girls travelling through the area who told us it was on the market, so we formed a partnership with them, put in an offer and bought it.' It was 1991 and, with two small children, Jane and Ross left the two women to run the pub for the next couple of years until they all realised they had quite different ideas about the way in which the business should be developed. Unable to reach agreement, they put the hotel back up for sale but, when there were no offers, Jane and Ross decided to buy the other pair out.

'The timing wasn't all that great as our two boys were still young and to have me working in the pub and still on the station entailed enormous sacrifice to family life,' says Jane. 'I spent a lot of hours there since the business wasn't really big enough to employ a lot of staff.' The strain grew even more when the children were ready to start school. Jane was determined they not be denied the normal social interaction of the schoolroom, so she and Ross shared the daily 220-kilometre round drive to and from school at Leigh Creek, to the north.

Three years after buying the hotel, Jane realised there needed to be a major investment of funds in order for it to grow. There was a lot of structural work required: a new roof and the addition of ensuite bathrooms to offer a more civilised option than the existing single-shared bathroom out the back. An architect drew up plans that didn't compromise the character of the original hotel rooms, but when Jane and Ross approached the banks for a loan they hit a brick wall. Outback hotels, in those pre-pokie days, weren't providing good returns, and no financial institution was prepared to take a risk on the potential of one that hadn't performed at all well up until then. For a while, Jane's dream of running an Outback pub with excellent food, quality wine and good old-fashioned – but immensely stylish – Outback hospitality, looked doomed.

It was a long and painful wait but, eventually, one bank agreed to lend money, although only with the station as surety. 'It was quite ironic,' says Jane, a short figure with a mop of cropped dark hair, who gives the impression of a tight coil of energy. 'We'd decided to diversify because life was so unreliable on the land, but it was our life on the land that gave the bank the security it needed for us to make it safe!' There was also some resistance in the community itself to the expansion plans, with the fear that locals would be driven out in preference to tourists being serviced. 'They didn't realise that, to be sustainable for everyone, we needed to have money coming in from outside the area,' says Jane. 'I've always maintained an optimistic approach.'

The redevelopment finally took place over 1997 and 1998, giving the pub new bedroom suites (one metre below ground to achieve natural temperature control and thermal efficiency) and a much smarter interior, while lovingly preserving the original brick, corrugated iron and sandstone façade of the old place. Even that wasn't all smooth going, however. The building works went on longer than expected and were extremely stressful, with the budget blowing out from $1 million to $1.2 million. An investment at about the same time in Opera of the Outback – a series of events in the Flinders Ranges that culminated in a performance by international opera star Dame Kiri Te Kanawa – lost the hotel $50,000. But, undeterred, Jane continued with her vision of an Outback pub offering visitors new standards in accommodation, food and hospitality.

Mim Ward, a former nurse who first met Jane in hospital after her waterskiing accident, says everything her friend tried to do with the Prairie was made so much more difficult because of the remoteness of the location. 'But she's so energetic, and is so committed to what she wants to do, she refuses to give up,' says Mim. 'I used to joke that she even has ideas in her sleep as she always seems to wake up every day full of them. She's a real doer. She'll say, "We can do that!" and everyone around her cringes, but then you get fired by her enthusiasm, and you all get on with it. She works extremely hard, but she's a lot of fun too. And her ideas are usually good – she could see the potential of the hotel straightaway, and to have the guts and the confidence in herself to do so much with it . . . Her attitude is always, "You can do anything!" and I really admire her for that.'

One of Jane's early ideas was to create a point of difference with other Outback pubs, so she employed top Aboriginal chef Danni Murray to design an extremely innovative menu, including 'Flinders Feral Food'. At the time, South Australia was the only State that allowed kangaroo for human consumption, so it became a well-known cuisine option – the feral antipasto, then the feral mixed grill, finished off with quandong pie – that people would often travel long distances to sample. 'We explain the kangaroo is sourced through a program monitored by National Parks in the controlling of kangaroo numbers, so it's not like we are shooting them out there in the wild,' says Jane. 'And emu is farmed for the plate. It's only in recent years that these meats have been introduced into restaurants throughout Australia.

'Overall, I think we probably pioneered a new level of comfort in the Outback. Some of the local establishments, like the one around Wilpena Pound in the Flinders, is purpose-built for tourists. But the interesting part of this business is that we've created modern comfortable accommodation here, where people are still able to experience life in the Outback in authentic surrounds.'

Very soon, a new kind of customer was being attracted to the Prairie Hotel. The vast flat plains of Flinders red rock had long entranced film-makers, but the lack of good facilities in the area had made projects extremely difficult. Jane made sure that the hotel started to offer flexible catering and bar hours for casts and crews who needed to make the most of the sunlight hours; accommodation packages and even an in-pub production office. As a result, location scouts were increasingly suggesting the Prairie as an excellent base to make use of the incredible surrounding landscapes.

The first big Hollywood movie to arrive was *Holy Smoke*, Oscar-winning Jane Campion's tale of a young woman who falls under the spell of an Indian guru whose family sends a 'deprogrammer' to save her. Both the stars, Kate Winslet and Harvey Keitel, checked into the hotel. Others followed, including Phil Noyce's Golden Globe-nominated and multiple AFI Award-winning *Rabbit-Proof Fence*. In 2001 alone, the Farghers were involved in the production of two feature films and eight commercials. After plenty of experience in location scouting, Aboriginal liaison, artwork and construction, Ross was even employed as an assistant director with the second unit for *Rabbit-Proof Fence*.

The plaudits started rolling in for the pub from the critics too. In 1998, the Prairie Hotel's growing reputation for style, an inventive gourmet menu and standard of service took out two categories in the Yellow Pages South Australian Tourism Awards: one for the Tourism Development Project of the Year and the other for Best

Hotel, while the renovation won an 'Award of Merit for Energy Efficient and Ecologically Sustainable Development' in the 2000 design awards of the Royal Australian Institute of Architects (SA). But in 2001 came the most welcome acclaim of all: a recommendation in American travel and design guru Herbert Ypma's ultimate international style guide, *Hip Hotels: Budget*. The Prairie was singled out as one of only three recommended Australian hotels – the others being the prestigious W Hotel on Sydney's exclusive Woolloomooloo Wharf, now trading as BLUE; and the fastidious Kirketon Hotel in Darlinghurst, Sydney. As a result, the Prairie now nestles among some of the most stylish retreats in the world, including the gorgeous Art Deco Albion in Miami, the ultra-cool Advokat in Munich and the fabulous Nilaya Hermitage in India's Goa.

But running the Prairie to such high standards hasn't been easy. 'It has been a really tough time financially,' says Jane. 'I guess we were fortunate that interest rates remained fairly low when we were stretched. But while we've been committed to investing back into the hotel and upgrading our facilities, we've just grown the business and done little to reduce our debt. It is still hard. There are a lot of expenses associated with running a hotel in the Outback. It's difficult to attract staff, accommodation for them is very limited, and freight costs are high as everything has to be brought in. Although our renovation was also aimed at making us more energy-efficient, and we have some solar lighting and heating, we're on a metered remote power scheme here, paying up to three times the city per-kilowatt rate. And with refrigeration and airconditioning in the summer, if anyone complains about prices out here, I have to remind them how many schooners of beer we need to sell just to be able to afford to pay our power bill!'

*

Jane Fargher is serving a little group of Italians at the bar of the Prairie Hotel. In broken English, they're asking if she's Italian. She smiles and shakes her head. But it's little wonder the thought crossed their minds. They're drinking surprisingly good espresso, they're looking at the antipasto on the menu and marvelling at the range of homemade speciality bush-flavoured gelatos served under Jane's own brand name 'Flinders Range', including pistachio and red gum honey, desert lime and lemon, quandong and roast almond, and wild rosella and berry. In addition, on the sound system, Andre Bocelli is singing his heart out.

Afterwards, Jane, now fifty, says it's a regular occurrence. 'There's nothing better than serving a good coffee to an Italian who's completely taken aback,' she laughs. 'To them, we must seem at times like a little taste of Italy in the Outback. But that's the most wonderful thing about this whole enterprise. We're now managing to attract a lot more people to the Outback, and getting them to appreciate it.

'Some people might think it's a fairly harsh environment but when you combine the comfort of modern cars and the standard of accommodation that we are now offering – combined with quality food, wine and good coffee – it becomes a really pleasant experience. It's helped tourism to South Australia too. We're probably the nearest stretch of Outback to any capital city in Australia and close to the city and the wine regions, so it's very convenient. And we offer a dual experience: the desert landscape to the west of the Flinders Ranges and the beautiful ancient landscape of the Ranges themselves.'

One of the biggest drawcards, however, is the warm hospitality Jane always provides. She learnt early on that, as well as good accommodation, quality food and stunning landscapes, visitors are looking for an authentic Outback experience, and to meet real people in their natural environment. These days, Prairie guests mingle happily with locals, the numerous visitors from overseas as a result of European marketing campaigns, and all the workers from the local zinc mine, now undergoing an unprecedented expansion because of the resources boom. She makes it a policy to recruit staff more on personality than experience, she meets as many of her guests as she can, is always happy to chat with them and often parties late into the night.

'Her stamina is quite ridiculous,' says friend Cate Spurling. 'She's like an android; she just goes and goes and goes. I remember one morning hearing the door of the pub closing and wondering if that was Jane having an early breakfast – or a late night. When I went back in, there she was, cooking breakfast for everyone. She'd thrown her swag down in the office for two hours and then was bright and ready to go once more.'

The Prairie's manager, Margii Caldwell, agrees absolutely. 'You learn early never to try to keep up with Jane in the energy stakes,' she says. 'For events, it's not unusual to start at 7.30 a.m. and go through to 3 a.m. keeping everyone fed, watered and stocked up. Usually, after that, I'll have a couple of drinks and hit my bed but Jane . . . she's on the dance floor, up on the stage with the performers if she can swing it, getting home at 4 a.m. and is then back at work for breakfast at 7.30 a.m. She can do that for at least three days, no problems!'

While never expecting guests to match her stamina, the greetings note to guests arriving at the Prairie sums up Jane's philosophy. 'Welcome to the remote bush Hilton,' it begins:

We offer more stars than any swanky city hotel. Shake off your conventional city values and indulge yourself in the relaxed style that the Prairie has become so renowned for . . . We apologise for the lack of TV and phones in the rooms, but it's a Prairie tactic to flush you out of your rooms and soak up the environment. A setting sun is worth more that the evening news!! And guess what? The paper is delivered daily at 7.00 am anyway . . . Why do people fly in from all over the world to stay or eat here? You'll just have to see for yourself. Thank you for choosing to stay at Australia's most awarded Outback pub. But don't just stay here, join us! We want the Prairie to be more than an Outback bed. It is beer o'clock!! See you on the verandah. Jane Fargher, your elusive host.

Drinking beer out on the verandah to watch the sunset has become a regular ritual at the hotel, with Jane and Ross even having their own brand of lager, Fargher Lager, brewed especially for them. One visitor, singer-songwriter John O'Dea, was so taken by the experience, he wrote and recorded a song about it, *Parachilna Sunset*. Margii always laughs at the description of Jane in the song as 'a mosquito on speed'.

But Jane is serious about the intent. 'It's not a plan to make people spend money at the bar; it's more to flush them out of their rooms to enjoy life here,' she says. 'We're not a typical hotel by many measures. We don't have pokies or a pool table or even a TV – we love the arrogance of not relying on that kind of distraction. We've also been a non-smoking pub for years, and don't even sell cigarettes. I think because we're all so passionate about the experience of the Prairie Hotel it rubs off on other people.'

While the incongruity of a sophisticated oasis at such an isolated spot in the Outback never fails to startle people, Jane continues to introduce other dimensions to the Prairie experience. Close by the hotel, she's developed a separate budget-accommodation complex out of the old railway accommodation, now named the Parachilna Overflow, for whenever there simply isn't enough room at the inn, or when people are looking for a cut-price place to sleep. Recently, she signed a deal with a national backpacker-bus company, Adventure Tours (previously Oz Experience) that brings in buses six nights per week, fifty-two weeks of the year, with around one hundred backpackers a week on tour, rising to 150 in summer.

A marquee has been bought to extend the restaurant for outdoor dining, functions or weddings, and a catering company, particularly for groups on tour or film productions, has been created. Jane's also tireless in organising special events, including a Lee Kernaghan concert that recently attracted 2300 people; a night with Outback comedian Fiona O'Loughlin; outdoor movies; and big New Year's Eve parties.

'She can see the potential in anything,' says Lisa Pearson, formerly the marketing manager for Flinders Outback. 'If you have an idea, she'll make it ten times bigger, and she'll make it work. She has no fear of overloading herself. You can say something as a joke, and Jane will say, "Mmm . . . we could do that!" while the rest of us are thinking, Oh my God!

'But she can make things happen. If a group wants to see some cattle, she'll gather a big mob together with stockmen and put on a show for people at a moment's notice. She makes it look so easy. Her passion is just infectious, and others then want to be involved.'

The local area has also benefited from that passion. There are now between twelve and twenty-five staff on the payroll at any one time, with the annual wage bill exceeding $350 000. That has a flow-on to many other local and regional businesses, while young people who'd otherwise leave the area as soon as they were ready to look for work now have the opportunity to stay. For the five permanent locals and surrounding station owners the hotel also acts as the post office, newsagent, bank and general supplies store. It's also acted as a catalyst for other tourism ventures in the area, with many former workers leaving to set up their own enterprises, a number of other pastoral families taking tourists on their stations, and the local Iga Warta Aboriginal community running cultural tourism tours.

On a personal level, despite the years of intensive hard slog and the difficulties of combining a fulfilling family life with a hectic work schedule, the experience has only helped Jane and Ross grow closer. 'I couldn't have achieved anything without so much support from Ross,' says Jane of the husband friends admiringly refer to as a 'SNAP' – a Sensitive New Age Pastoralist. 'He's helped so much with bringing up the children, the domestic chores – everything. He's also been a really steadying influence on me. This has only happened with the support of an amazing guy on the land.'

Along the way, the Prairie has proved a huge adventure for Jane and Ross's two sons also. The eldest, Lachlan, now twenty-one, initially chose a career in hospitality, with a traineeship at the Prairie. 'It was great to have him home and enjoying the industry that has compromised our quality of family life for so many years,' Jane smiles. 'I have thoughts about some of the lost time we've had with the family but, at the same time, both boys have been exposed to some pretty interesting experiences through the hotel too.' While Lachlan has now taken a break to work for retailer R. M. Williams, he's likely to return to hospitality sooner rather than later. Edward, now twenty and working in mining exploration, was able to explore a love of film surrounded by working professionals, and his first pay cheque – for $500 – was from producing a film about the making of a car commercial at the Prairie.

In recognition of Nilpena Station's early leg-up to the hotel, the hotel has now repaid the favour. Income from the pub has enabled Jane and Ross to buy, with Ross's parents, another property in the south-east of South Australia that adjoins Jane's parents' property. As well as giving Ross's mother and father an easier retirement, it's also effectively drought-proofed Nilpena Station by providing a dry-land lucerne property.

Jane also negotiated a two-year lease on the old Leigh Creek Tavern, renaming it the Flinders Outback Resort, with twenty-four motel rooms and forty-two cabins, aimed at the family market. The extra accommodation, rated as three-star, successfully lured other film companies to the area, with many of the action sequences of the fighter-bomber-pilot movie *Stealth,* starring Jamie Foxx, Jessica Biel, Josh Lucas and Sam Shepard, filmed in the area.

Recently, that was overtaken by another enterprise: a lease and complete renovation of a sister hotel to the Prairie, the beautifully stylish North Star Hotel in Melrose, 217 kilometres south of Parachilna and three hours north of Adelaide. A broker approached Jane when it went up for sale to ask if she might be interested in taking it over. Cate Spurling's family's business, the Southern Flinders Ranges vineyard Bundaleer Wines, was looking for a cellar door at the time, so the pair agreed to go into business together.

'Jane trusts her gut a lot with business, and she felt this was a good venture,' says Cate, who now manages the North Star. 'Of course, she has so many ideas; some of them don't work, but she doesn't brood. It's more a case of, "Oh, bugger!" and then moving briskly on. But she's always looking for something new. She's like a magpie.'

So far, Jane's very happy with how things are going, and is currently working on reducing the obligations of the North Star's hotel licence to establish a more boutique-style hotel. 'We've got to establish the gallery café experience with retail space and really pursue the function and conference markets, and concentrate on the restaurant business on the weekends,' she says. 'We've attracted some big national events to Melrose, among other things, to introduce quality entertainment to the region and give youth the opportunity to perform. It's going very well.'

As if these weren't enough, Jane and Ross have also just launched a new-style houseboat, the *Parachilna Sunset*, which will be based on the Murray at Mannum, three hours south-east of Melrose, towards Waikerie. 'It's like a floating luxury apartment,' says Jane. 'It'll cater for a maximum of four people who can cruise slowly up the river, find themselves a mooring spot and build a camp fire on the riverbank. It's beautiful, with a sunken spa on the rear deck, beneath a retractable roof canopy. We're particularly promoting it for the honeymoon market and internationally.

'It'll be an exciting addition to the whole tourism enterprise. While it's been tough at times, I've never had any negative thoughts about the business; I'm always optimistic. I feel we've only really touched the surface in the potential of what we're doing. There's so much more to do . . .'

12

Swags on the Ground, Salt Beef, Spuds and Storytelling

SANDY THORNE, *Lightning Ridge, New South Wales*

Sandy Thorne is striding energetically backwards and forwards across the stage, the spotlight darting to keep up with her, barely pausing for breath midst the torrent of words. Her audience in the packed theatre is hanging on to every one of them, sending wave after wave of warm laughter rolling through the room.

> So you'd like to learn the lingo of the Aussies from the bush
> Where the men are tough as gidgee, far from the city push
> Where the women muster blowflies in the blazing Outback sun
> And the children crack big mulga snakes like stockwhips, just
> for fun.
> Where you ride all day to travel from one boundary to the next,

You'll find the dinkum Aussies, a way out in the west.

Sandy's grinning from ear to ear. This is one of her favourite parts
of her work: talking, cracking jokes and reciting bush poetry on a
theme that's forever been closest to her heart: Outback Australia.

Now fair dinkum means ridgy-didge, or genuine, or true
And if you've made a big mistake, mate, you've made a blue
But if some mug bungs on a blue, he's tried to start a fight
He's a nong, a galah, a drongo . . . a ratbag al' flamin' right!
– probably not the full quid – just nineteen 'n' six up top
– mad as a bag of cut snakes, a few wallabies loose in his crop.

As Australia's first, and perhaps still only, female professional
yarnspinner and bush poet, it's the kind of material Sandy loves.
This is also one of the most popular of her self-penned verses,
and one that's won her admirers not only from around Australia,
but from all over the world.

She's recited it in places as diverse as her current home in the
rough, tough frontier New South Wales town of Lightning Ridge,
800 kilometres north-west of Sydney; on the theatre set of the
David Letterman Show on New York's Broadway; before some of
Australia's biggest cattlemen at the Beef Festival in Queensland's
Rockhampton; and in the studios of the *Michael Parkinson Show*
in London. And sometimes she's kicked it off in a style that's seen
her billed as everything from 'Crocodile Dundish' to 'the oldest
jillaroo in the west': she casually bites off the top of a stubby with
her teeth.

*

226

If some of Sandy's tales sound a little tall, that's only because her own adventures, from which most of her material is drawn, have been a great deal larger than life. She began by running away from home in the bush near Brisbane to the wide open spaces of the Australian Outback at the tender age of just fourteen, to fulfil her dream of becoming a jillaroo on a big cattle station.

A tall, strapping girl who passed herself off as at least two years older, Sandy had grown up around horses, and so instantly impressed the station owners with her riding skills. What took them more aback, however, was her daring. Ending up at the remote, sprawling 1350-square kilometre Inkerman Station, north-west of Normanton on the mangrove and saltwater crocodile-lined Gulf of Carpentaria, no one could believe a sixteen-year-old girl was up there alone, looking for work. If she'd have confessed her true age to anyone, they would have been horrified.

As it was, though, she carried off the deception handsomely, and was quickly given a job as a jillaroo, working with some of the country's toughest bushmen and accomplished horsemen from the indigenous Kowanyama people. 'Working with them was a highlight of my life,' says Sandy. 'They taught me a lot. I was so lucky to be accepted by people who were part of that land and had lived there forever. The men, especially the old fellers, were real gentlemen, and horrified that a girl wanted to ride the roughest, wildest horses on the place. But that came as naturally to me as breathing. I loved the experience of handling those big mobs of cattle which, back then, were very toey, and taking them across those huge open plains. It was such an exciting world.'

Jillaroos were an extremely rare commodity in those parts, and when she arrived in 1966 she was the first the men had ever

227

encountered. Initially they worried that she'd get badly hurt or lost – or both – and end up in serious trouble. To prove herself, she thus had to constantly volunteer for the most dangerous of tasks, in a bid to win their respect.

As a result, as well as the fond memories, she has plenty of other mementoes from that time too, including a large scar on her left leg and knee after she was bucked and then dragged by her horse until she lost consciousness. When she came around, there was a gaping hole where her knee had been, full of meat ants, feeding. 'But I recovered!' she laughs. 'It was just one of those things. I was always getting on mad horses that no one else would ride, and I ended up covered in scars from the top of my head to my toes. At the last count, I've had 174 stitches from being dumped off, dragged and rolled on. Horses have done everything to me. But the men finally realised I could ride just as well as they could, and relaxed. It was a thrill a minute. The wild cattle were mad, absolutely mad, then we'd go brumby running, catching and breaking in the horses that were any good.'

After three years in the Gulf of Carpentaria, the then seventeen-year-old Sandy Sefton was ready for a fresh challenge. At that time, there was a lot of work on the fishing trawlers off the Gulf, and deckhands were paid handsomely for their labour. Sandy went along to see a recruiter, again lied about her age – this time saying she'd just reached their minimum of twenty-one – and was immediately offered a place. She worked long days and often nights too, cleaning the decks and polishing the rails of the mother ship and, when the four trawlers in the convoy behind brought in their catch, she joined the men to process the prawns as fast as possible, sorting them into ammonia plate freezers to be frozen, ready for export.

That year, however, there was a newcomer in the Gulf, the massive Russian Supertrawler, the *Van Gogh*. With its powerful vacuum equipment, it would enter a prawn boil and suck everything into its hull, leaving nothing for anyone else. One night, the crew of Sandy's ship grew so exasperated that, much to her amazement, they pulled out .303 rifles and fired across the bow of the *Van Gogh*. Their actions sparked an international incident. When the diplomatic tsunami had finally settled, pickings were so slim from the ruined fishing grounds that the Australian trawlers were all put in dock for the season, the crew paid off and dropped in Cairns.

There, Sandy saw an advert in the local paper for a position as a jillaroo on the Cape York peninsula, one of the last great wildernesses on earth. A vast landmass at the north-east tip of Australia full of savannah grasslands, rocky hillsides where gold was once mined, tropical rainforests, pristine wetlands and bleached white sand dunes – it promised her all the adventure she still craved. Virtually uninhabited except for isolated cattle stations, several Aboriginal communities and a number of tiny settlements along the route of the telegraph line, it felt like the country's last untamed frontier. Sandy's job originally was to look after the quieter horses and cattle closer to the homestead, but she wanted to join the ringers out in the bush mustering camps, where the real action was.

'Back then, it was absolutely unheard of to have a woman out in the camps,' says Sandy. 'It was extremely dangerous mustering the wild cattle in such rough country, with living conditions ultrabasic. But the manager was a modern thinker, willing to give a girl a go at what had always been a man's job. It was a case of swags on the ground, salt beef and spuds.'

Acceptance by the men again took some time. The trick was never to show fear, whether riding at full pelt through thick scrub with barely a metre's gap between the trees, or on horses that continually bucked and reared without warning. And the scrub cattle did everything to evade capture. They had huge horns, hated people and were highly dangerous to handle. Racing down steep hillsides and leaping over gullies provided many a thrill when the chase was on. 'I loved it,' says Sandy. 'Once I proved to the men I could ride as well as them and handle the rough conditions, I was accepted as an equal workmate – even though women were paid a lot less.'

She also enjoyed secretly writing about it, over the dying embers of the camp fire every night. Today, her verses about jillarooing conjure up the scent of freedom, along with the discomfort and the exhausting hard slog.

Up north on Cape York, where crocodiles talk
And songs of the black men are sung
Where the men are true blue, the women are few
I went there when I was young.

On the top of the nation I worked on a station
duffing calves that were grown by a neighbour
As a green jillaroo, for a company who
recruited a force of slave labour.

We started at five on a long cattle drive
But on Sundays, slept in 'til dawn
Working 'til dark, we'd dip, brand and mark

Never filled in a union form.

We ate beef that was tough, the cook was as rough
as his tucker that churned in our guts
When hitting the booze, he'd serve 'mystery stews'
of onion peel, gristle and butts.

At night we lay fryin' in galvanised iron
quarters that leaked in the rain
The frogs that resided, quite often collided
with snakes, in a screaming refrain.

As if the days weren't quite action-packed enough, Sandy soon discovered another fun pastime at night: crocodile shooting. When the stockmen on Starcke Station, north of Cooktown, had accepted her as 'one of the blokes', they agreed to take her with them at night to the lagoons. Sitting in a small aluminum boat in the pitch dark, listening to the massive saltwater crocodiles slithering down the banks into the water, was always an adrenaline-pumping experience; no one knew just where they were going to surface.

Their red eyes in the spotlight made them a fairly easy target at first but, when they dived under after being shot at, it was any-one's guess at how badly injured they might be, and whether they might come up again under the little boat and tip everyone into the bloodied water. Fortunately, that never happened. But then came the biggest challenge of all: dragging the crocodile back to the banks in order to skin it. The incentives, however, were huge. A stockman's average wage, back in 1969, was just $40 a week, with a jillaroo earning $5 less. The skins brought in 55 cents a square centimetre and, with the biggest croc Sandy ever saw shot measuring nearly 5.8 metres, a good haul could prove a handsome income bonus.

'I look back now and can't believe the stupid risks we took, but we were all in our late teens or early twenties and quite mad,' admits Sandy. 'The extra money you could earn was quite an incentive for our insane nocturnal hunting. I took a little "stuffer" – a small, metre-or-less live croc that I planned to send away to a taxidermist – back to the homestead one night to show the station's owners. They were due to visit the next day but were held up. The only place I could keep it comfortable was in my shower recess, which had a high edge filled with water. It ended up there for three days. At the dinner, finally, at the manager's house, I brought it out to show everyone but one of the owners, a big man, dropped it with a shriek and it ran around the dining room snapping at all the furniture. The men were all up on chairs until a jackaroo was able to help me catch it and put it back in its box. That was a lively dinner!'

Occasionally, Sandy would be given the odd weekend off, and a whole gang of workers would descend on Cooktown or Cairns for a 'blow-out'. One night, at a party, Sandy was asked to give her mates a song. She was reluctant but, fuelled by their enthusiasm and not an insignificant volume of beer, she finally relented, singing her old school hymn, 'Oh Joyful Light', to the mournful tune of 'Danny Boy'. She had a beautiful voice, and someone drinking in the same bar overheard her. 'You know, you should do something with that,' he told her. 'You're really talented. With a bit of proper training, you could do great things . . .' He gave her the address of the Sydney Conservatorium of Music, which he said was auditioning for new singers in a few weeks. Sandy laughed, but his words played on her mind.

Before her next break in January 1971, she called the Conservatorium, which comes under the auspices of Sydney University, and booked an audition. To her shock, after singing for a panel, she was told they were happy to offer her a place to train as an opera singer. When would she like to start?

It was yet another monumental change in Sandy's life, but she was nothing if not game. She handed in her notice up in Cape York, found a small apartment in Mosman, on Sydney's North Shore, and brought all her worldly possessions – which didn't amount to much, since she'd been on the move herself for so long – down south.

Her new lifestyle proved a shock to the system. She'd never lived in a big city before, and found it hard to get used to the crowds, the traffic and the never-ending concrete. Her yearning to be back in the bush grew stronger all the time. But she knuckled down to her three-days-a-week studies and worked hard, training her voice. Her tutors were enthusiastic about her prospects, and she was keen to prove to herself that she could stay the course. She found two part-time jobs to support herself and tried to make the best of the situation, taking emotional refuge in her weekly copy of *Queensland Country Life*.

One morning at the newsagent's she struck up a conversation with another customer who'd been picking up his copy of the racing guide, and they soon became mates, chatting regularly about their shared love of horses and rural life. He turned out to be a member of a big Sydney racing family, and invited her along to Randwick one day to the races. Once there, he introduced her to his nephew, grazier Stephen Thorne, and the pair hit it off immediately. Stephen was from one of New South Wales' most established 'old' families, which had properties at Lightning Ridge, Bourke and Cootamundra. As their romance developed and deepened, Sandy was torn – on the one hand, she dearly wanted to complete her studies, but on the other, she was dazzled by her handsome, refined and fun-loving suitor. And then came the complete circuit-breaker: her old boss visited Sydney from Cape York, took her to dinner and urged her to return to help on Starcke Station over the Christmas holidays. Sandy knew she had to make a decision. She ended up following her heart.

The wedding took place in June 1972, at Stephen's grandmother's beautiful old home in Orange, with its formal sitting room transformed into a chapel. The couple then divided their time between the different properties, and the vast family station between Cootamundra and Wagga Wagga. Sandy was always happiest, however, in Lightning Ridge, that isolated settlement close to the Queensland border, pretty much in the middle of nowhere and famed for its reserves of some of the best black opal in the world. It still had the air of a rough-as-guts frontier town where anything goes, and its residents were often known only by their first names – 'Don't ask, and we won't lie' was a regular refrain. The sun-bleached, pale grey lunar landscape, pitted with small opal mine claims and piles of dirt scratched up from the earth, had always drawn colourful characters from all around Australia; battlers eager to seek their fortune for the cost of a $2 licence.

While Stephen's property was nearly an hour out of town in the red dirt, Sandy loved nothing more than trying her luck to strike opal. She dug her own mine – a claim in the opal fields of Lightning Ridge – and then worked, in her spare time, 15 metres underground for a year, alone with her pick and shovel. Luck was never with her, however. In all that time, after all that digging, she found just one stone, value: $30. And then she dropped it on the way back home from the valuer. But she didn't waste too much time mourning her loss. One of the couple's closest friends sold his sheep property that he'd worked for over twenty years, only to have the buyer sink a shaft in the sheepyards and pull out $30 000 000 worth of opal. Losing $30 of opal was never going to win you much sympathy.

Sandy had two children in that time, Sam and Marie, and predictably proved herself a rather unconventional mother. As a little girl, Marie vividly remembers hurting her arm the night before a big gymkhana. 'You'll be right, mate, just ride with one hand,' Sandy told her when she complained, and Marie went on to win a huge haul of ribbons and medals. It was only later they discovered she'd been riding all day with a broken arm. 'We used to joke, ironically, about her being Mother of the Year,' laughs Marie, now twenty-seven. 'But she was so tough on herself, she didn't really indulge us. We always used to think it was funny. She's done so many amazing things in her life, we just used to find her inspiring.'

But slowly, Sandy's marriage was breaking down. Her husband's old-moneyed family's formal lifestyle felt stifling and, although superficially she looked as though she fitted in, their world was utterly foreign to a young woman who'd grown up in the bush, barefoot, wild and free. Her dad was 'Snow' Sefton, the Queensland motor-sport pioneer who'd raced a modified WWII Jeep powered by a Ford V8 engine and who'd famously 'borrowed' some local council machinery to tar an old wartime airstrip to create the site of the State's first post-war motor race in 1946. He himself was a world championship motor racer and a popular stunt driver at Queensland shows and his genes passed on a real love of speed and daredevil escapades to the youngest of the three children borne by his wartime bride, Pearl.

Sandy's childhood was spent surrounded by cattle and horses in a sleepy farming area, not far from either the city or the beach. Always the rebel, however, she was constantly in trouble at school. She was expelled from her first after a clash with a teacher, which ended in her setting fire to his clothes; she was kicked out of the second after an altercation with a rail inspector when she'd forgotten her student pass; she was asked to leave her next, a private business college from which she continually played truant to ride showjumpers; and then ran away from the fourth, a strict Anglican boarding school, at age fourteen, to make her own way in the Outback.

So to be back within the strict confines of a family, particularly one where breeding and good manners were so important, and where belonging to the right clubs, afternoon tea and dressing formally for dinner were *de rigeur*, felt stultifying to a woman who'd always managed to live as a free spirit. 'God! It was such a complete opposite to what I was used to,' she says now. 'I found it so hard, but I genuinely believed that once you're married, it was for keeps. You stick with it, no matter what. But all the time I was finding it harder and harder. In the end, I started thinking I had to get my own money again, so I could regain a little bit of my independence. Whenever I told people about my experiences up in the Outback and the characters I'd met, they kept telling me I should write a book. I'd always loved writing – I was good at essays at school and used to write people long letters when I was away. So I decided to try.'

Sandy locked herself away for hours at a time to write her book. Gradually, it grew and grew. Thinking no one would believe a female had mixed with such wild characters, she wrote as if she were a bloke knocking around the bush. Her publishers kept writing to her as 'Mr Thorne'. Finally, with the colourfully irreverent title, *I've Met Some Bloody Wags!*, the book was published in 1980.

Launched on TV on the *Mike Walsh Show*, a friend confided to the program's producer that, in the Outback, Sandy would routinely bite the top off a stubby. She was urged to do so on air, much to the horror of her husband's family. It spelled the beginning of the end of the marriage.

The book was an immediate success and propelled Sandy into a whole new career. Suddenly, she was in demand all around the country to tell her yarns, recite some of the bush poetry she'd written in secret over the years, and crack jokes at corporate dinners, ladies' luncheons, festivals and shows. TV and radio chat and variety programs were hungry for good talent to brighten up their shows and, always a natural talker, performing came easily to the vivacious brunette, and the invitations to return came thick and fast. She started being billed as the new ambassador for Australia's Outback women.

'Women loved to hear a female being funny, and handling drunks or bad sound systems with natural ease,' says Sandy, who separated from her husband soon after. 'But, as always, the men were harder to win over. When I started out as a stand-up humorist, you could see the skeptical looks on the men's faces as I'd walk out on stage, and you could tell they were thinking, What's this bloody Sheila going to do? I quickly learnt you had to get an audience laughing in the first minute, with a never-fail, slightly outrageous short-short yarn. Then you had them in the palm of your hand. If they were drunk or the sound system was dodgy, it was a huge challenge to win them over immediately. Delivering humour for a living turned out to be no job for the faint-hearted.'

The challenges were many and frequent. Asked to entertain a convention of 3000 British travel agents at the Gold Coast, Sandy wrote a special poem for them to explain bush slang, called 'Learning Australian': *So you'd like to learn the lingo of the Aussies from the bush . . .'* It later turned into a huge hit, an ice-breaker at events all over the country and her entrée to major events, where she was constantly introduced as 'Australia's answer to Pam Ayres'. But that first evening, it couldn't even be heard. The agents were so drunk following a long, long lunch they'd all attended, Sandy was almost completely drowned out by the clamour. In the end, she got through it by concentrating on the twelve people sitting right at the front who appeared a great deal less inebriated than the rest and who were, at least, trying to listen. She also thought of her two kids left back at home, and the fact that she wouldn't get paid if she didn't see it through.

As she finally left the stage in relief, the organiser couldn't stop apologising. 'That must have been so terrible for you,' he sympathised. 'What can I do to make it up to you?' Sandy didn't hesitate. 'How about a free trip to America?' she replied. He looked startled for a moment, then smiled. 'Done!' he said.

He was as good as his word, and organised a deal, in conjunction with the Queensland Tourism Commission, to send Sandy over to promote the Australian Outback. Leaving her children with her sister, she went to the US, where she was invited to address the National Press Club. She received a standing ovation and was invited to appear as a guest on the *David Letterman Show*. 'Now tell me,' he said to her in front of his worldwide audience, 'do you *really* bite the tops off beer bottles with your teeth in the Outback?' Sandy had no alternative but to oblige. 'Oh my God!' he exclaimed. 'How about that, folks!' Larry King, on his show, called her 'One of the most entertaining people I've had in my studio' and implored, 'Sandy, come back next time you're in the US!' The *New York Post* ran a photograph of her on page 3, biting the top off a Heineken bottle on the top floor of the Empire State Building. The headline made her cringe: *Crocodile Dundish Bites into the Big Apple.*

The American tour was such a hit it was extended to London, where she went down just as famously. London Aussiephile Michael Parkinson pronounced himself an instant fan. 'Listening to Sandy's hilarious explanation of Aussie slang, "Learning Australian", made me want to get back there immediately,' he said. 'Brilliant!'

Meanwhile Sandy continued to write her bush stories, poetry, and columns in newspapers and magazines, and was appointed a World Ambassador for World Expo '88. In 1991, she had another book published, *Laugh Yer Guts Out*, this time a collection of bush jokes, stories and verse, which broke publishing records with 35 000 books sold in the first six weeks. She was just a natural, with an instinctively colourful turn of phrase. 'I remember phoning her up one day and asking her how she was going,' says old friend former jockey Jim Pike who, as a youngster, renamed himself after Phar Lap's jockey. 'She said, "Oh, mate! I'm as busy as a one-legged man at an arse-kicking contest". Another time, explaining she'd been out on the town the night before with her sister, she said they'd "played up like second-hand chainsaws". She's just funny without even thinking about it.' Her son Sam, now thirty, agrees. 'She can write verse anywhere, even while she's driving a car, she's ripping something out, or in a plane scribbling on an airline sickbag,' he says. 'We grew up watching her doing verse, and went to sleep listening to her tapping on the typewriter. Mum can't help being funny. She doesn't have to try too hard at all.'

Many other people thought so too, and demand continued to grow for her personal appearances. 'She's a natural storyteller,' says close friend Jackie McCabe. 'We were having lunch in a restaurant in South Australia once and she was telling us about what she'd been doing, and we turned round and discovered everyone in the restaurant was listening. She was so taken aback, but they all said, "No, carry on, *please!*" She often doesn't even realise what a gift she has.'

But some performances could be hard work. On a tour of New Zealand universities, she received an enthusiastic reception at all the rural stops, but in Auckland no one would stop talking, shouting and heckling her. Out of the corner of her eye, she was horrified to see a student sneaking up behind her with a noose, obviously preparing to throw it over her neck as a joke. Just as he prepared to loop it over her head, she wheeled around and yelled to him at the top of her voice, 'Get off this stage, you stupid bastard!'

Completely taken aback, he went to jump down off the stage and, at that moment, she gave him a hearty kick up the backside. The student audience roared as one and cheered . . . finally won over enough to listen, rapt, to every word.

Yet while Sandy's professional life was going great guns, she was still lonely. Then, in 1981, as she toured the country promoting her books, she kept bumping into the same man who was also travelling on a similar schedule, this time to set up branches of a new bank. Every time they met up, they'd have a chat and soon became close friends. Kim Smith was the son of former radio and TV star Keith Smith, of *The Inventors* and *Pied Piper* fame, working in banking – and hating it. Gradually, their relationship developed and, when he won over Sandy's children, he won her too. They married in 1983, settling on a small cattle property at Baffle Creek, near the picturesque seaside village of 1770, birthplace of her beloved Queensland, halfway between Gladstone and Bundaberg.

They decided to build their own house on the land there, something daughter Marie remembers only too well. 'It rained every day for five months, so we couldn't start building in all that time,' she says. 'So basically, we camped for five months. But Mum made the experience seem like fun. We were outdoors and she told us this was how the pioneers lived, and made it all into a real adventure. As kids, we fell for it! I don't know how on earth she cooked two hot meals a day over open fires and sent us to school in clean uniforms under those wet and muddy conditions.'

Jim Pike remembers visiting them when they finished and was amused to hear how Sandy had been lying in their little tinny one day, bobbing on the water, writing and fishing at the same time, when Kim had noticed a long, eastern brown snake, one of the world's most venomous reptiles, swimming straight for her hand, which was holding the line above the water. He yelled at her to watch out. Then yelled again. And again. Finally, Sandy looked up, just as the snake reared up out of the water, ready to slither into the boat. Casually, she whacked it on the side of its head with her wine glass, saying, 'Bugger off!' Dazed, it vanished from sight. She was just as nonchalant the day she noticed a snake's tail hanging down from a crack in the ceiling above where she was writing. Naturally, she simply yanked it, trying to pull it down.

'She's quite fearless,' says Jim. 'Sandy's a real bush person, someone who's done it all, and many times. She's quite incredible. She's so much at home in the country, then you see her equally relaxed in the presence of real dignitaries doing one of her shows. You can put her in front of anyone and she'll entertain them.'

After new husband Kim became her full-time manager, the marriage started to go sour. Sandy was miserable, and the effort of being funny on stage became even harder. Finally, at Easter 2000, she simply packed a suitcase, put her cattle dog Deadly Dudley and cat Mad Max into the car, and drove off into the sunset.

She went to stay with her helicopter-pilot sister, Lesley Webber, for a time while she figured out what to do next. Daughter Marie was nineteen and having a wonderful time jillarooing, just as her mother had done, while her son Sam, twenty-two, was travelling around Australia, pearl-diving in Broome and mustering cattle in the Kimberleys. 'I tried to live up to Mum's adventures and it nearly killed me,' he laughs. 'With cattle that knocked you around and horses that would try to throw you off, you'd wake up every morning wondering if you'd end up in hospital. Most people did. But it gave me a real appreciation for what she'd done.' Sandy herself, however, fast approaching her fiftieth birthday, was feeling utterly lost. 'I felt really jaded and that I needed a real change, to do something different,' she says. 'I needed a fresh challenge.'

One morning, reading a newspaper over breakfast, a job ad caught her eye: 'Good Communicators Needed'. She looked closer. Wardens were needed for detention centres, where asylum-seekers from Iraq and Afghanistan were being increasingly held. She had a laugh over a misprint in the ad – 'Applicants must be prepared to do shit-work' – but then started thinking seriously about the job. 'It said you should be prepared to work with people from other cultures and undergo riot control training, and I thought I've never done anything like this in my life. It sounded so exciting.' Sandy applied, and was given a job working in the detention centres at Woomera, 488 kilometres north of Adelaide, and at the Curtin Centre, in Derby, north-west Western Australia. 'I went into the jail on my fiftieth birthday and started learning all this incredible stuff, I found it just amazing,' she says. 'Halfway through the course, I realised I had to start writing things down, so I began a diary.

'Because of the danger of being hurt, we were earning huge money and I promised myself I was going to buy a unit on the Gold Coast; then when I went back for my next rotation in Derby, the government announced it was stopping the boats from coming in, and they wanted to close detention centres down as fast as they could. We casuals on big money were the first to go. It had been another great adventure. I loved every minute. There were a lot of very violent people in there, but there were a lot of nice people too who I enjoyed helping. I loved telling them all about Australia and about getting work in the Outback.'

Even though the job finished, the material provided Sandy with enough work to keep her going for a further year, writing another book about her experiences, *Beyond the Razor Wire*, which is now being adapted for a movie. Working for so long behind barbed-wire fences had been yet one more astonishing adventure, but she was ready to return to the wide open spaces of the Australian Outback, where her heart truly lay.

An old friend and neighbour at Lightning Ridge rang Sandy just as the job at the detention centre was finishing up. Tony Dowton had been having a hard time and, once the third-biggest wool producer in the entire region, family difficulties and the havoc wreaked by the long ongoing drought had knocked him for six. 'Mate! I wish you'd come out and cheer an old bloke up!' he told her. Sandy, hearing an uncharacteristic note of desperation in his voice, immediately rolled her swag and drove out to see him. He was the larrikin character on which her *Battler* series of novels had been based, twenty years earlier. Now in his early seventies, she was horrified at his situation.

Beyond the green lawn around the homestead, kept alive with bore water, the land had dried to a hard, cracked ochre. With no rain to speak of, the sheep were living on the leaves blown from the trees, with Tony hand-feeding them grain three times a week, plus cutting scrub several hours a day with a chainsaw. Most days, he worked so hard and long, he was too exhausted to prepare a meal, and would simply collapse into bed at night, ready to wake at dawn for another day's hard slog against the elements.

He was delighted to see Sandy, and her two-day visit turned

into two weeks, then two months, and then two years as the long drought continued. Now having been there for six years, she still feels she needs to stay on to keep up her old mate's spirits, and help his sheep stay alive. 'Sandy always cheers everyone up,' says Tony. 'She's so happy and brainy and so very, very funny. She always likes to be positive about everything all the time. Everyone loves her for it.'

As for Sandy, she was happy to reconnect with the 'back country'. 'The drought just kept on, and I'm still here,' she laughs, loving being in the Outback again, dividing her days between mustering the sheep in the red dirt of the property and spending time over on the sun-bleached white landscape of the Ridge itself. 'I got back into the groove of life out there. So I'm quite happy living here, performing, travelling to gigs, writing and feeding sheep.'

She's also found herself, almost by accident, as an unofficial ambassador for Lightning Ridge. So often on her travels, people hear she's living there and say how much they've always wanted to visit. And she understands that completely. 'It's a real, genuine Outback place,' she says. 'There's so much to see and do; so many real characters around the place. Someone's constantly trying to get opals somewhere, or starting a rush or a rumour, and someone else is invariably being caught ratting on another bloke's claim, then copping instant bush justice. It's free and easy, yet friendly and exciting. There's nowhere else like it in the world.'

That's certainly true enough. Coming into town, all visitors pass a huge sign reading: LIGHTNING RIDGE, POPULATION? – a local joke about the numbers of people living in the area. There are only 1800 people registered on the electoral list, but the membership of the town's bowling club alone numbers more than 2000.

Locals put the population, conservatively, at around 7000. With the numbers swollen by runaways, desperates, fortune-seekers, hermits and those eager to get away from it all – and never be found again – it's little surprise that the majority of people have so little time, or regard, for officialdom . . . and anything remotely connected with it.

But, essentially, Sandy feels the town, and its community, really embody the heart of the Outback. 'To me, the Outback is all about the freedom and the people,' she says. 'You don't have the restrictions and the hassles that city people have with commuting and traffic lights and noise. It's just a much more free-and-easy atmosphere to live in, which is reflected in the character of the people: easy-going, friendly, less stressed. The Ridge has also been a successful multicultural society for a long time, giving lie to the impression urban people have of intolerant rural rednecks. This country has a real romance to it. Even the huge red claypans with their weird stunted broombushes I used to think were so ugly, I now love. I honestly feel it's the real Australia out here.

'Of course, there are extreme difficulties with the isolation and drought, but people are starting to accept now that drought is a season – a natural season – that you've got to ride out. You have to always remember it will rain some day, no matter how bad it is now. Here, without rain for so long, there aren't even any burrs left for the stock to eat; everything has dried up and blown away. But it's incredible to see how animals adapt to survive. You see the sheep go along through the paddock like vacuum cleaners, licking up the leaves, and rearing up on their hind legs pulling down branches. The sheep here have never even seen grass. They wouldn't know what grass is. This country is only for tough survivors, both people and livestock.'

Apart from those rural hardships, which Sandy naturally finds heart-rending, life is pretty good these days. At fifty-six, she's just had reprinted a biography she wrote of self-made multimillionaire grazier and sheep dealer Arthur Earle, *On the Shake of a Hand*, while still constantly penning her bush poetry and performing it on radio and around the country. While she split from Kim eight years ago, she's never bothered to get a divorce – 'I purposely haven't because I don't ever want to make the mistake of marrying again,' she explains. Her two kids are now both settled and happy: Sam's an ex-Naval officer who works on computer systems for warships, and Marie is a policy officer for AgForce, Queensland's peak rural lobby group. 'I still learn new things about Mum all the time, especially over a few wines,' says Marie. 'Her achievements have been just amazing. She's really taught a lot of people about the bush, and bush values.'

That's a contribution experts in the area hold most dear. Warren Fahey, social historian and folklorist, says Sandy's voice and typical bush humour has always sounded out loud and clear. 'As Australia hurtles towards the inevitable "global culture" it has become vital that we preserve our unique Australian identity,' he says. 'I see Sandy's work, like my own, of tapping Aussies on the shoulder and reminding them of our past, especially the role of the bush – past and present – as being vital. Humour is a great way of identifying culture.'

Certainly, Sandy's bush poetry is constantly making people laugh – and cry – while an unexpected side effect is that many women have told her that until they took one of her books home, their son or husband had never read a book before or been interested in them. 'But the covers of my books have attracted them, and they've picked them up, started flicking through, and the next thing . . . hey presto! They're reading a book for the first time,' she says.

The other thing Sandy's most proud of is giving laughter to both bush people – who deserve all the laughter they can get – and city people, who gain an understanding of Outback life and spirit through her writing and performances. 'So, in a nutshell, I am extremely proud that my knack for humour has introduced many rural men and boys to the wonderful world of books, and, in turn, many city people to the wonderful world of the Outback. That makes it all worthwhile.'

13

Learning to Love the Country

SHARON OLDFIELD, *Cowarie, South Australia*

Sitting in a rented house in Adelaide one day, newly-widowed Sharon Oldfield looked at her three young children playing at the dining table and realised that, at last, it was time to go home.

Eight months had passed since her husband had been killed in a light plane crash and she'd gathered them up and fled their home, away from the painful memories of the happy times they'd shared as a tight-knit family in one of the most isolated places on earth. But now, finally, it was time to go back.

'I needed to go home,' she says today. 'It was our family home and I needed to go back to grieve among the familiar day-to-day reminders of our life together. It was something I couldn't do in town. I needed to be there, and the kids needed to be there to grieve properly as well. So that's what we did. It was tough, but we had to do it.'

Indeed, it proved heartbreaking walking back once more onto Cowarie Station, the incredibly remote 3900-square kilometre cattle property in the far north of South Australia, just off the Birdsville Track. The pastoral lease had been in Sharon's husband's family since 1943, with the Oldfield name synonymous with the area. But now, for the first time, Grant Oldfield wasn't by his family's side. 'It was probably the hardest thing I've ever had to do,' says Sharon. 'But I knew it was the right thing for us all.'

Grant's presence was still in every room of the house, around every corner, in every shed and across the paddocks. It was painful to remember that he wouldn't walk in at any moment, with that radiant smile that lit up his eyes and a laconic 'G'day'. Gradually, however, the anguish began to fade just a little, and Sharon was able to relax and talk to the kids, aged two, five and six, about the man who'd brought such joy to all their lives.

'People said to me, "Oh, you're so brave making a decision to stay on to manage the property", but, really, I didn't make that decision,' she says. 'I just couldn't make *any* decision. The only one I could have made would have been to sell it, and I couldn't do that at that stage. So after a while, I thought, Oh God! I'm actually managing it! Then I thought I'll go on managing it, I understand it a bit more now. So that's how it happened.'

That was thirteen years ago and today Cowarie Station, run by an ex-Sydneysider who had absolutely no idea about living in the Outback until she fell in love with one of its favourite sons, has become a hugely successful venture.

*

Never in a million years did the young Sharon Kelly ever imagine she'd end up on a property surrounded by desert, at the apex of three of the most hostile stretches of terrain on earth: the Tirari, Simpson and Sturt's Stony deserts.

Living in Sydney's western suburbs, the Scots-born nurse planned herself a future in midwifery in Britain, and then jetting off to explore the rest of the world.

But first, the 21-year-old decided to consolidate everything she'd learnt in a quick, one-year Australian country posting. She chose Birdsville. 'I had no concept of where Birdsville was, what it was, and what the job there might entail,' she confesses. 'I just thought it sounded nice and would be good. What did I have to lose? I had all the confidence of youth that everything would work out well. My mother was horrified.'

Very soon, Sharon's confidence began to evaporate too. With no experience at all of the vast Australian Outback, and as the sole passenger on the small plane heading there, she began growing increasingly uneasy as the towns ran out and the desert began. After a while, all she could see far below was an endless vista of blood-coloured sand ridges. As her heart went into free-fall, the pilot called her into the cockpit to sit with him. 'Look down there,' he told her, pointing to a vague spot on the horizon. 'Can you see Birdsville?'

She squinted into the blazing sun, but could see nothing. 'No . . .' she answered uncertainly. The pilot smiled. 'Well, see that line of trees?' She could see a couple of green dots against the sand. 'Yes,' she said in triumph. 'And you see where that line bends?' She nodded; she thought she might just be able to see a kink in the line. The pilot glanced at her. 'That's Birdsville,' he said. Sharon was horror-struck. She couldn't see any buildings, any houses, shops or even a hospital. She felt a lump in her throat.

It stayed there as the plane landed on the small airstrip with the giant sign that seemed to mock her: 'Birdsville International Airport'. It was still there when she was greeted by a reception committee organised to welcome the new nurse into town. And it was only when she was shown into a room near the corrugated-iron shed serving as the town's hospital that it finally went. For it was then that she burst into tears. 'And I cried for the whole of the next week,' she says. 'I was devastated. I thought, What have I done?'

Things didn't get much better when Sharon started exploring her new posting. It was 1984 and Birdsville was tiny, perhaps only a third of the size it is today. The hospital was extremely rudimentary compared to those Sharon was used to back in Sydney, with the nearest doctor 850 kilometres away to the east, in Charleville. One of her duties was to drive the hospital's lone ambulance – another problem, since it was manual and Sharon had only learnt to drive with automatics. Anyone coming in with a fracture always similarly caused trouble, since the only X-ray machine belonged to the Flying Doctors, and it was always too hot for the films to be developed. Meanwhile, the hospital didn't even have a phone; just a party line that only worked from 8.30 a.m. to 5 p.m. Instead, any would-be patients at the far-flung stations would radio in at certain pre-arranged times to describe their symptoms over the airwaves and there were regular 'clinic runs' where the nurse on duty would go off on a two- to three-day trip to visit a number of stations.

It was Sharon's turn just two weeks into her stay. That morning, she dressed carefully and packed for the trip. When she came out to get into the car, however, ready to go on the long, lonely drive into the deserts of the south-west, the other nurse in town stared at her in amazement. 'I'd dressed in my white uniform with epaulettes, and all my badges, my white stockings and duty shoes,' laughs Sharon, shame-faced. 'And I had an apple, a couple of cans of Coke and some chocolate biscuits for the journey. She told me to change immediately.'

More suitably attired and armed with more extensive provisions, yet still with no concept at all of how bleak the terrain was going to be and how empty the landscape, Sharon eventually set off. 'I must have driven for six hours, and I didn't see another vehicle or person or building,' says Sharon. 'I thought I'd gone to hell! I'd come straight from Sydney – where could you possibly travel and not see another sign of life? All I could see were eagles circling, and I thought, Oh God! They're vultures! I'm going to die! It was terrible, it was all so frightening.'

At one of the stations, Cordillo Downs, owned by the Brook family of Birdsville, some ringers had recognised she was new to the area and decided to have a bit of fun with her. They told her to be careful not to stop when she was driving in the dark, as dingoes tended to bite the tyres off cars. The warning had its desired effect. When darkness began to fall that first day, she needed to stop to fix the spotlights on the car but was too terrified to halt in case the dingoes attacked.

'I didn't know any different,' explains Sharon. 'I was fair game for anyone. I was so lucky that trip. I got a flat tyre, but someone was with me at that time, so they changed it for me. But when I finally got back to Birdsville, David Brook, who ran the council, found out I'd been on that isolated run on my own, not knowing how to change a tyre and not even knowing how to work the radio – although I probably would have worked it out if things got desperate – he couldn't believe it. In the end, he taught me how to change a tyre himself! He also talked to the people who'd sent me out to Birdsville and said any future candidates should be taught basic mechanics.'

Yet in every way, Sharon felt hopelessly out of her depth. Early on, she'd spotted a steaming hole in the ground near the centre of Birdsville and asked what it was. 'It's a bore,' came the answer from a local, who'd grown up thinking nothing of the near-boiling water that's forced up from the Great Artesian Basin under the town. 'Ah!' said Sharon, knowingly. 'A boar!' All that day, she thought with relish of the pit-oven feast obviously awaiting everyone in town.

Gradually, Sharon started getting into the rhythm of life in Birdsville. 'The people just envelop you,' she says. 'Coming into the community as a nurse, you're automatically greeted with respect and acceptance, then you have to earn it. You're included immediately in the life of the community, yet there are obligations that go along with that. I had lots of invitations and soon found myself on the Parents & Citizens' Association and on the sports club committee. Part of my duties for the sports club was to help run the weekly chook raffle, selling tickets, drawing the raffle and presenting the winner with the chicken. The first time I did it, no one actually told me I was supposed to cook the chook too; I didn't even know how to cook a chicken! I just gave the winner a frozen chook. No one said anything.'

There were aspects of Birdsville life that proved challenging, especially everyone knowing everyone else's business in such a small town, but Sharon was continually struck by the locals' warmth and willingness to have a go. Any time she found a task problematic, she was spurred on by the thought that everyone else had faced similar difficulties in the past, and coped. Besides, there was always someone around happy to lend a hand.

'Your admiration begins to really grow for these Outback people, and you learn to manage too,' says Sharon. 'You end up growing as a result. You also learn not to sweat the small things, to become more tolerant of people and go with the flow. In a place like that, you wake up in the morning with a plan for the day, but it's guaranteed everything will have changed by lunchtime. You learn to get on with life. You grow up.'

The first time Sharon met cattleman Grant Oldfield from Cowarie Station, 320 kilometres to the south-west, along the treacherous Birdsville Track and then off on a dirt track barely marked, she was less than impressed. A friend had arranged for the pair to get together for a blind date at the annual Jundah Races, 500 kilometres to the east. He was wearing a blue satin shirt with drainpipe trousers, and she wrote him off almost at first glance. Then he smiled, and started to talk in a beautifully laidback drawl, and she was immediately won over.

They started dating in secret, not wanting to provide fodder for the gossips and, besides, the great distances between them (as well as Grant's constant travels between Cowarie and the family's other property, Currawilla, 670 kilometres north-east over the border in Queensland) meant they didn't have much opportunity to see each other anyway. When it finally came time for Sharon to leave Birdsville in May 1985, she unveiled their relationship at her farewell party, to everyone's shock – and pleasure. Then she went and stayed with Grant for three weeks at Currawilla before returning to Sydney to do some agency work, and deciding what she was going to do next.

The pair had so little in common, they surprised even themselves with how well they got on. Grant's family had been on the land forever, his grandparents Marree-born Claud Oldfield and his wife Dora setting up a home in sheds on uninhabited Crown land north of Cowarie in 1938, calling it Mona Downs. 'My mum was moaning about the terrible ants there, and having to wear kerosene rags around their ankles to stop them biting,' says Eric Oldfield, the third son of their seven children. 'And then the men were moaning about the women moaning, so my mum said, "Let's call this place Mona Downs!"' The couple then bought and moved to Cowarie in 1943, with the station's name coming from the Aboriginal word for a marsupial rat. Eventually, Mona Downs was merged into Cowarie. After Claud's death, the eldest son Claudie, took over. Grant was, in turn, his eldest son.

With Sharon migrating from Glasgow as a small child and growing up in Sydney, they were from completely different backgrounds, had utterly diverse lifestyles – and their taste in clothes were from opposite ends of the spectrum. Yet, somehow, they were good together. 'I don't think we had a lot in common,' says Sharon. 'But he was so different to any blokes I'd ever met in the city. He came across as very confident. I suppose he grounded me while I livened him up – added a spark to his day and showed him a whole side of the world that he didn't know about. So we found we could lean on each other, take from each other and give to each other.'

Indeed, Grant fared much better than his clothes. Sharon gradually cleared out his wardrobe, hiding the items she didn't like, until she finally became game enough to throw them all away.

On her last day at the property, just as the pair were about to say goodbye, Grant took a deep breath. 'Well, I suppose we'd better get married,' he said casually. Sharon looked back at him, astonished, but her voice stayed calm. 'Well, yes, I suppose we'd better,' she smiled. He grinned back. 'Do you think you can?' he then asked, with a new note of gravity in his voice. 'Do you think you could live here? Because this'll be it. I can't give you the city, I can't ever do that. This would be it.' Sharon, not trusting herself to speak, nodded. To herself, she thought, 'Yes! With you by my side, I think I can. I'm sure I can.'

Arriving back in Sydney in June 1985 was a shock for Sharon. There'd been a lot of changes in nursing in the year she'd spent away. The way in which nursing was administered had been completely overhauled and a great deal more red tape introduced, which contrasted sharply with the way she'd been able to work in Birdsville completely off her own bat. She'd got used to making her own decisions; now she found she had to account for almost every move. In some ways, she'd slipped behind in current medical practices, although in diagnostic skills and in her practical knowledge, she'd developed hugely. And while she fondly imagined she'd love being back in the buzz of a big city, her reaction wasn't quite what she'd expected. 'I hated it!' she laughs. 'It was so noisy and busy and smelly and rude. I just had a completely different perspective when I came back. I didn't enjoy it at all.'

A few weeks after she left, Grant flew to Sydney to meet Sharon's family, and asked her mother for her daughter's hand in marriage. Everyone was taken by his old-fashioned gallantry and charm. But after she'd said yes, he turned to Sharon. 'I've got to go back to Cowarie tomorrow,' he said. 'We've got half a day to buy an engagement ring.' Sharon looked stricken. 'I can't buy a ring in half a day!' she protested. He shrugged. 'Well, if you don't, you'll have to wait till I come back in October,' he said, bluntly. They found a ring and took photographs so he could show his family.

It wasn't long before Grant phoned and asked Sharon to come and see Cowarie for the first time. She was due to finish a contract in October that year, so arranged to fly up then. The homestead was large and low with an airy verandah and a beautifully green garden at the back, surrounded by a corrugated-tin fence. To the front was the vast horizon of red dirt with an occasional light dusting of green that seemed to go on forever, relieved only by the thin blue slash of the Warburton River running through the middle of the property. At that time, Cowarie was extremely dry, having received only a fraction of its annual 13-centimetre rainfall, and was running about 2000 cattle, with a fair number of poddies being handfed just outside the house.

Grant's family welcomed Sharon warmly but, while she was there, Grant's grandmother in Perth fell ill, so his mother Barbara went off to nurse her. Sharon unexpectedly found herself as the lone female of the house, a position that conferred on her some nerve-wracking responsibilities. 'They asked me if I could cook while she was away, and I said, "Yeah sure!"' recalls Sharon. 'But I'm thinking, I don't even know how to cook! And then they wanted cake. I'd never made a cake that hadn't come out of a packet. I asked where the cake mix was, but they just all looked blank. So I asked Grant what you'd put in to make a cake and he said, "I dunno, I guess flour, eggs, butter and milk. There must be a book here somewhere . . ."'

Even worse, Sharon's prospective mother-in-law made all her own bread, so they didn't have any bread in the house. 'I realised I'd have to make some, but had no idea how to do that either,' she says. 'Barbara even made her own yeast! So I had to learn to make it out of potato and sugar, and then make the bread. It was a real case of keeping-the-home-fires-burning type of thing. They'd all get up in the morning and eat and go, and I'd be there all day thinking, What do I do now? Cook? Cook what? What do I cook? I'd go in the cold room and there'd be chunks of meat everywhere, but I had no idea what was what, what I should roast, what I should stew . . . I had *no* idea.'

Then there was the washing. The house had what looked like an old cement mixer, which Sharon couldn't even work out how to turn on, and Barbara still also used a copper. Sharon asked Grant what his mum usually put in the copper, and he looked blank. 'I don't know, everything I suppose!' he eventually replied. 'How long for?' asked Sharon. He shook his head. 'I don't know. Just make a really big fire and boil the guts out of it.' So Sharon did. She boiled everything – the gabardines, jeans, shirts, towels – nothing was safe. It took her a day and a half. She found out later, of course, that Barbara only boiled the tea towels and the handkerchiefs. Her heart sank when she eventually pulled the garments out of the copper, all hopelessly misshapen and shrunken, and everything the same muddy-brown colour. 'It was horrible,' she says glumly.

It was thus something of a relief when, after four weeks, Sharon had to return to Sydney to work. She stayed there until the wedding on 21 February 1986 at a Catholic church in Merrylands, in western Sydney. Then, Sharon, twenty-four, and Grant, twenty-six, went to Singapore and to the Maldives for their unexpectedly exotic honeymoon before returning for good to Cowarie Station.

There was a difficult start awaiting their married life, however. It was one of the driest seasons on record which was causing problems on the property, and they were only back three weeks when Grant's father Claudie was diagnosed with terminal cancer. He went to hospital in Adelaide for treatment, and all the family went along with him. Sharon was left alone in the homestead, with not even a phone, while a stockman was brought in to look after the animals. Claudie eventually died in January 1987.

As the oldest son, Grant was taking over the property, and spending a great proportion of his time away, looking after the stock. For Sharon, it meant staying home and perfecting her cooking skills. He'd once jokingly threatened to make sure she'd be barefoot and pregnant all the time, and he was as good as his word. Their first baby, a daughter named Ashlee, was born on 28 August 1986, and was only a few months old when Sharon fell pregnant again. The second pregnancy was a difficult one and Sharon was flown out from Cowarie in an emergency airlift after going into labour only five months into her time. Baby Craig was eventually born full-term on 27 September 1987 in Adelaide, with Grant by Sharon's side. Three years later, Christopher arrived on 6 May 1991.

Back in Cowarie, Sharon made good friends with other married couples, including Nell and David Brook in Birdsville, who became close confidants. Another friend was Jenny Stevens, who'd been working as a governess at Marree and then married a Cowarie ringer and came to live on the station. 'Sharon and Grant were just brilliant together,' says Jenny. 'Nobody's perfect together, but they were as close to it as any other couple I've ever come across. He knew how to keep her cool and calm and when to stir her up, and she was the same with him. They came from absolutely different backgrounds, but Grant was a brilliant personality who was so comfortable with himself, he was comfortable with everyone else.

'It was phenomenal how well Sharon adapted to the life. It couldn't have been easy: it was a huge cultural shock and she was living with Grant and her in-laws, her father-in-law was dying and she was pregnant and cooking for station hands, not to mention dealing with the isolation and the kind of daily things she'd never have come across before. But she dealt with it all.'

For, just as Sharon had imagined, with Grant by her side she could cope with virtually anything. 'I missed my family and my friends, and I missed the hairdresser's and going to the movies, but life was so full,' says Sharon. 'We were married, we had a young family, we were always busy doing things, so I never really felt like I was missing out on anything at all. I did miss nursing at first, but those skills came in quite handy, living in a remote area with medical assistance so far away, especially with children, and with several nasty accidents over the years. I learnt to manage.

'Besides, the difficulties only strengthened our relationship in a way. We were mates and we'd talk everything through. You have to pick the good things about a place and work with that. It doesn't really matter where you are. Where you're happy with your husband and your family, that's where your home is – it doesn't really matter whether it's in a beautiful apartment in the city, in Antarctica or in the middle of a desert. It doesn't matter – it's what you have with you, not around you. I was learning to love this country through Grant – the colour of the land, the colour of the sky. He was teaching me this life, and I was very happy.'

The morning after the couple's eighth wedding anniversary, on 22 February 1994, Grant woke early and went straight to his plane to go mustering, saying he'd be back for breakfast at 9.30 a.m. But when Sharon called him on the radio at 9 o'clock to check everything was all right, as per normal, there was no response. When there was no answer again at 10 a.m., and then nothing at 11 a.m., she immediately called on neighbours for help. Tom Mackay flew out over one side of the property to look for Grant's plane, while Malcolm Mitchell and Danny Oldfield searched the other. The latter two came upon the wreckage just as it was growing dark. It was too stormy to land, so they returned to the homestead and Malcolm and Sharon drove out to the site. Grant's passenger was still alive after the mystery crash, but badly injured. Grant was dead at the age of just thirty-three.

Completely in shock, Sharon moved herself and the children to Adelaide for some time by themselves. A month later, Sharon's mum Maureen died. 'Life was a bit of a mess at that point,' says

Sharon softly. But, after eight months in the city, Sharon decided it was time to go back. It was heartwrenching to return home without Grant; it took six months to stop seeing him everywhere she went on the property, but slowly she managed to cope. 'I suppose I just needed the familiar by that stage,' she says. 'I needed to go home to our memories and wallow in everything we'd known.

'We asked family, friends and workmates to write letters after Grant died for the kids, how they knew him, what he was like, the funny things he did . . . His family and this community have been very good at doing that – sharing their memories of him. So the children know he blew his nose a certain way and could be bad-tempered about certain things. It's interesting, you hear them say, "Dad did this, Dad did that", but those aren't even their memories. They've taken them from other people, honed them and made them theirs. It's nice.

'I didn't want him immortalised in their minds as some sort of god that could do no wrong. I think that tends to make things a bit unhealthy as they grow older. But they were very young at the time, yet they've got a little bit of insight into their father now – fuller, better and more rounded.'

The harsh reality of a land stricken by a terrible drought and crashing beef prices forced Sharon to focus on the property too. She couldn't even entertain perhaps what would have been the most obvious solution – to sell Cowarie Station – and eventually she realised she was actually running it instead. As the months passed, she began to understand its survival demanded drastic measures and, slowly, she worked out what would have to be done. She'd picked up much more than she'd realised from her years with Grant; not only a love for the land, but a deeper understanding of how to manage it. She responded by totally destocking the station for a fourteen-month period, with the remaining core herd sent away on agistment.

'She's an extraordinary woman,' says John Payne, a retired tourism operator who helped organise the Year of the Outback's 2002 cattle drive through her property, and subsequently became a close friend and honorary 'grandpa' to the children. 'She had the terrible loss of Grant to deal with, but she still never chose the easy way out. Instead, she carried on with Cowarie, and made an absolute success of it. I think she needed to remember Grant and to honour his memory in the best way possible and that wouldn't have been to sell Cowarie. Instead, she wanted to create something for Ashlee and her two boys, and to pay her respects to Grant and his vision.'

There'd been talk in the area about the possibility of running an organic beef operation and Sharon met with a few other producers to discuss the viability of such a project. She was excited about the plan, and her enthusiasm proved infectious. She became one of the first beef producers to sign up to the fledgling OBE organic beef operation.

'Sharon was one of the most enthusiastic members from the start,' says Peter Schmidt, the current director of the now-flourishing organisation. 'When I first met her, she had just been through the terrible tragedy of losing her husband, so it was a big call for her to pull everything together. But she came through with flying colours, reared her children and took that extensive property and made a real go of it. You have to hand it to her!'

Sharon re-stocked, started running the station along environmentally sustainable principles and had soon wrested the property out of the mire. In May 1996, the rains came and in 1998 Cowarie was given full organic status and, with 4500 head of organic beef cattle, suddenly the way ahead looked assured. 'I believe we have something very special,' she says. 'This country is inherently organic anyway – we don't need pesticides.'

Still the sole one-woman producer at OBE – the other women are all in partnership with their husbands – Sharon has played a major role in the company. Recently, she took part in a four-person delegation to the United States to showcase their products. 'She was the obvious choice,' says Peter. 'With so much enthusiasm and passion for both organic beef and the Outback, she's a wonderful ambassador. She's great at interacting with the public, a good talker, very warm, and also a good cook now, so she could demonstrate cooking our burgers and meatballs. She's involved in so many aspects of the Outback that she had to leave a couple of days early to attend a Landcare conference. She gives a great deal of time to many causes, like natural resource management groups, soil conservation – anything you can think of.'

Sharon believes strongly in an holistic approach to managing Cowarie, where no one part of the property can be managed in isolation from the rest. As a result, conservation management has become an underlying principle fundamental to the whole operation. 'And it's a way of bringing the spotlight to this amazing region of Australia and the world,' she says.

A complex system of 240 kilometres of pipes on Cowarie now enables water to be carried all around the property to ensure stock don't all gather in specific areas and damage the fragile earth. It's hard work to maintain it, but that's something she's always happy to do. John Payne remembers going out with her one day to fix a major burst in a pipe near a new bore. As the hot Artesian water bubbled up – close to a temperature of 100 degrees, boiling point – it hit John's boots and ate through the leather. 'We were in the middle of absolutely nowhere,' he says. 'It was baking hot and the water was so hot, it was burning us. We were covered in steaming water and mud and there was a lot of swearing and curs- ing going on. Then she suddenly looked up and said, "I suppose a cold shandy is out of the question?" It was so ridiculous, it was very funny. She has a great sense of humour, and never seems to lose it, no matter what.'

In addition, Sharon has made a huge effort to retain as many varieties as possible of native vegetation, which, in turn, has led to a sharp rise in the number of species of birds and lizards on the surrounding land. Cowarie reaped the rewards in 1999, winning that year's Commonwealth Development Bank State Ibis Award for combining excellence in wildlife conservation and farming, and now also has a Cattlecare Accreditation. 'I just wish I had a little of whatever it is that keeps her going,' says John. 'She's a tireless worker for the pastoral industry, for this area, and for the Outback in general.'

Yet despite Sharon's success, there are still constant challenges. 'This drought has actually been harder for me,' she says. 'We were in quite bad drought when my husband died, but this drought has been much worse. Before I was quite ignorant – I didn't really understand. Now I understand the full consequences, so I feel a bit more stressed. But Grant said to me once, "It's no good looking behind you all the time, because you can't change what's behind. You've got to look ahead, see what's up front and see where you're going". I think he was quite right.'

Onlookers say she's proved an expert in looking forward, combining the station management with whatever's new and useful in technology. She'll usually look for any advances in science, seek out advice and then filter anything that might be useful to plough back into her land. 'She's become a real trailblazer,' says John Payne. 'She's got great business acumen, works hard and is persistent. This country is so changeable, things that worked yesterday might not work tomorrow. She's able to change with it, too. She's a great bushwoman in that she's able to be all alone at Cowarie and feel quite comfortable. And, above all, she's stubborn. She never gives up.'

That's an assessment Jenny Stevens agrees with wholeheartedly. 'She was pretty much a zombie after Grant died, and so low it was hard to believe she'd take it all on so successfully,' she says. 'It isn't her natural lifestyle but she's adapted so well to it. I didn't doubt that she'd come back to Cowarie. I think she felt responsible to keep it for the children. And she's such a smart and cluey woman.'

Now aged forty-five, Sharon divides her time between Cowarie and Adelaide, where her youngest, Christopher, sixteen, is still at school. She didn't want to send him away to board; she wanted to be there for him. Her daughter Ashlee, twenty-one, is at the University of New England in Armidale studying agribusiness, and has just started her own Shorthorn cattle stud; while Craig, twenty, is currently working on Currawilla, now owned by Grant's brother Roger, and intending to travel overseas to learn more about the cattle industry and maybe one day coming back to take over Cowarie. When she's away, Sharon manages to run the station from a distance with the support of her manager John

Germein and his partner Cathy Morgan. 'John has given me an invaluable opportunity as well as providing me the chance to learn from him through his lifetime of experience, insight and general outlook on life,' says Sharon. But she relishes every opportunity to go back home herself.

One of her greatest admirers is Grant's uncle, Eric Oldfield, also a cattle-station owner until he retired, and who was the boss drover on one of the cattle drives that passed through Cowarie. 'Sharon's one in a million,' he says. 'She's done a marvellous job, she really has. She came from Sydney and had a young family when Grant was killed. Any normal young girl would have said, "I'm out of here!", sold up and nicked off with a couple of million dollars to spend. But she hung in there and made a fantastic job of it, looking after the place and bringing up her kids. I take my hat off to her.'

As for Sharon, sitting on the verandah at Cowarie, it was a choice that today she's very happy she made. It's been difficult dividing her life between the station and Adelaide – as well as studying a master's degree in rangeland management through the University of Queensland – but she's determined to make the very best of it.

'It's pointless sitting down in Adelaide, focusing on what you miss so much about Cowarie,' she says, wiping a film of red dust off the table and smiling into the sunshine. 'Now, I feel I have the best of both worlds. I have the city and I can still come back here any time I like. I have the best as well as the worst, believe me!' She laughs and looks away towards the distant horizon.

'I've had a lot of help – I call it "picking old brains" – trying to gain an understanding of how to manage things. Over the years, a lot of people have been prepared to listen and provide advice and, at other times, listen and then let me work it out on my own.

'But it was Grant who taught me to love this land, and I think he'd be quite proud of me and how it's all working out. We have three wonderful kids, and we have this place. Yes, I miss him, but I have a lot to be thankful for.'

14

The Outback in All Australians

TERRY UNDERWOOD, *Riveren, Northern Territory*

It was in a new white crimplene suit with white stockings and high heels that eighteen-year-old Sydney nurse Terry Augustus made her first foray into the red billowing dust of one of the most remote parts of the Northern Territory. As she stepped out of the plane into the ferocious heat and swarm of black flies, the local Aboriginal kids shied away, thinking she was a ghost, and as soon as the dyed-in-the-wool cattleman she'd gone to visit drove up in his battered old truck, she was immediately covered in a sticky film of red earth.

'I'd wanted to make a good impression but, in retrospect, it was ridiculously inappropriate,' Terry now laughs. 'Then I looked at this man unwinding himself from the bull catcher and I just fell in love with him. I only had eyes for him.'

It might not have been the most auspicious of beginnings but today, forty-five years on, Terry is completely at home in her isolated cattle station, 600 kilometres south-west of Katherine, the nearest town. Happily wedded both to husband John Underwood and to Australia's last frontier, she's become one of the nation's best-known champions of the Outback.

'You somehow become a part of the Outback, and it becomes a part of you,' says Terry, now sixty-three. 'I wouldn't want to be anywhere else.'

At first, she did find it hard to adapt to bush life in such a lonely spot in the heart of the Territory, especially making a home of a tent beside a dry river creek, without electricity, running water or any form of communication. There was plenty of heartbreak to overcome too, like the death of her first-born from leukaemia at the age of just nine months, a later miscarriage, the devastating discovery that the local bore water wasn't good enough to drink, and plagues of rats, cats and even owls.

But eventually, she and her beloved husband, the man she first met at her Sydney hospital where he'd gone for treatment for a back injury, developed their massive cattle station on 3000 square kilometres of land, an area bigger than Luxembourg. There, Terry brought up four healthy children, teaching them at home by correspondence via the School of the Air, before sending them off to boarding school in Sydney to make sure they had a big-city education too.

'I loved the man, I loved the solitude, and I loved the place,' says Terry, whose autobiography about her life at Riveren, *In the Middle of Nowhere*, has sold more than 100 000 copies, becoming a much-loved modern Australian classic.

'You can't define the Outback. Life's hard there – one minute you can suffer terrible drought, and it feels like the next minute you're flooded with twelve inches of rain in three days – but it's a lifestyle that's inherent in all Australians. It's about our beginnings, and it's vital to keep it alive.'

It's been ten years since Terry's book captured the hearts of so many Australians, followed up by a book of her photographs, *Riveren: My Home, Our Country*, but life in the meantime has just continued to get better. The most exciting development has been the return of her children to the land, one by one, and being able to welcome a fourth generation of Underwoods into the world – and on to Riveren.

At a time when so many youngsters born to bush families choose to make new lives in the cities, it's all credit to Terry and John that their children's lives are so inextricably entwined with the Outback.

'They've all been away and done lots of things, but they're always happiest when they're on the ground,' says Terry proudly. 'They all love life on the land and we're pleased they seem to cherish it just as much as we do.'

The eldest, Marie, after a career working in Darwin for the world-famous Paspaley Pearl company, has settled at another of the Underwoods' properties, Midway, a couple of hours south-west of Darwin. Still working from home for Paspaley, she and husband Chris have a baby, Jock, born in October 2007. 'It's exciting that we've all come back to the land, and are so committed to it,' says Marie, thirty-seven. 'It's amazing when you think how many families are walking away because it's all too hard, or the drought is too bad or the stresses are too great. But our parents have really taught us to be very resilient and not to throw in the towel when things get tough, and to also be very passionate about the Outback.'

After university and four years of accountancy, the second-eldest, Patrick, became CEO of the Northern Territory Livestock Exporters Association before joining Meat & Livestock Australia (MLA). In the middle of 2007, however, a neighbouring property to Riveren came up for sale: the 2400 square kilometre Inverway Station. Once part of the original 1950s landholding of John Underwood's father Pat, it had been left to John's sister. Terry, with her heart in her mouth, immediately convened a family conference and was over the moon when everyone agreed that they should buy it, to keep it within the family. As a result, Patrick handed in his notice to the MLA and took his wife Susannah and baby son Archie back to within 75 kilometres of the Riveren homestead where he'd grown up, to run it as another branch of the Underwoods' Outback empire.

The media reported the sale of the property as 'one of the most significant rural property sales this year, the outstanding Northern Territory cattle holding, Inverway Station, sold at auction in Darwin for $17.65 million'. 'It was a big move for us, and means we have a lot of debt, but it feels right,' says Terry of the purchase of Inverway and its 11 000 Brahman and Brahman-cross cattle. 'It also allowed Patrick to come back.'

Patrick, now thirty-six, was delighted with the move. 'This property was very important to the family,' he says. 'It's great to

274

be there. I've always loved the open spaces and skies and the land itself. Mum's always said you grow up as a part of the Outback, and I think that's very true.'

Terry and John's third child, Michael, has long since returned to Riveren to help with, and ultimately take over, the running of the station. With his wife Georgia, their baby son Xavier and another child on the way, Michael, now thirty-five, never had any doubt that he'd be back. 'The decision to return for me was the most natural thing in the world,' he says, from his own homestead, 50 metres away from the main one. 'Growing up here as the third generation on cattle stations, I always wanted to come back.'

The youngest, thirty-year-old Becky, is the only one yet to return to the land, although she's already deeply entrenched in the cattle industry, working for the MLA. With a boyfriend from the land, however, she is determined to return to a property, and probably sooner rather than later. 'We've had every opportunity *not* to go back but, despite that, we're all choosing to do so,' she laughs. 'I'll definitely be back. I never really even left it in spirit.'

For Terry, it's another dream come true that her children have chosen to keep their own love affair with the Outback going, just as she once did. And being able to share in the upbringing of her grandchildren is an absolute joy. 'Being a nanna is fabulous,' she says, shaking her head in wonder at it all. 'Georgia will bring Xavier over in the morning and ask, "Are you busy?" and I say, "No, no! He can stay with me". It's just lovely. His dad Michael is so like John in that he's huge, tireless and fearless, and always has this big smile on his face. He loves his little baby boy, and Xavier responds accordingly.

'For John and me it's like reliving our love, our coming together, our children. It's so beautiful, it's just the best time for us.'

Nowadays, Riveren supports 18 000 head of Brahman cattle, in addition to the 11 000 next door at Inverway, and plays a critically important part in the live export market. Terry, a small, perfectly groomed figure against a massive and wild landscape, continues to take an active role in that industry. When we next speak, for example, she has just visited a small Indonesian village in Central Java, where some of her Riveren cattle have been sent as part of the burgeoning live-export trade.

The family she visited were operating a small feedlot for cattle, and the women were thrilled to see Terry arrive with the little delegation from Australia. They were even more delighted when she crouched down with them in the dust to show them a photograph album of their new steer's old home far away, then talked about the care and love with which it had been reared. 'The grannies and the aunties were all so excited to see me – a woman!' smiles Terry. 'It's nearly always such a man's world, like it is back home. I showed them photos of when the steer was born, and talked about how we look after our animals, how we feed them. Our relationship is now such an educational interactive program, it's wonderful.

'It's a great industry and there's wonderful interaction whereby the Indonesians or the Filipinos come to our Territory conferences, they visit our properties, they have a meal with us, they see where the cattle are born. It's good for us, it's good for them, and it's good for the cattle. Now, travelling out of Darwin on the boats, they actually put on weight. So it's the best outcome for the beasts, and for all the people involved.'

While controversy from time to time flares over the live-export trade, Terry and her family are convinced that these days, with all the safeguards and programs put in place, it works extremely humanely and well. Patrick, with all his past experience of the Asian end of the operation with the MLA, says that those last few months of the cattle's lives, when they disembark the boats and then spend a minimum of seventy-five days on an Asian feedlot until they're slaughtered, are often among their happiest times.

'They're so well fed and looked after, whereas at home they can struggle for a feed at certain times of the year,' says Patrick. 'At some places over there, they can put on a kilo and a half a day with unlimited feed. The live trade conjures up some negative images, particularly with sheep going to the Middle East, but the way we do it is something we're totally comfortable with.'

Terry too has come to embrace the industry and do everything she can to promote it both overseas and back home. She's one of the few honorary life members of the Northern Territory Cattlemen's Association, the peak primary industry lobby group in the Territory, and its lone female life member. 'Terry knows the industry as well as any man brought up here,' says Executive Director Stuart Kenny. 'She plays a major role, and she's wonderful at promoting the industry to the key people, particularly in the cities. She has an incredible ability to tell the story, to tell it like it is, and at the same time convey her real care and love of the landscape.'

As part of that role, Terry enjoys travelling to Asia to talk up

Australia and its products, recently visited Washington DC as part of a delegation to represent Territory pastoralists, went over to a conference in South Africa on Brahman cattle, and invariably relishes meeting the locals and forging new bonds of friendship each time.

'It's a great privilege to be able to do that,' says Terry. 'Now, it's so multi-dimensional, there are a lot more opportunities. But we have to keep working at it; we can't afford to be complacent. Our industry is clean and green, we haven't had any outbreaks of disease, and we are very blessed in Australia. We just have to keep on doing what we do, and doing it well.'

Everyone constantly marvels at how Terry manages to find the time for all the projects she's always undertaking. Her kids point to the fact that she doesn't seem to need much sleep, and wrote her book exclusively between the hours of 3 a.m. and 6 a.m., while the rest of the family were in bed. Even today, her energy and enthusiasm don't seem to have waned at all.

'She's got an incredible ability to get things done, which has always been a great example to us all,' says Marie. 'She always taught us that there's no such thing as "can't", and that if you want something done, then you should just get on and do it yourself. Mum's very, very determined in everything she does.'

That's stood not only Terry in good stead but others around her too. When Bruce Campbell came up with the idea for a Year of the Outback to take place in 2002, Terry was one of the first people he canvassed. When she embraced it with real gusto and was happy to become an ambassador, he knew he had a winner on his hands, and it ended up one of the most important events the Outback had ever seen.

'She was one of the speakers at the launch in Longreach, and she just captured the audience,' says Bruce, the Chairman of the Australian Outback Development Consortium, who followed it up with another series of events in 2006, and has Terry on board for the planning of the next in 2010. 'She told the human story of her family, of going to the Northern Territory, and everyone was captivated. She'll do anything for the Outback, and is a wonderfully committed person.'

Terry wanted to do more to commemorate the Year of the Outback, and came up with the idea for a stockman's tribute statue to be built in Katherine, then set about raising the funds to make it a reality. She chose Sabu Peter Sing as the role model for the Katherine icon, a man born of the Wardaman tribe, who she felt epitomised the unity that could be achieved between the different races and cultures. Soon after, through the generosity of eighty-six sponsors worldwide, she unveiled the larger-than-life-sized bronze statue of the stockman on horseback by Outback sculptor Archie St Clair, a lasting tribute to the pioneers of the pastoral industry.

'A gentle, humble man, Sabu was our mate,' Terry said at the ceremony. 'He rode beside my husband John and many of you gathered here today. His outstanding skills as bushman, horseman, stockman and cattleman were widely recognised and acclaimed . . . Now through Sabu, the chosen representative of all people – blackfella, whitefella, yellafella – our history and heritage will be immortalised. We are all inextricably linked.'

Bruce Campbell was astonished by how quickly and efficiently

Terry made the statue happen. 'She said she wanted to do something small for the Year of the Outback, and that 'small' thing must have cost the best part of $200000!' he says. 'If anyone had any doubts about her capacity to drive people . . . It was an extraordinary endeavour.'

Bruce was just one of many to recognise Terry's hard work. In 2005, she was awarded the Medal of the Order of Australia for service to the community, while in mid-2007 she was asked to become a member of the Australian Government's Northern Australia Land and Water Taskforce, which is working out the best way forward for everyone in the top half of the nation. Meetings to plan the priorities took place in Canberra, Darwin, Perth, the Kimberley, Brisbane and Queensland's Gulf Savannah country.

At first, Terry was hesitant to become involved, living so far away from everyone else. Then she came to the conclusion that her position was exactly why she'd been invited into the fold. 'You know what you're talking about *because* you live there,' she says. 'You have a role, and you've earned your place. It's a huge agenda because it's all about the changing face of Australia and we've all got to be able to adapt to change. I think people like us have to be out there fighting, having an influence on the future.'

For her family, it was no surprise that Terry accepted this new challenge, once again as a lone female member. 'She's not slowed down at all as she's got older,' says Marie. 'She's very generous giving her time to the community and to charity. She and Dad will often drive 1000 kilometres up to Darwin for just a function or a meeting. It's quite ridiculous. But she loves to burn the candle at both ends.'

Old friend Jim Dominguez, a former financier and chairman of

St Vincent's Hospital, remembers vividly the time he and a group of mates went up to stay at Riveren. After enduring a rough plane ride and then the rutted red-dirt track, they arrived bedraggled to find Terry waiting for them in a cocktail gown, card tables spread with delicate white lace tablecloths and covered with the most exquisite tiny canapés and bottles of chilled champagne, against a backdrop of curious Brahman cattle. After an evening of eating delicious food and drinking good wine, the group retired to bed. 'But half-an-hour later, Terry ran through the house, turning every light on,' recounts Jim. 'Then she shouted, "Come on, you pikers, you've come here to party, not to sleep!" So we did party. She's quite a lady!'

Terry's under continual pressure to carry on writing. With letters and emails from people who've read her books constantly flooding in, a follow-up is eagerly awaited. One day, she says, she will write it, but not just yet. First, she wants to write a book about people in the country called *Bush Souls*. She's also busy with public-speaking engagements, people asking her to take photographs for them, and was one of the first ports of call when the Northern Territory branch of the breast cancer survivors' charity Dragons Abreast asked her to take a page in their fundraising calendar. The resulting photo shows her in an evening gown, with a glass of champagne, among her cattle at Riveren. 'I wanted to show us celebrating life in the bush,' laughs Terry. 'So I loved being Miss April!'

Every day, Terry still springs out of bed in the darkness, quickly dresses, calls to her four dogs and slips out of the front door of her homestead. Then, as day slowly breaks, she takes a long walk over Riveren, communing with the land and with nature.

'There's just barely enough light to see without falling over as I pound off eastwards,' she says. 'As I head home, the sun is just tipping the horizon, like a gold blanket wrapped around your back. It's so beautiful. That's how much I love this place!'

Of course, it still has its difficulties, with soaring fuel costs now reaching around $200000 a year, cyclical drought and the constant vagaries of the weather. While bores throughout the property protect against dry years, even a good wet season can bring problems: too much rain can easily cause a protein drought in the grass. Finding staff to work on such remote properties is also an annual headache. There's still a tradition of city kids coming to jackaroo or jillaroo for a year, or backpackers coming out for a real Outback Australian experience, but usually after their allotted time they'll all return home and to their chosen careers. 'Long term, maybe we're better off breeding our own stockmen,' Terry laughs, thinking of her three grandsons and the next on the way. 'But that'll take a while!'

For family has always been, and remains, a top priority. Bringing new members into the close-knit fold naturally has its challenges, but everyone's working hard at that too. 'It was a very important learning curve for me to make sure that my daughters-in-law feel this is their home,' says Terry. 'You just have to work through relationships together, with no support systems, no counsellors, no distractions, and when everyone is trying so hard – too hard, sometimes – you can have mini-volcanoes.

'The other challenge is to make sure John and I slip into the background and hand over the reins, which is the reality of modern multi-generational families in the bush. Michael's now the one who makes the decisions, he's the one that gives orders, while Georgia is the one who he consults with. That can be hard, having been queen of your world, but I'm now just the backup. They run Riveren.'

Succession planning is a process that's started, but with a long way yet to go. At the moment, all the Underwood children want to stay on the land but Terry's well aware of some of the big money now being offered for family properties by the major investment companies and superannuation funds. Someone asked Terry the other day, 'What if you were offered $50 million for Riveren, what would you do then?' Terry immediately shook her head, 'No, we wouldn't sell,' she replied. Then a family member said, only half-jokingly, 'Wouldn't we?'

Terry shrugs her shoulders. 'What price heritage?' she asks. 'We are very aware of the fact that two family properties we know of in Central Australia sold recently, and another two in the Top End. But you just never know. These are all the issues that are affecting me as a mother, wife, advocate for the bush . . . there's a lot on the table. John says, "Oh well, we've had our day – they've got to work it out now". We've all got an equal vote, including our daughters-in-law, whom we treat as our children, and we know that if at any time John and I are outvoted, then we will have to accept that, because we have had our time.'

Whatever happens in the future, however, it's most likely that the Underwoods will continue to build on their Outback dynasty. Patrick says he can't imagine anything else. 'It's great to step outside and look around and know that the land for 100 kilometres all around you belongs to the family,' he says. 'It's a pretty special thing. It can certainly be tough and frustrating and isolating here, and you're always looking at the sky and wondering whether the rain is coming, but I always think that while the lows can be very low, the highs are so very high. If you work in the city, sitting at a computer all day, I see it as more of a flatliner existence. Here, it's much more of a roller-coaster.'

With all the children having had a mother so keen to instill in them a real appreciation for the Outback, it's now become an integral part of each. Marie says Terry's influence has been huge. 'She's quite remarkable, and a great role model. She taught us to reach for the stars and that we could achieve anything we wanted to, as long as we wanted it enough. She's always extremely committed and one of the most important things in her life is to promote the bush and Outback, so everyone can better understand it. She realises lots of people don't have any concept of the hardships and the joys, so she wants to bring the Outback to the cities too.'

Becky agrees. 'Mum is just such an Australian Outback icon,' she says. 'From the moment she made a decision to love Dad, she embraced everything.'

As for Terry herself, every day she counts her blessings. Someone commented to her recently that she was very lucky to still be so in love with the man who first brought her to the Outback, with little more than a dream and a huge heart brimming over with determination to make a life for the two of them there. 'And yes, I am so very lucky,' smiles Terry. 'John and I are still very strong partners, loving being together, and loving seeing our family grow here.

'And the Outback is just so glorious and so powerful. It's the wide open skies, the air, tending the animals . . . I want to share the Outback with everyone. I'm lucky enough to have it in my veins now, and I see my ongoing role as bringing the Outback into the minds and hearts of all people.'

ACKNOWLEDGEMENTS

This book came about after Jo Wiles, the indefatigable deputy editor of the *Australian Women's Weekly*, asked me to write about the five finalists in their Inspiring Women Competition, run in conjunction with Meat & Livestock Australia. The women were so inspiring, in fact, that Ali Watts at Penguin Books contacted my agent with the idea of my writing a book about some of Australia's most amazing Outback women. Thus my first thanks go to Jo who, over the years, has become a great friend as well as a mentor, and magazine editor-in-chief Deborah Thomas who has given me so many opportunities. My gratitude is also, as ever, with my agent and friend, Selwa Anthony, who never fails to see the funny side of sending a long-standing vegetarian with absolutely no sense of direction and who has only ever lived in big cities, into the vast Outback among all those cattle and sheep producers.

For her faith and vision, I'd similarly like to thank my publisher

Ali Watts, and my editor Saskia Adams for all her hard work knocking this manuscript into shape.

My mum, Edna Williams, deserves a medal too, for typing up the transcripts of many of the interviews I did with the Outback women, despite knowing even less about the Outback than me. Naturally, I couldn't have done it without my partner Jimmy Thomson either, who cheerfully travelled to many of the Outback destinations with me, did the lion's share of driving and reassured me when the charter plane turned out to be much smaller than I'd imagined – and with only one engine. A mention too to Angie Kelly, a fabulous support, and Catherine Chan for her incredible help and generosity.

But my most sincere gratitude goes to the subjects of this book, many of whom have been through enough traumas for a lifetime, who welcomed me into their homes, cooked me more vegetable lasagnes than I've ever seen before in my life and shared their stories with incredible warmth, honesty and generosity of spirit. These women I simply can never thank enough. It was an enormous privilege to step into their lives for a short time and to be entrusted with their stories. I salute them as some of the most courageous, resilient, determined and inspiring people I've ever been lucky enough to meet.